PRAISE FOR

CREATING YOUR OWN MONOLOGUE

WITHDRAWN

"This is the perfect book for actors willing to take on the challenge of creating their own monologues. Every aspect of character development and dialogue writing for solo material is handled. There is a gold mine of information here."
> —**Peter Askin**, Director, John Leguizamo's *Mambo Mouth* and *Spic-O-Rama,* and *Hedwig and the Angry Inch*

"Finally, a book that truly empowers actors! *Creating Your Own Monologue* offers you everything you need to know about writing your own material. Any actor serious about writing monologues MUST get this book!"
> —**Charlayne Woodard**, Actress and Monologist, *Pretty Fire* and *Neat*

"Learning how to effectively corral your memory and put those thoughts into words are important skills necessary for writing autobiographical monologues. Glenn Alterman's book offers invaluable techniques and tools that can assist you each step of the way. I HIGHLY RECOMMEND IT!"
> —**Spalding Gray**, Actor and Monologist, *Swimming to Cambodia, Monster in the Box, Gray's Anatomy,* and *Morning, Noon, and Night*

SECOND EDITION

Creating Your Own Monologue

GLENN ALTERMAN

ALLWORTH PRESS
NEW YORK

09 08 07 06 05   5 4 3 2 1

Published by Allworth Press
An imprint of Allworth Communications, Inc.
10 East 23rd Street, New York, NY 10010

Cover design by Derek Bacchus
Interior design by Joan O'Connor
Typography by Integra Software Services

ISBN: 1-58115-429-1

Library of Congress Cataloging-in-Publication Data

Alterman, Glenn, 1946-
   Creating your own monologue / Glenn Alterman.—2nd ed.
      p. cm.
   Includes index.
   1. Monologue—Authorship.   2. Monodramas—Authorship   3. Acting—Auditions.
   4. One-person shows (Performing arts)   I. Title.

   PN1530.A48 2005
   808.2'45—dc22

                              2005018576

Printed in Canada

Dedication

*I dedicate this book to all solo performers
who have ever had the courage to stand
alone on a stage and perform their
own material.*

*I dedicate this book to every monologist
whose work has inspired me to create
my own monologues and to write
this book.*

*And finally, I dedicate this book to the
memory of Spalding Gray and
Quentin Crisp, two extraordinary men
and wonderful monologists.*

CONTENTS

Part II

interviews with monologue writers and performers

Part III

interviews with directors of one-person shows

Appendixes

ACKNOWLEDGMENTS

I wish to thank: Kathleen Russo (Washington Square Arts), Seth Gordon, Abigail McGrath, Doug Barron (Plaza Desk Top Publishing), Andre DeShields, David Pace, Greg Phillips (CSTAR—Creative Stage Artists Management), Eleanor Speert, and Nicole Potter-Talling.

INTRODUCTION

to the
second edition

Since the first edition of this book was published the world has changed a great deal. September 11th occurred and many lives have been dramatically affected. Art reflects people's lives and the world we live in. There have been a great many one-person shows dealing with the effects of 9-11. James Cartens's harrowing solo show *After* is one that immediately comes to mind. In trying to deal with their feelings about this disaster, a large number of other solo artists have found the solo show a platform to express their painful feelings. There are many other shows being performed around the country right now that specifically deal with the effects of 9-11, terrorism, and the war in Iraq.

In the last few years there has been an abundance of one-person shows at theaters all around the country. There are many reasons for this. For one thing, the solo show is much less expensive to produce than a typical play. Also, today's audiences have learned to accept and appreciate solo shows. Many regional theaters now include at least one solo show as part of their season. Broadway has never had as many solo shows as it presently does. And there are plans for even more solo shows on the Great White Way in the upcoming seasons. HBO, Showtime, and other cable networks are now including more solo shows in their lineups. Some of these shows were originally produced in theaters around the country and later optioned by the networks. Sarah Jones's solo show *Bridge and Tunnel* originally premiered off-Broadway and is bound for Broadway in 2005.

The future of the one-person show looks bright. More and more actors are finding it a satisfying venue to express their talent. As you'll discover in the interviews in this book, many of the actors wrote their solo shows because they were unable to connect with material they were auditioning for. A solo show should never be written just to showcase your talent. There must be a strong need to express your feelings and thoughts. That being said, a solo show can be one of the most profound experiences an actor can have. It is you as an artist standing alone, saying what you want to say about your life or the world as you see it.

As an additional benefit, if you're an actor looking for new, interesting, original monologues for upcoming auditions, you'll discover that this edition has quite a few pieces that have never appeared in any other monologue book before. Feel free to use them for your auditions.

INTRODUCTION

I am an actor; I have been for over thirty five years. About twelve years ago I became a writer—more specifically a monologue writer. How? Why? Well, like many actors I was constantly looking for new monologues for auditions. It was a tiresome process. Each monologue that I'd find seemed to have something wrong with it, something that eliminated it from my being able to use it for auditions. Some were overused, some were too long and couldn't be cut (while keeping the story cohesive), others were too reliant on the plays they came from, others . . . well, it went on and on. It was a very frustrating situation, to say the least. I was constantly monologue-hunting when I could have been better spending my time looking for acting work.

Basically, what I was looking for in a monologue was something that I could hook into, a monologue that had a story that engaged me, characters that touched me, a situation that interested me. I must have logged hundreds of hours over the years looking for that one perfect monologue. On the rare occasion that I found one I could use, I'd do it so often that it would become stale in no time, and I'd be back once again looking through monologue books and plays, trying to find another one.

One day, on a whim—well, actually out of total frustration—I decided to bite the bullet and try to write one myself. Considering that I'd never written creatively before, I knew it was going to be a challenge. After all those years of monologue hunting, I certainly knew what I wanted. The monologue that I was going to write would have a beginning, middle, and end; a conflict of some kind; and a character who interested me and whom I could identify with. But most importantly, it had to have a good yarn, an engaging story.

It was trial and error for quite a while, lots of looking at the walls, throwing crumpled sheets of paper into the wastebasket. But one thing I gradually began to realize was that I could use my acting skills to help me write monologues. I could use some of the same skills that I'd used as an actor to create characters in plays to create characters in monologues. After a few very long, trying weeks I completed my first monologue. I felt a tremendous sense of achievement. This was something I had never done before. I had now become a monologue writer! There was nothing left to do but try it out, to see if the monologue worked.

I was studying acting at that time with Wynn Handman in New York. I brought my new monologue to class one night and nervously performed it. It went over very well. Everyone wanted to know where I'd found this great new monologue. After confessing that I'd written it, about five or six actors asked if I'd write one for them. I agreed to, and began writing monologues almost every day after that. The more I wrote, the more I realized I was on to something. I started to develop a more efficient way of working. Over the next few months I turned out a lot of monologues. That's not to say that every one of them was a gem; no, not at all. Actually, there were more flops than hits. But I learned more from my mistakes than from my successes. On any given night in Wynn Handman's class, I'd have up to three new monologues being performed by different actors for the first time. At the end of that first year I had completed nearly eighty monologues (not to mention the dozens of discarded ones). Each night in class when the monologues were read, I was always open to any comments, any criticism that anyone had. I took notes, kept records, and created a file. Over the years, that file has grown extensively. It is the basis for my monologue classes as well as this book.

Since writing that first monologue over fifteen years ago, I've written several hundred monologues, had six successful books of monologues published, and had dozens of my monologue plays performed all over the country. In my classes, I've seen actors who never thought they could write suddenly develop into skilled and successful monologists. I've written this book for actors—actors who are fed up and tired of spending countless hours looking through plays and monologue books for that one perfect piece.

The American theater has experienced a resurgence of interest in the one-person show. Coming out of diverse backgrounds and disciplines, many artists today are creating and performing full-length solo works. Obviously these appeal to presenting organizations in part because of economics; it is usually much cheaper to produce one actor on a bare stage than to mount a lavish musical. But clearly, these producers would not continue to present solo shows if the audience didn't support them. Perhaps these performances appeal to viewers because they often permit an intimacy that is missing from other forms of entertainment. Perhaps they are popular because they showcase the virtuosity and versatility of the actor—attributes that can disappear in the sauce of special effects and editing that comprise other popular media. Perhaps solo shows captivate audiences because they contain such clear, quirky, and individual worldviews.

This book is also intended for actors who are seriously thinking of creating their own one-person shows. As you will notice in the monologist interview section, the artists I interviewed have many different points of view, many different reasons for needing to speak their minds. Quite a few were frustrated actors who, tired of waiting for their phones to ring, decided to take matters in their own hands and create their own shows. Once that decision was reached, the roads that these performers took in building and shaping their own material were almost as diverse as the artists themselves. But all of them had to go through the process of discovering what they wanted to say and how they were going to say it.

I hope this book will guide you in finding a working method that clicks for you and ultimately results in a finished piece. I've tried to cover every possible aspect of creating your own monologue, and I have included sections on marketing and performance venues for your finished piece. I think that you'll find the interview sections with the solo artists and directors helpful, inspiring, and informative.

A final side note: In writing this book, my editor and I struggled to find an appropriate and inoffensive way to use pronouns. Since "he/she" is awkward and "them" is incorrect, we have settled, in the main, on pairing "the actor" or "the writer" with forms of the third-person masculine pronoun "he." Although this may be considered gender biased, it was my editor's feeling that we should sacrifice political correctness for the sake of simplicity and clarity.

I'm not saying that writing your own monologue will be easy, but I can almost guarantee that if you can commit to it, it can be an incredibly empowering and artistically satisfying experience.

Glenn Alterman

New York City

SIX WAYS

to get the most out of this book

1. I suggest, at first, that you *don't* read this book nonstop from cover to cover.
2. The best way to get the most value out of this book is to first look through the table of contents, then skim through the book, stopping at particular chapters that you feel are pertinent to the monologue you're presently writing or thinking about writing.
3. Next, I suggest that you read through the entire book, taking notes on whatever you feel will help you specifically with what you're working on or about to work on.
4. Once you have begun work on your monologue, I suggest that you occasionally refer back to the chapters dealing with process: "Starting to Write," "Beginning Your Monologue: Structure and Process," "Developing Your Monologue," and so on.
5. Reread some of the excepts by the monologists used to illustrate points in this book. You may find their material helpful, informative, and inspiring.
6. In addition to the monologue excerpts in this book, it's always helpful when working on monologues to browse through material from other monologists or writers whom you respect. Their work may be a source of inspiration during difficult periods.

the monologue: writing, rehearsing, performing

CHAPTER 1

a definition
of terms

For our purpose, in this book, solo art refers to one actor/artist alone on a stage before a live audience, performing material that he has created.

What Is a Monologue?

Webster defines a monologue as "a dramatic soliloquy" and as "a long speech." In a play, a monologue is an uninterrupted speech. Monologues can be quite flexible as to the form they take. Some monologues are delivered directly to the audience. Some try to create the impression that the actor is alone, talking to himself. Other monologues occur when the actor (in character) is talking to an imaginary person (or people). When speaking to an imaginary person, the character may be saying things that he always wanted to say but didn't get the chance to say, or didn't have the courage to say, or perhaps is preparing to say. In many if not most audition monologues, the actor (in character) is speaking to another character. The actor is imagining the other character and his responses. An example of this would be Linda Loman's "Attention Must Be Paid" monologue from *Death of a Salesman.* In this case, Linda is actually speaking to her sons, even if the actress is imagining them on the back wall.

The short monologue generally runs from two to ten minutes. It has a relatively uncomplicated story with not too many characters. Successful short monologues are highly condensed experiences that can be thought of as the theater's equivalent to poetry. Generally these monologues are written for auditions, acting-class work, or to be a part of a larger play of multiple monologues. Casting directors and agents pride themselves on their ability to make snap judgments, so when you write for auditions it is best to remember that brevity is the soul of wit. An audition piece that unfolds slowly will still be folded when the agent says "thank you." For this strange format, your material ought not to exceed three minutes.

A long monologue or monodrama is a one-person play. Monodramas can be a powerful form of theater. Quite often the writer uses elevated language and strong images to create a poetic enlargement of the characters and subject.

Monodramas are like all plays in that they have a beginning, middle, and end; contain concise dialogue; and express the writer's personal vision. They vary as to style, content, and time. What make monodramas so exciting and challenging to work on are the flexible forms they can take. Although there is only one actor on stage, he can bring many characters into the piece by assuming their personalities and voices. Although many monodramas incorporate conflict, it's not always necessary. The writer can rely on interesting characters, choice of words (dialogue), a dramatic situation, and so on to make his piece theatrical.

Types of Monologues

It's difficult to categorize monologues and monodramas because quite often they are hybrids of style. The following categories are somewhat arbitrary, but hopefully will be of some use in identifying specific characteristics of both monologues and monologue plays.

THE AUTOBIOGRAPHICAL NARRATIVE MONOLOGUES

In these plays, the artist recalls actual stories and events from his life. The actor/writer generally is the narrator in these pieces. There may be little or no attempt to perform different characters in the story. The emphasis here is on the telling of his own personal tale. Billy Crystal's autobiographical journey, *700 Sundays,* tells of growing up in Manhattan, and the people who influenced his life. Spalding Gray's *Swimming to Cambodia* is an example of this mainly narrative storytelling style. In this monologue, Gray recalls his fascinating experiences while working as an actor during the making of the movie *The Killing Fields* (see interview).

Another example of an autobiographical monologue is Evan Handler's *Time on Fire* (see interview). In his play, Mr. Handler tells the story of a time in his life when he was dealing with a life-threatening cancer. His story reveals the helplessness patients quite often feel when dealing with medical bureaucracy.

AUTOBIOGRAPHICAL CHARACTER MONOLOGUES

Some autobiographical monologue plays are character driven, relying mainly on dialogue rather than narrative. The actor/writer acts out his story with multiple characters to propel the story.

Chaz Palminteri's *A Bronx Tale* is based on his recollections of growing up in the Bronx. At the age of thirty-six, Palminteri wrote and performed this thirty-five-character, one-man show. It was a major success and was later turned into a film starring Robert De Niro (and many other actors). William Gibson's *Golda's Balcony* is a fascinating portrait of Israel's fourth prime minister, Golda Meir. Mr. Gibson uses one actress (Tovah Feldshuh in the original Broadway production) to play all the roles. Doug Wright's Pulitzer Prize– and Tony Award–winning play, *I Am My Own Wife*, tells the true story of Charlotte von Mahlsdorf, an East German transvestite. Once again, one actor (Jefferson Mays in the original Broadway production) plays all the characters in this fascinating play. John Leguizamo's *Sexaholix* tells the personal and hilarious story of his high-octane sex life.

CHARACTER-DRIVEN, FICTIONAL MONOLOGUES

In these plays, the actor/writer creates multiple characters to express a theme, display a lifestyle, or tell a (sometimes) imaginary story. In many cases the characters have a common connection. For instance, John Leguizamo's plays *Freak, Spic-O-Rama*, and *Mambo Mouth* deal with his childhood, his life, and growing up in Manhattan using real and imaginary characters.

Danny Hoch portrays mainly urban characters types, many living on the edge, in his character monologues (see interview).

Sometimes one character acts as the spine of the piece. In Jane Wagner's *The Search for Intelligent Life in the Universe*, Trudy, a mad bag lady, serves as a narrator who has befriended aliens from outer space who have come to study a "planet in puberty." Lily Tomlin, who premiered this play on Broadway, inhabited twenty-four characters during the course of the evening.

Whoopi Goldberg's recent revival of *Whoopi* uses characters to express Ms. Goldberg's point of view on humanity, politics, and the world as she sees it. The recent production was updated for the post 9-11 world.

REALITY-BASED DOCU-MONOLOGUES

These pieces are created from real-life events. The monologist uses the exact words of the people involved. In her play *Twilight: Los Angeles, 1992*, Anna Deavere Smith relates the experiences of forty-six real people in the wake of the Rodney King verdict and the riots that followed. Ms. Smith portrayed all of the characters. She obtained her information by tape-recording the actual people and taking notes on their speech tics and vocal inflections. For more information on reality-based docu-monologues, see Christopher Ashley's interview later on in the book. (He was Ms. Smith's director for her play *Fires in the Mirror*.)

Another American: Asking & Telling, Marc Wolf's one-man play, was distilled from over two hundred interviews conducted with members of the military culture (including gay and lesbian service members and veterans, their family members, and the people who oppose their right to serve). Mr. Wolf portrayed a series of characters struggling with the government's ban on gays and lesbians in the armed forces.

TOPICAL MONOLOGUES

These monologues rely heavily on the events of the day as seen through the eyes of the monologist. They are part autobiographical, part observation, and part opinion. There is a thin line between topical monologues and stand-up comedy. Both generally incorporate anecdotes, jokes, and personal observations. I feel, however, that there are differences between the two. For one thing, the topical monologist's intention isn't only to get laughs from his material. His stories generally have a wider sweep, and usually there is more of a cohesive quality to his piece. Stand-up comics primarily tell jokes, although on occasion, they will also include some anecdotal material. Kate Clinton's funny, feminist topical monologues express her particular view of the world as she sees it (see interview and excerpt). She has done both stand-up and theatrical topical monologues. Mario Cantone's *Laugh Whore* allows him to express his acerbic point of view on current events and the world of celebrities.

STORYTELLING MONOLOGUES

These are fictional stories performed by the actor/writer. They are generally written in narrative form, in which the actor serves as storyteller. During the telling of the story, the actor will occasionally break the narrative form to momentarily become one of the characters, and then immediately return to the narrator/storyteller role. *St. Nicholas* by Conor McPherson is an excellent example of this form. In this monologue play, a fictitious character tells an intriguing imaginary tale of vampires and late-night debauchery.

What Is Performance Art?

An agreed-upon meaning of the term "performance art" is very difficult to find. Unlike the word "monologue," there is no dictionary definition. Performance art can be described as an expression of an artist's creativity through visual art, drama, multimedia, dance, or music. Performance art is to theater what poetry is to prose. I asked several solo artists and directors of solo shows how they would define performance art.

Director Jo Bonney said, "The label 'performance art' has always been applied to things that are elusive and flexible. The very term 'performance art' actually came out of the visual arts scene. Artists were creating happenings. These happenings usually took place in galleries. They took place in real time. They generally were a way an artist could explore something, a concept, a visual idea. They were not just for some entertainment value, to entertain an audience. They were generally attended by members of the art community. Basically, what I'm saying is that 'performance art' is just a label. It seems that many artists who come out of a theater background don't choose to use that label for their work. Dancers, cabaret performers, visual artists tend to use it more often to describe and identify their work. But basically it's a very elusive term."

Penny Arcade, a performance artist, asserts, "My work is a combination, I suppose, of very personal and very political, which is, in a sense, performance art. It's hard to say where one ends and the other begins."

Dael Orlandersmith defines a performance artist as "someone who technically breaks the fourth wall with the audience. It's a form of storytelling that relies heavily on the audience in some way."

Because of the amorphous definition and the variety of forms that performance art pieces can take, it's difficult to provide general guidelines for approaching them. In this book, for simplicity and clarity, I will mainly be dealing with the textual aspects of performance art pieces. For a more in-depth discussion of creating performance art, I refer you to such books as *The Art of Performance: A Critical Anthology*, edited by Battcock, Gregory, Nickas, and Roberts. This book offers a fascinating collection of essays by performance artists as well as by established critics of performance art.

CHAPTER 2

a brief history
of the one-person
show

Most people believe that the one-man show is a recent phenomenon that started here in America. They might be surprised to learn that it actually began back in the eighteenth century.

Samuel Foote (1721–1777) Creates the One-Person Show

Samuel Foote was a British satirist. Foote wrote *The Rehearsal*, a burlesque, in which he mimicked some of the political figures and well-known actors of the day. *The Rehearsal* was an extremely popular theatrical piece.

In April of 1747, Foote opened a new play, *The Diversions of the Morning*. I should mention that originally, Foote's shows were not totally solo. There were other actors on the stage with him. But it was his solo work as a mimic that audiences enjoyed most. Foote continued his solo satires for the next thirty years. At times, his plays could be quite offensive. Nevertheless, they were the "must-see" shows for the audiences of his day.

Over the years, there were many others who followed in Foote's tradition of solo mimicry. Among the most well known were George Saville Carey, who was famous for his impersonations of other actors, and Harry Woodward, a comedian who wrote solo topical skits.

George Alexander Stevens, the Father of the Monologue

It wasn't until 1764, when George Alexander Stevens wrote *Lecture Upon Heads* that the monologue as an art form truly came into being. By all accounts, Stevens's monologue ran about two hours. During the monologue he poked fun at many things, but mostly at many of the great statesman of the day. He also lampooned common stereotypes and social behavior. Stevens's shows were a major success and had very long runs (nearly a thousand performances each).

Stevens's success opened the floodgates for copycats, spin-offs, and imitators. These imitations were not just limited to England. Quite a few other countries, including America, had their own versions of Stevens's *Lecture Upon Heads*. The copyright laws at that time were very limited and could not protect his work.

Charles Mathews

During the nineteenth century, Charles Mathews, a comic actor and mimic, wrote *The Mail Coach Adventure*, which later evolved into what became his very popular one-man show. Eventually Mathews developed an entire group of solo shows called *At Homes*, which he toured in both England and America. Like Foote's monologues, Matthews's monologues mimicked many of the famous actors of the day, but unlike Foote's, Matthews's were not offensive.

By the early 1900s, monologues were quite often used to "cover" while scenery was being changed during a play. Also, if some minor technical disaster occurred during a play's performance, the monologist would be out in front keeping the audience entertained. Today's warm-up entertainers do a similar job both before and during the taping of sitcoms and late-night talk shows.

Ruth Draper Perfects the Monologue

Perhaps one of the most famous monologists of all time was Ruth Draper. Draper, an actress, performed many of her one-woman shows during the 1920s, 1930s, and 1940s. Her first show of "monos," as she called them, was performed in England in 1920. The two-hour-long evening was composed of an assortment of well-developed characters created totally from her imagination. From the very beginning, the critics raved about her work as a monologist. She spoke many languages and performed her monologues all over the world.

Draper's characters ranged from the very poor to the extremely wealthy, and they had a true-to-life quality to them. Through her characters, she developed her monos into mini-plays with a beginning, middle, and end. She never used a script, but relied totally on her memory. Her characters were constantly changing and evolving. She was never content with her work and was always looking for new ways to express herself. She tried to work as simply as possible, without too much clutter. A prop as simple as a hat or a handbag was all that was required. Add to that a chair and a table, and she was ready to create magic—"Draper's magic," as it was called. Draper had a tremendous belief in the actor's ability to pretend.

She felt that if she truly committed herself to her imagination in creating her characters, the audience would believe in them.

Cornelia Otis Skinner

A contemporary and admirer of Draper was Cornelia Otis Skinner. When Skinner first began performing her one-woman shows, there were many similarities between her work and Draper's. Eventually however, her taste ran toward more sumptuous costume dramas. In 1937, she performed an adaptation of *Edna, His Wife*, a bestselling novel of the day. This further distinguished her from Draper, who primarily did "character-created plays." Skinner also made a very comfortable living as an actress in regular plays, and was a well-respected writer and essayist.

Historical Monologues

As I mentioned earlier, solo shows went through a period of decline, but historical solo shows continued being popular even during that period. Some monologists created shows based on real rather than imaginary characters. Emlyn Williams played Charles Dickens, Paul Shyre played H. L. Mencken, James Whitmore performed in *Will Rogers U.S.A.*, and Hal Holbrook was *Mark Twain Tonight!*. These are just a few that come to mind.

Some solo plays have been written by playwrights for specific actors. Samuel Beckett wrote *Krapp's Last Tape* for Patrick Magee; Cocteau wrote *Le Fantome de Marseille* for Edith Piaf; William Luce wrote *The Belle of Amherst* for Julie Harris.

The Solo Show Today

Over the last few years there have been many successful one-person shows to hit the Great White Way, such as Elaine Stritch's *At Liberty* (for which she won a Tony), Eve Ensler's *The Good Body*, Tovah Feldshuh in *Golda's Balcony*, John Leguizamo's *Sexaholix*, and Rob Becker's *Defending the Caveman*, to name just a few. In the last year or so, many solo shows have opened on Broadway. They include *Dame Edna: Back With A Vengeance*, Billy Crystal's *700 Sundays*, Mario Cantone's *Laugh Whore*, and Whoopi Goldberg's revival of her one-woman show, *Whoopi*. Off-Broadway there have been some new and exciting solo shows. They include (among many) *The Syringa Tree, Squeeze Box, Bridge and Tunnel, Nine Parts of Desire*, and *Belfast Blues*.

Eric Bogosian, Laurie Anderson, Danny Hoch (see interview), Anna Deavere Smith, and John Leguizamo are just a few of today's many solo artists who have made hugely successful careers for themselves with their solo work.

There are probably more monologists and solo artists performing their work today than ever before. Because of the high cost of regular play productions, solo shows are welcomed in many regional theaters, as well as off-Broadway and on Broadway. It seems like every Broadway season now has at least one solo show.

If you are interested in a more detailed history of one-person shows, I highly recommend *Acting Solo: The Art of One-Man Shows,* by Jordan R. Young (Moonstone Press, 1989). I personally found this book to be an excellent source for the research that I did on this subject.

CHAPTER 3

a preliminary look

Before you begin working, it's very important to ask yourself, "Exactly why am I doing this?" Obviously the answer is going to be different if your intention is to write a short monologue for auditions versus if you're planning to commit yourself to writing a solo show. If you are planning to write your audition piece, it may well be because you are frustrated with the material that is out there, and you think you can showcase yourself better than a playwright who doesn't know you or your special talents. Audition pieces have specific guidelines that you will probably want to abide by, mainly in terms of length and arc. I will deal with the particular demands of the short/audition monologue in chapter 6, but in general, most of what I have to say about creating a solo show can be applied to a short monologue as well.

If you are thinking about creating a solo show, you, like many of the actors interviewed in this book, may have decided, out of frustration and unemployment, "The hell with them, I'll write my own show and star in it!" You will learn, as they did, that creating your own show requires a tremendous amount of work. If your only reason for writing is to provide yourself with an acting job, perhaps you should consider what's ahead of you. The commitment level for writing a solo show is quite extensive. There's a tremendous amount of work involved. Some solo shows can take many months, even years to complete.

Questions to Ask Yourself before Starting Work on a Solo Show

- Am I really committed to doing this?
- Am I willing to work on this for however long it takes?
- I realize that I'll be alone on stage for each performance. Can I handle that responsibility and pressure?

- Do I believe that I have the talent to keep an audience entertained for up to two hours?
- If I chose to use my own experience as the basis for the show, what do I want to share with the audience?
- Are there painful or funny stories from my life that I want to reveal to the world?
- If I'm planning on writing character monologues, do I feel that I'm a versatile enough performer to carry them off with variety, allowing for each character to be fully realized?
- If I don't have the technical skills now (dialects, etc.), am I willing to work as hard as I can to develop them while working on my show?

If, after answering all these questions, you are willing to commit yourself to all the work involved in creating your own solo show, all I have to say is, Congratulations, welcome aboard! I'll do the best that I can to help you find the answers to questions that inevitably will come up along the way. At this point, my only advice is:

- Try to stay focused on what you're doing.
- Keep your goal constantly in mind.
- If it gets uncomfortable, even frustrating, at times, don't give up; just work through it.

The Similarities/Differences between Being an Actor and Working as a Writer

The most obvious similarities between the actor and the writer are that both are creative artists and both use their imagination in their work. That ability to use your imagination as an actor will be very helpful in the work we'll be doing here.

Generally, the actor interprets and performs what the writer/playwright has written. The interdependence of both professions should be obvious. However, the actor's creative life involves constant collaboration with other artists (the director, other actors, etc.) early on in a play's production. The writer generally does his initial creating alone. After he's written the play, he collaborates with the production team (producer, director, actors, etc.). Since this book offers guidance for actors in creating their own material, we'll be looking at techniques and approaches that merge both of these professions.

As you will note in Part II, not all actors/creators work as the traditional writer does, although some do adhere to a more "writerly" process.

As an Actor, Do I Have the Necessary Skills to Create My Own Material?

I personally feel that anyone can write, tell stories, create monologues. If you've lived and had experiences, then you have stories like no one else. Your stories are unique, yours and yours alone. How you'll tell your stories is as individual as you are. No one else has lived your life or knows the things that you've seen or felt.

- The secret to writing *autobiographical monologues* is learning how to access your private stories, your memories, your point of view, and put them into words.
- The creation of fictional *character monologues* requires keen observation of people, a good ear for dialogue, and a healthy imagination.
- *Performance art pieces* require a commitment to a purely personal vision, a good imagination, and, quite often, a variety of performance skills.

As I've mentioned, actors interpret and perform what writers have written. As an actor, if you've worked on plays, you're already familiar with all the ingredients of playwriting, character, dialogue, scenes, drama, comedy, etc. It's therefore safe to assume that you already have some basic knowledge of the mechanics of playwriting, and more importantly, of character development. Writing your own material may not be as difficult or as complicated as you imagined. It's much like going through to the other side of the mirror. Now, instead of being merely the instrument of a writer's vision, you will create the world that you're going to inhabit, perform, play in.

Pluses and Minuses, Assessing Specifically Where You Are Now

It's helpful here at the start to know the type of solo work you're interested in working on. It may be that the material you are thinking about seems to require a specific presentational style, or it may be that you, as a performer, want to explore a particular form. Either way, you now need to determine whether you have the necessary skills to create the work ahead of you.

If you're planning on doing *multiple character monologues*, do you feel capable of creating and playing a range of characters, quite often in quick succession? If not, do you know where you can get the necessary help? You should be able to play characters of different ages and both sexes. You should also know how to do dialects comfortably. Also, being flexible and agile with your body is very helpful with multiple characters. If you need to take some classes in bodywork, I suggest starting prior to the rehearsal of your show.

For *autobiographical monologues*, you should be a good storyteller. Can you and are you willing to access (sometimes painful) memories from your past? Do you feel that your story will be of interest to an audience? Why? And ask yourself, why do you need to tell this story?

Your Sense of Truth

To be a good actor, you have to develop and rely on your own sense of truth in your work. That sense of truth is also a major asset in the creation of your own monologue material, no matter how long or short it is. It's the thing that will help you to honestly say what you want to say in the most personal way.

As an actor, I'm sure that you've had definite opinions and feelings about the material you've worked on. Certain characters may have touched you more than others. Some moments, some lines of dialogue, may have seemed more real to you. I'm not talking about judging a playwright's work; I'm talking about how you've responded to the material, from your personal sense of truth. *That sense of truth is like a divining rod in the work we'll be doing. Much of what this book is about is learning about your sense of truth, and how to access it and utilize it as a writer.*

CHAPTER 4

ways to work, selecting your tools

There are many tools that you can use to create your own material. They include writing it out with pad and pen, using a computer or typewriter, working with a tape recorder, working improvisationally, and working orally. Whichever way feels most comfortable to you and facilitates your work is the best way. I write on paper and/or use the computer to create my monologues and books. But for many years, I worked with pad and pen, and then on a word processor. How you work and what you choose to work with is as individual as who you are. You should experiment with several of the suggested ways to find out which works best for you.

Writing

This is the old pad-and-pen way of working. Many solo artists prefer this medium because of its tactile quality. There's a sense of your creative energy starting in your brain then going directly through your arm, to your hand, down into the pen, then onto the paper. It's quick, spontaneous, efficient. Many writers feel that this is the best way for them, particularly during the exploratory stages, when they're just starting out on a new piece. As soon as an idea or some dialogue hits them, they can immediately jot it down. Many artists are intimidated by complex word processors and the perfunctory nature of computers, so they find writing more actor-friendly.

Still, for many solo artists, the day begins with sitting in front of their computer, typing away in creative abandon. Word-processing programs such as Microsoft Word and WordPerfect can shift phrases around, rearrange whole sections, catalogue what has been developed, and so on. There is no need to endlessly rewrite what has already been written, no carbon-stained fingers, no pages lost or thrown out by mistake. It's an orderly, systematic, high-tech way to work.

The Internet can be a tremendous source of information for material that you're working on. By connecting with chat rooms, you can have discussions with other writers and monologists who may be experiencing some of the same problems that you're trying to overcome. Also, today there are several monologue Web sites that you can connect to.

While we're talking about writing, it is important to mention that many solo performers carry a pad and pen with them at all times to take impulse notes (see the discussion of journal-writing later on in this chapter). A great line of dialogue, an inspired moment for your monologue, or a keen insight should not be left to one's memory alone. You can be on a bus or walking down the street when you are struck with a great idea. It would be a shame to forget it. Just jot it down in your pad.

What Is Creative Writing?

Throughout much of this book, I'll be discussing writing in the creative sense of the word. At this point, I'd like to briefly discuss writing not so much as an activity (using paper and pen), but as an artistic process.

Writing is kind of like talking to yourself. Writers get to re-experience and even rethink moments of their lives. Writing is a way of understanding incidents and memories. By doing this, you quite often get a new perspective, a new point of view of where you've been and what you've experienced. When you reveal different parts of your life in your work, your audience may learn something about their own lives. *Writing is a form of communication, sharing, informing, and enlightening.*

HELPFUL BOOKS ABOUT CREATIVE WRITING

For those of you who would like to get some more information about the craft of writing, I recommend these books:

- *If You Want to Write* by Brenda Ueland (Graywolf Press)
  Like me, Ms. Ueland believes that "everybody is talented, original, and has something important to say." This book is very inspiring, informative, and helpful, especially for those who feel a bit intimidated by the idea of writing.
- *Three Genres: The Writing of Poetry, Fiction, and Drama* by Stephen Minot (Prentice Hall, Sixth Edition).
  This book explores the fundamental aspects of creative writing, including fiction writing, playwriting, and poetry.

Fear of Writing

There is always the fear that if you expose yourself in your writing, your audience will sit in judgment of you and your life. That fear is one of the great crosses all writers (and performers) have to bear. One of the secrets to quality writing is to not be too concerned about who you're writing for. It should *always* be just for yourself. You can never second-guess any audience, so why waste time worrying about the people you're writing for? If you honestly find that what you have to say is interesting or funny, it is more than likely that your audience will, too. Jot it down.

Journal Writing

While working on your solo piece, you may want to keep a journal. Basically, a journal is like a diary. You put in it whatever interests you as you go through your day. Perhaps some of the material that you enter in the journal will be relevant and helpful to the piece that you're working on. Many monologists keep a journal with them at all times.

In the journal, you will want to keep a record of such things as *your dreams.* Dreams are wonderful sources of subconscious information. Many artists rely heavily on their dreams for their creative work.

Observations are your day-to-day perceptions of the world around you and how you feel about things. The more descriptive you are about the things you see and feel, the more useful they might be later on.

Also, look at *your imaginary world.* We all have a fantasy life that pops in and out of our consciousness throughout the day. It can be very helpful to become aware of your fantasies on a conscious level. One way to use your imagination is to observe people and then imagine what their lives are like, where they're from, what they do for a living, and so forth.

You may find *photographs and ads* to be of use in your work. If you see an ad that interests you or triggers your imagination, paste it in your journal. If you come across a photo that brings up an old memory, paste it in your book.

Looking at *paintings* can be very useful. Sometimes we respond to other artists' works and are inspired by them. A painting of a man sitting in a bar can trigger a strong idea for a character monologue. A painting of a quiet street can remind you of the street you grew up on, which can bring up all kinds of memories that can be useful in your autobiographical monologue.

Newspaper articles can also be of value in this type of work. Today's headlines can be terrific sources for new ideas and interesting stories. Many TV and film writers rely on the daily news as fodder for new material.

Using a Tape Recorder

Some monologists prefer not to type or write out their material. For them, the tape recorder is the most efficient way to work. They just turn it on and talk, more or less the same way that writers write and typists type. One bit of advice for those of you who plan on using a tape recorder: Make certain that all the tapes are very clearly marked. You should be able to locate any section of your recorded work. It's also been suggested that at some point you have someone type out the material from the tapes. You will need a script of some sort that can be used by the production teams at the theaters in which you'll be performing.

Improvising: "Are You Talkin' to Me?"

Many actors enjoy the freedom of working totally improvisationally. If you've worked as an actor, you know that improvisation is a form of theater where no scripts are used. There are many different ways to approach and set up improvisational situations, from the highly structured to the completely freeform. The really great thing about using your improvisational skills to create a monologue is that in improv, you give your mind permission to go wherever it wants and your mouth permission to say whatever comes out. When you improvise, you ignore the tiny censor in your head that sits in judgment, criticizing your every effort. The secret to successful improvisational work is to not put any restrictions on yourself, but leave yourself open to any impulse, physical or verbal. As you start working this way, you may want to tape-record your work. To some degree, much of the work we'll be doing on monologues incorporates some aspect of improvisation.

HELPFUL BOOKS TO LEARN ABOUT IMPROVISATIONAL WORK

- *Improvisation for the Theater* by Viola Spolin (Northwestern University Press)
  This is an essential book for those who want to learn improvisational work. Spolin works with theater games, which can also be a very useful way to develop material. She was one of the founders of modern improv.

- *Impro: Improvisation and the Theatre* by Keith Johnstone (Methuen)
  This is a wonderful book for those actors who are just starting out in improvisation. Johnstone explores the "nature of spontaneity," which is essential in the work we'll be doing.

- *Improv! A Handbook for the Actor* by Greg Atkins (Heinemann)
  This book, like the other two, focuses mainly on the theatrical application of improvisation in theater. Atkins has some wonderful improv exercises and offers some very interesting tidbits. This book is recommended for the beginner as well as those with some improvisation in their background.

Working Orally: In Front of an Audience

Some solo artists prefer to live their creative lives dangerously. They like to create their work on the edge of the sword. They develop their material improvisationally each night in front of a live audience. They "riff" (improvise) or ad-lib their dialogue in character (if they're doing character work), improvising completely from moment to moment. The dialogue that their character(s) speak changes nightly; a word here, a phrase there, sometimes even long sections are totally added or subtracted from the text. After each night's performance, the artist evaluates what he's done. Based on experience (and perhaps the director's feedback), the play changes, sometimes dramatically. It's not unusual for characters to be added or dropped and entire sections to be totally reworked.

Spalding Gray always said that he preferred to develop his autobiographical material in front of a live audience (see interview). The audience in the first preview of a new Spalding Gray show would always see something quite different from the audiences that came later on. Some members of his audience would come back several times to see how the work progressed. Generally, Gray started out each show with just an outline of what he'd be talking about, and then let the piece evolve night after night. How the audience received the material each night was a factor in how it changed. His original show would sometimes be up to an hour longer than the final performances. Even after it opened, Gray said that he continued working on the material, refining it and reshaping it (but to a lesser and lesser degree) indefinitely.

Danny Hoch riffs his character monologues each night in front of his audience. He says that he knows the general subjects his characters will be talking about, their themes and ideas. But as he works in front of the audience each night, like Spalding Gray, he lets the work evolve. Also like Gray, he hones and develops material based on audience reaction. Hoch says that in his case, his director, Jo Bonney (see Jo Bonney's interview), is also a major contributing factor to his rewriting process.

Working Orally: Developing Your Stories Throughout the Day

Another way monologists develop their stories is by telling and retelling the same story to different people throughout the day. They repeat this process over a period of weeks or months. By constantly retelling the story, they hone it down, refine it, perfect it. They edit out unnecessary phrases or sections that they've noticed didn't work in prior tellings.

They bring the developed story to small audiences. They continue refining the piece, first in workshops, then during previews, right until the show's opening.

Charlayne Woodard (see interview) mentioned that for up to a year before she creates one of her solo shows, she constantly tells different people the same story, "sometimes at dinner parties, sometimes to friends on the street." Usually her stories are anecdotal recollections of her childhood with her family. She watches listeners for their reactions to the story, especially noticing any emotional response. Ms. Woodard says that she'll tell the same story dozens of times before deciding whether or not she'll actually include it in her show.

CHAPTER 5

preparing

In the beginning, there's just your will and determination. But for many actors, facing that blank sheet of paper or that empty cassette in the tape recorder can be intimidating. One thing to keep in mind when working on your own material is that the better prepared you are early on, the easier your work will be later.

For Those Actors Who Know Which Type (Style) of Monologue They Want to Create

If at this point you know the form that you want your short monologue or monologue play to take (e.g., character monologue, autobiographical narrative monologue, etc.), then look at the list below. This list can also be of use to those of you who have a specific story that you want to tell in your monologue.

The purpose of this outline is to jump-start your thinking about the piece that you'll be working on. It's just an eye opener, a preliminary look at future possibilities. We will be working on a detailed outline later on:

- Start out by listing any ideas that you now have regarding the piece. Put down whatever comes to mind, no matter how ridiculous it might seem to you. List your intentions, your goals, your dreams for the piece. Let yourself go as far as you can with this wish list.
- List any things that you feel you may need to research later on. If you're working on character monologues, list any ideas that you have for potential character material (and anything that might connect these characters).
- This is a very early phase of your work. Don't be too concerned if things go in a very different direction as you actually begin working on the piece.

For Those Actors Who Don't Know What Type of Solo Material They Want to Create

Some actors start off on a project knowing that they want to do a solo show, but they don't know what form or even what subject they'd like to explore. For those of you in this category, perhaps the following material will be of help.

Spend some time exploring, researching, opening yourself up to new ideas that may be fodder for your monologue. Take as long as you need for this research—a few weeks, months, whatever. You might also want to reread the earlier section in this book on keeping a journal. Keep the following thoughts in mind during your search:

- There's no shortage of ideas; they're everywhere, all around us, all the time.
- Keep an ongoing list of all possibilities for your piece. Don't be stingy; put down anything that comes to mind, no matter how ridiculous it may seem.
- Become a people-watcher. Go to parks and malls. Noticing how and what people are communicating to each other can inform your work tremendously, especially if you decide to develop character monologues. As you watch people, listen to what they're saying; notice what they're *not* saying. Be aware of their body language, their movement, their rhythms, even their wardrobe.
- Let your imagination run wild as you watch people. Ask yourself as many questions about them as you can think of. Who are they? Are they married? What do they do for a living? What is their family life like? What do you think their secrets are?
- Other things that you can use to inform your work: music, theater, even TV. These may be things you've always been aware of, but now your perception, your intention, your focus, is different.
- Start to search your memory. Think about what your life has been like so far. Your memories can be of great value to you in this kind of work. Some of your stories may be very funny, some embarrassing, and some very painful. Tennessee Williams, Arthur Miller, and many other great playwrights created some of their greatest works based on actual events from their childhoods. One thing that certainly makes you different from anyone else is your personal memory, your past experience.
- Try to imagine what your future will be like. Think about what you'll be doing in ten years, in twenty-five years, or longer.
- Read works by other monologists. See what types of monologues personally interest you. If someone is performing a one-person show in your area, try to see it. Also, there are several one-person shows on videotape. Spalding Gray in *Swimming to Cambodia* and Julie Harris in *The Belle of Amherst* are just a couple.

Perking with an Idea

Perhaps you've had an idea for a piece and don't yet know how you want to express it. Sometimes it's better not to do anything for a while—just let it perk. Many artists talk about an initial gestation period before they do any actual work on a new piece. This is very different from using delay tactics to avoid work. By letting an idea perk, you're trusting that your subconscious mind will collect the necessary information for you. Like little elves in the night, the subconscious instinctively knows how to gather and organize the material you've been looking for.

Looking at your dreams and keeping a journal during this time may also be very helpful.

Cheryl King, writer and performer of the solo show *Not a Nice Girl*, is a New York City producer, and teaches acting, writing, and comedy nationwide. What follows are some exercises Cheryl devised for her students. I found them interesting and hope that they may be of value to you.

Exercises to Help You with Your Solo Show, by Cheryl King

We work on what I define as the two main forms of solo show writing: direct address (monologues), in which the actor speaks directly to the audience, and enactment, in which the actor plays a scene as one or more characters.

Of the seventy exercises I created for the workshop, I have constructed a number that focus on dualism—inner forces that drive us to do the things we do. They can be utilized to work from any character's point of view, and they produce both monologues and scenes. Here are two examples:

TOPIC: FEAR AND ANGER

Most of us are unwilling to acknowledge, or at least to display, our fears. The experience of feeling fear often makes us angry.

Oral Warm-up: Tell a story in which one character's fear makes another character angry.

Writing Prep: Make lists. Create a Column A and B for each of two or three characters. In Column A, list a fear and in Column B, list the anger that would correspond to that fear. For example: Martha fears looking stupid. She would be angry with the person who witnessed her looking stupid or she would be angry at a situation she might look stupid in (like asking for information or making an assumption).

Timed Writing: *Monologue*—Character is confronted with a fearful situation and tries to talk herself through it.

Dialogue—Two characters in a scene. One of the characters experiences a fear and gets angry at the other character for witnessing it.

Scene—Event occurs that is extremely frightening to at least one of the characters. One character owns up to her fear, another one instead behaves angrily. They pay the consequences for their behavior.

TOPIC: POWER & HELPLESSNESS

Power: Does your character have it? In what way? Is she using it? In what way? Conversely, are there areas in which your character exhibits helplessness? How does it affect the character to be helpless? Is there an internal conflict? Is it repressed (buried in the unconscious)? Is it suppressed (consciously held at bay)?

Oral Warm-up: Tell a story about a moment of power.

Writing Prep: Make Lists. Create a Column A and B for each of two to three characters. In Column A, list ways in which the character has power. The character need not be fully aware of this power. In Column B, list ways in which the character feels helpless. The character's helplessness may be real or imagined. For example: Martha feels her power as the authority figure over her two children. When one of them is ostracized by other children at school, she can do nothing to alter the situation.

Timed Writing: *Monologue*—The character is in a situation where helplessness is experienced.

Dialogue 1—A situation where power is exercised by one character; the other character may or may not experience helplessness.

Dialogue 2—A scene in which the powerful character from Dialogue 1 experiences helplessness.

Deciding When to Begin

The right time to begin is obviously when you feel ready, when you know that you'll have the time to put into the work ahead of you. But perhaps out of fear, many writers procrastinate, putting off the starting date with one excuse after another. If writing your own monologue is really something that you want to do, then my advice is to just do it, just begin. It's amazing how things fall into place once you get the ball rolling.

CHAPTER 6

guidelines for creating short or audition monologues

Now that you have selected the tools you'd like to work with and have some preliminary ideas of what you think your piece will be about, let's discuss some of the technical aspects of monologue writing. As I mentioned earlier, the monologue form is a very flexible form, with flexible rules. However, since the short monologue and the audition monologue have more strictures, especially when it comes to time, I'd like to give you some of the basic rules. While rules are made to be broken, I offer these because I have found them to work.

There are several attributes that a good short monologue (audition monologue, character monologue) should include. It should generally be two to eight minutes in length. Because of its brevity, your story shouldn't be too complex or convoluted. I don't advise spending too much time on exposition in a short monologue, since it tends to drag the piece down and bore your audience. Although narrative short monologues do work, monologues that include strong, immediate dialogue and have an intense, passionate, and exciting story are generally much more effective, especially for auditions where you want to wow them.

Generally, a short monologue doesn't include too many characters. Having too many characters tends to confuse the listener. Also, it's difficult to develop multiple characters in a short amount of time.

The short monologue, like all monologues, should have a clear *beginning, middle,* and *end.* I know that this seems obvious, but by being aware of this rule and adhering to it, you'll be able to avoid structural problems while developing your piece. I'm sure you've seen monologues that seem to hop all over the place, losing the audience along the way. Or monologues that seemed to just *stop* rather than *end.* Monologues that set out to handle a large issue and then suddenly end, without sufficiently dealing with that issue, generally need a stronger middle. Each one of these three portions of your monologue must be given its due. Your sensitivity to your own material is the guiding force that allows you to know when each section has sufficiently expressed what your character(s) needs to say. In most (but not all) monologues, the main character wants to achieve some goal. In the middle section, we see him struggle to get what he wants. By the end of the monologue, he'll either get it or he won't. Generally speaking, the middle section of your monologue will dominate because it deals with action and plot development.

Your monologue should include an obstacle, an objective, and an arc. Just to clarify, an *obstacle* can be described as any obstruction, hindrance, or opposition that stands in the way of a character getting something that he wants. The character's *objective* is what he wants, what he feels he must have. (The action of a piece begins once we know what the character's *objective* is). The *arc* is the shape the monologue takes. It is the through-line from the beginning to the middle to the end. The arc is determined by the journey that the character takes to get what he wants or needs.

If you are writing a performance art piece, you still need to have a beginning, middle, and end. You want your audience to be able to somehow follow the progression of the monologue, no matter how abstract or non-narrative the piece is. Since you are not telling a story in the conventional sense, it is your job to create your own set of ground rules and structure and then to diligently maintain what you've set up. How you choose to express yourself (i.e., with dance, multimedia, music, etc.) is very much a part of the selection process of a performance artist. The canvas may be different from that of a conventional storyteller, but the challenge and demand to tell some sort of story, express some sort of message, is still the same.

Unlike a play, a monologue does not always have to have conflict in it. Strong characterization and dialogue are sometimes enough to keep the monologue interesting and theatrical. It should be able to answer the following questions:

1. **Where am I physically when I'm delivering this monologue?**
   Letting the audience know where you are (in the context of your story) is helpful in their understanding and sharing of what it is your trying to tell. In the case of autobiographical monologues, you may be back in the house that you grew up in. If you can clearly establish this location for your audience, you set a mood and bring them into your world. In some monologues, you may be acting as your story's narrator. There may be no pretense that you are in a make-believe location. You are just in the theater, telling the story of your monologue to the audience. Often, during monodramas, there is little or no scenery. It is therefore your job as the storyteller to fill the stage with images that will somehow create the world that you're trying to evoke.

2. **If I'm talking to someone in this piece, who is this person in my life?**
   The secret to dealing with this aspect is to not bog down your monologue with a lot of facts about the person you're talking to. How you

relate to them, what you're saying, and how you say it will give the audience most of the important information. Certainly some relevant facts about the relationship may be necessary. But by calling someone "Mom" or "Honey," you immediately give obvious clues about the relationship.

3. **Why am I telling this story?**

This information is central to any monologue. The audience must get a sense of why you're standing there in front of them in the first place. This need to express yourself is central to the storytelling aspect of any good monologue. The need to tell this story cannot be general; it must be specific. Your character may need to rid himself of some pain from his past, or he may have this hilarious story that he must tell someone or he'll just burst. Or it may be some profound insight that that he feels must be shared with the rest of the world, now! Whatever you select, remember, the need to tell, the urgency, should be a propelling force. Think of a short monologue as a miniature one-act play.

If the monologue that you're working on is specifically for audition material, there are certain things to keep in mind. Many of the items listed below deal mainly with the marketing aspect of audition monologues, but since the purpose of an audition monologue is largely marketing, these are significant considerations.

You should create characters that you know you're capable of playing and that are within your grasp as a writer. Take into consideration the pressure you'll be under while auditioning. *This is not a time to emotionally stretch. Work on characters that show off your best assets as an actor.* If you're not good at physical comedy or gut-wrenching emotions, don't create characters you will need to portray these things with.

While it may seem like overkill to repeat this, it is particularly important that an audition monologue have a clearly defined beginning, middle, and end. In a bare rehearsal hall, with no lights or costumes to help you, you will only have your words, your body, and your voice to indicate to the viewers when you've started performing, when you've reached the high point, and when the piece is finished. You want to indicate to the auditioners that you are professional enough to accomplish this, in a tight time slot, with no technical support.

Remember that auditioners, who often see dozens of actors, usually make these decisions quickly. You don't want to be cut off before you show your stuff. Try to keep the monologues down to about two minutes in length. (Less is more.)

You should develop an assortment of monologues, each of which will be appropriate for different audition situations. *As part of your repertoire, you should have a comedic monologue, a dramatic one, and, if you feel so inclined, a surreal or stylized one.*

CHAPTER 7

fundamentals of all good monologues

I'm listing these particular attributes here because I believe that most good monologues contain them. Before you build the bridge, I think it's always a good idea to know where it's going to go. But don't think that these are absolute or unbreakable. *The only rules that you must follow for your monologue writing are the ones that you create, that work for you.*

Good monologue plays, no matter what form they take, should have a well-defined structure, just as a good play would. Even a performance art piece that doesn't follow some of the basic rules of form should have its own truthful structure.

In his monologue play *St. Nicholas,* Conor McPherson has his character recall a chilling story of a particular night of drinking when he encountered a vampire. The story takes a narrative form. Occasionally, the man will reenact a moment with present-tense dialogue. The story has a very clear beginning, middle, and end. It builds in tension as we experience what our main character tells us about this very scary night. In some ways, this is similar to a bizarre bedtime story. We, the audience, go along with our storyteller as he takes us from one moment to the next in a kind of "and then . . ." suspense, discovering what happened next along the way. The structure (and arc) of this suspense-filled monologue is as old as storytelling itself.

In his most recent solo play, *Sexaholix,* John Leguizamo creates a series of character monologues centered around memories of his high-school gang (the Sexaholix). This gang was always on the prowl, looking for sex. His play features stories about family members, his girlfriend, and friends from his past.

You can see that these two examples, *Sexaholix* and *St. Nicholas,* employ very different styles and structures to tell a story to an audience. There is no one rule as to how a monologue must be structured. I'm constantly asked, "How should I structure my play?" The answer, quite simply, is that *the story should always dictate the form.* Let your story guide you as to the style of your piece. Some parts may be naturalistic, some parts more poetic, and some parts may even be surreal. Trust your impulses and go with your instincts. It's your play; there are no rules other than the ones that you create.

Like the short monologue, monologue plays should have a clear beginning, middle, and end. Remember: No matter what form it takes, your monologue play is a way of telling a story, and all good stories have a clear through-line.

The story that you're telling should be able to sustain interest for however long it takes to tell. This doesn't mean that you need to concern yourself solely with the entertainment value of the play. But keep in mind that there is an audience out there. *Make sure that the story you're performing is theatrical and not something that the audience could have stayed home and read. Always remember, you're writing for the theater.*

Your play, like the short monologues discussed in the previous chapter, should usually include an obstacle, an objective, and an arc. Like the short monologue, the monologue play doesn't always have to have a strong conflict for it to work theatrically, but having one can certainly be advantageous.

You may create as many characters as you want. Just be sure that each one of them is necessary to your story; you don't want to overpopulate the piece. Each character should be fully developed and different from the others.

You may have as many scenes and settings as you wish, but be sure that the audience can follow your story line.

At some point, your audience should become aware of your point of view, of what you're trying to say. I hate to say that you should have a "message" because that conjures up some sort of didactic sermon. But for any play to succeed, the audience should have some sense of why the writer took the time to create it in the first place. If you'll recall, I mentioned earlier that one of the main reasons to create your own monologue should be a need to express something that deeply concerns you. It may be a burning issue or some event(s) in your past that you need to personally resolve. The important thing is that during your monologue you attempt to come to grips with the issue or the meaning of the events. You don't have to resolve it, but you do need to at least show us why you've decided to discuss it in the first place.

John Leguizamo has said that one the of the main reasons he wrote *Mambo Mouth* and *Spic-O-Rama* was so that he could better understand his family and the neighborhood he grew up in, and share this with others.

Evan Handler wrote *Time on Fire* to reveal how we can become victims of medical bureaucracy when dealing with doctors and hospitals during the treatment of serious illness.

I feel I must once again mention that the most important thing to keep in mind is that all monologues and monologue plays must have *an interesting story to tell, a good yarn, a reason for us in the audience to want to be there in the first place.* Actors quite often tell me that they don't think that their personal story will be interesting to others. If it's truthful and heartfelt and you feel an urgent need to tell your story, you can trust that others will want to hear it.

The bottom line is that the only way you can really find out how interesting your story will be to an audience is by doing it.

To Whom Is the Character Speaking?

This is a very important question to answer when working on a monologue. Many actors, when asked why their character is speaking will answer, "Because he feels like it," or simply, "He needs to." When asked whom is the character speaking to, many actors are uncertain, and answer something like, "I guess to anyone." It is the monologue writer's job, at the very least, to provide some clues that will assist the actor in answering these questions.

One way of dealing with this is by imagining whom your character is speaking to. Is it to the actual audience in front of him? Is it to a specific character referred to in the monologue? Or is the character speaking "into the abyss"?

You must invent a dynamic character who absolutely must speak, must reveal his inner self. The character must have a powerful need to express his thoughts; that is why he is speaking.

In theater, as in real life, the words that people (or characters) say are influenced by whom they are speaking to. As an actor, you have surely discovered that what you are trying to get and whom you are trying to get it from influence your choice of actions. As a writer, you must create a character with strong, specific needs and desires. This is especially true in character-driven and narrative pieces.

Sometimes monologists place imaginary characters on the stage so that the character has someone to speak to. I strongly advise against having these imaginary characters speak back to your main character. It forces the main character to take pauses to listen, and then, quite often, waste valuable stage time repeating the questions just asked by the imaginary character. That device can become tiresome very quickly.

Questions Every Monologue Must Answer

Since monologues are stories, they must be held accountable for the basic ingredients that are true of any story. Answering the following questions in your monologue will give it detail, depth, and texture. Also, the more information you, the writer, have about what you're creating, the richer your work can be. I'm not suggesting writing information out in some factual way, but rather, being able to creatively reveal important information to your audience within the dialogue or narrative. I'm sure that as an actor, you were constantly trying to learn as much information as you could about the character you were playing. The same holds true here.

WHO?

This refers to the character. Who is he or she? You must know your character inside out. You should be able to improvise as that character if necessary. You should be able to imagine the character in situations other than the one you are presenting in your piece.

WHAT?

What problems or complications arise for this character? To make something dramatic there should be some sort of conflict, something that stirs the character to action.

WHEN?

Are we in the present, the past, or the future? What is the time of day? Is it four in the morning or three in the afternoon? Obviously these facts will affect how characters speak, move, and think.

WHERE?

What is the setting? Are we dealing with a character who lives on Park Avenue or a beggar on the street? Your audience must get a sense (preferably early on in your piece) of where they are. How does this location affect the character who is speaking?

WHY?

Through the character's dialogue, let us know why the character is saying and doing the things he is. The audience must have some sense of what motivates the character; otherwise, they will become confused and eventually disinterested.

HOW?

How does your character resolve the complication that you've set up? The way he goes about solving his dilemma or conflict is one of the main components of storytelling. Specifically, how a character resolves his problem is often an indication of whether we are watching a comedy or a drama.

About Autobiographical Monologues

Unlike fictional monologues, autobiographical ones require a somewhat different preparation. Since your life is the main source for the material, you'll need to access pertinent information from your past. Reviewing parts or all of your life for material will not only be informative to you, but can also be a source of inspiration and illumination to your audience. Sometimes the things that we consider to be the most private are in fact quite universal and can be understood by everyone in the audience.

IF YOU NEED TO JUMP-START YOUR MEMORY FOR MATERIAL

- Look through desks, drawers, and closets for any photos, letters, old diaries, old toys, or any other *memorabilia that may trigger some recollections.*
- Try to recall, in as much detail as you can, *that first romance that you thought you'd never get over.* What was it about that person that excited you? How do you feel about the experience now?
- Many people have *a turning point in their life.* Did you? Think about what your life was like before that event. How did it change afterward?
- Think about *an important job* you once had. What was important about it? How did it change you?
- Recall, as painful as it might be, *the death of someone you really cared about.* How did that affect you then? How does it affect you now?
- Think about *a relative, friend, or teacher who somehow influenced you,* changed your life in some dramatic way. What was so special about this person? How did he or she influence your life?
- Thinking about *past holidays* usually brings up memories. Was there a particular holiday that will always bring strong memories? What happened?
- There may have been *a dream that you had growing up,* something that you really wanted to do, but never got to (or perhaps did). How did that affect your life?
- At any point in your life, *have you or someone you loved been ill with some incapacitating or life-threatening disease?* What was the story surrounding that period?

As you can see, these suggestions are just memory triggers. If your monologue is about a specific period of your life, try to recall what was going on both internally and in the world around you in as much detail as you can. Recalling world events creates a context for your story.

Another thing to keep in mind is a list of the characters that you're going to include from that period of your life. Recalling the exact things that they said is ideal, but unfortunately we usually can't. But we can recall things such as what those characters wore. Try to remember every detail of their wardrobe. How their hair looked. Were they carrying a purse? Were they wearing earrings? What was their makeup like? Can you recall the smell of a specific cologne or perfume? Do you remember any specific mannerisms that they had? The way they held their head when listening to you? A look in their eyes when they ate something they liked? Their look of disapproval when they saw someone they didn't like? Try to remember any idiosyncratic things they did.

Try to remember how you felt about them back then. Have your feelings toward them changed? It's interesting how after people are gone, our feelings toward them change, sometimes dramatically. That change in feelings can be very helpful when writing about them.

Interviewing relatives and family friends can be a useful source for gathering information that you may not recall. Return, if you can, to the old neighborhoods that you grew up in. Walk around, look at familiar buildings and streets, see what it conjures up. See if people you knew still live there. Perhaps pay them a visit. Interview them if it feels comfortable and is practical to do so.

Cheryl King suggested the following approach to writing autobiographical material.

Another Way to Approach Autobiographical Material, by Cheryl King

In my experience both as a writer of my own solo show and as a director working with other solo show writers/performers, I occasionally see artists having trouble with the issue of writing about personal traumas and crises.

When writing in the first person about these issues, the author/performer often comes across as the victim. This stance does not sit well with the audience, nor is it a good approach for any performer who wishes to be a sympathetic character.

I often suggest that the writer produce a scene in which she plays both characters, herself and her antagonist, or that she write it as a narrative, but from a point of view other than her own. For instance, in my show *Not a Nice Girl*, I wrote a scene of my molestation at the hands of a cousin, not as my little three-year-old self, but from the point of view of the cousin doing the molesting, as he recounts the story to the prison shrink. This approach keeps me, the performer, from appearing on stage as the victim, and allows the audience to witness the perpetrator from a more secure point of view.

I think it is a good choice to write many of the stories in a solo show from several points of view, after which you can decide which one is the most powerful delivery vehicle to put in the final script. This "putting yourself in someone else's shoes" approach is not only good for writing solo shows, but can serve well for life in general.

A good solo show—specifically, a show written and performed by the same person (or occasionally by a very in-sync collaborative team, such as Jane Wagner and Lily Tomlin)—has the same qualities as a good play, plus a special quality produced by a virtuosity of spirit.

The lessons learned during the writing/performing/rewriting/reimagining process are more intimate, more emotionally risky, when the artist is both performer and writer. When the topic and the vehicle are the same, it's tempting to take it too personally. Add to that the often-necessary job of self-production and the situation is as fraught with complications as the planning of a wedding ceremony. Doubts set in—"My writing is better than my acting," or "I can't write a press release," or "I can't assemble the support staff or financial wherewithal to make it happen." These hazards, fears, and conflicted feelings have the power to stop the solo artist in her tracks.

Good guidance is crucial in the solo show arena. Many years ago, in my life in stand-up comedy, Rob Bartlett, a brilliant comic, told me, "When in doubt, question your delivery." It was one of the best pieces of advice I have ever received. The solo artist, creating her own text, can operate at this intersection of writing/acting in a way that is not possible for actors who are doing material written by others and who must be loyal to the text as written.

In the process of altering delivery, we find ourselves seeing clearly the ways to alter the text. This can be a very long process. It is important to be willing to continue to revise both the text and the delivery until it feels right.

These alterations in delivery heighten the value of the material, but even more importantly, they often seem to reveal or confirm some aspect of the performer's sense of self.

Storytelling Monologues

Actor Scott Robertson took the storytelling workshop led by the late Spalding Gray (see Gray's interview) at the Esalen Institute in Big Sur. Robertson recalls, "There were eight participants in the workshop. Their assignment was to 'tell a story that could engage the rest of the group.' They'd meet three times a day for eight days to tell their stories."

According to Scott, "Spalding believed that we all have a story in us. That story can be something that once happened to us, an event, something that changed our life. Or it may be our life story, what's happened to us along the way to make us become who we are today. The participants were assigned to tell their story in thirty minutes and then tell their story again in ten minutes. The purpose was for clarity, to eliminate extraneous information."

One thing Scott said he learned from his experience was that images are one of the main things that capture an audience. The more specific and descriptive you can be, the better. How you feel/felt about the event of the story that you're telling is another important thing to keep in mind. Storytelling is about saying something out loud to people who are listening. Words, images, and ideas are what we communicate to make our stories alive, vibrant, and interesting.

Narrative and Dramatic Style

I think it's important to describe the difference between narrative and dramatic writing, since both styles are interwoven throughout most monologues.

In the narrative style, a narrator (sometimes in character) *tells* a story. There is a great deal of background material with very detailed descriptions. Character, setting, and plot are developed in these detailed descriptions. Generally speaking, autobiographical monologues use more of the narrative style than other types of monologues.

In the dramatic style, *we're shown the story in strong dramatic actions, rather than told the story.* Quite often the monologist has the character start out in the middle of an action. For instance, the character may start the monologue by ranting about some issue, or appealing to the audience for something. The story is happening right there in the moment, before our eyes. While in this case there is no need to go through the beginning, middle, and end of the *narrative*, the piece itself still needs to have an *arc* to it.

Your Personal Style: Your Voice

Your "voice" is your style, your way of expressing yourself. Your voice stems directly from your sense of truth, which we spoke of earlier. It is your unique choice of words and phrases, your rhythm, the way you speak, your vision, how you tell your story. It is your trademark style. It is a major factor in determining the tone of your work. All good writers, successful monologists, and performance artists have their own distinct voice. Finding and developing your personal voice is an integral part of your work as a monologist. The trap for most beginning monologists is to try to emulate (whether consciously or not) their favorite writer's style. To avoid this happening, always stay focused on specifically what it is you want to say, on your need to tell your story, and on creating your characters exactly the way you see and feel them.

WHEN WORKING SPECIFICALLY ON CHARACTER MONOLOGUES

First, let your imagination take you inside the character's head as you see it. Stay there a while, breathe it in, live in his shoes. Imagine what it's really like to be him. Notice the differences/similarities between who you are and who he is. Notice how he thinks and feels about things. When you feel that you really know the character viscerally, let the character speak. Improvise different scenarios.

I was working on a character whom I called Lila for my book *Street Talk*. Lila danced on *Hullabaloo*, a 1960s TV show, and eventually became a go-go dancer in a sleazy bar. I'm not a woman, I never danced on *Hullabaloo*. When I started working on her, I recalled watching that TV show. I recalled thinking about what it must be like to have millions of Americans watching you dance on TV. I allowed myself to imagine a whole different world from my own. I allowed myself to feel what it might be like go-go dancing in a bar. As funny as it might seem, I danced around my apartment, pretending I was in a go-go cage. I tried to imagine what the bar must be like with men, many of them drunk, looking up at me, desiring me. The more I imagined Lila's world, the clearer the character became, and the easier it was to speak in her voice. The trap is to speak "in character" prematurely, to come from your head the way you think the character would speak. What happens then is that you create characters that are stereotypes, ungrounded, and ultimately difficult to perform.

Once you have found the character, letting him speak improvisationally, you'll find his story, what it is he has to say. Many playwrights mention that they really don't write their plays; rather, they say that the plays write themselves. Let your character lead you where he wants to go. Let your character tell the story that he wants to tell. Just get out of the way; just "play."

Always try to simplify things; bring them down to their basic truth. You can always elaborate later in rewrites. *There is nothing more boring on stage than long-winded, unnecessary narratives that could easily be stated in a line or two of dialogue.* Use the facts of what you're trying to say as a guideline for how you'll say it. Review the "Questions Every Monologue Must Answer" section of this chapter.

Even if there is a surreal, poetic, or stylized quality to the monologue that you're working on, initially try to say the lines as you would say them in your everyday life. As you become more comfortable in your monologue's style, you'll find that you're able to speak the "new language" freely, more appropriately to the style.

Once again, keep in mind that you are writing for the stage, not for a book. You don't want to become too literary, too cerebral; your audience will fall asleep on you.

To sum it all up:

- Write as you think
- Write as you feel
- Write as you speak

Examples of Different Voices and Styles

As I mentioned earlier, one of the main goals of this book is to help you find your own voice as a monologist. To give you some idea of how diversified this field is, I've reprinted some excerpts from some well-known monologists. Notice the differences in their styles. Notice their choices of words, phrases, and ideas.

From *An Evening with Quentin Crisp* by Quentin Crisp

I've been told that I equate wealth with style. I don't, but I would say this: To a physicist, money would be the solid state of style. There's no other connection between the two. And of this, also, I can give you an example.

Until recently there was in SoHo, the hooligan district of London, a woman known as "The Countess." But in spite of her imperial style, she had in fact no fixed address, no means of support, and her body was perpetually bent double from a life-long habit of looking in the trashcans to see if she could possibly find something there she could sell to a kind friend—or, if not, that she herself could use. And one day, in a trashcan in the most expensive part of London, she found a complete backless bead dress. She longed for night to fall, so that she could nip into a dark doorway and try it on. But by about half past six, her patience had worn out. It was barely twilight, but she went into a churchyard in the middle of London, and there she proceeded to take her clothes off. This caused a crowd to collect—and the crowd caused the policemen to collect. And the next day, in court, when the magistrate said, "And what exactly were you doing stripping among the dead?" she replied, "I was doing what any woman would be doing at that hour—changing for dinner."

So you see, however grandiose the style you may have chosen for yourself, you will not need any actual money to support it—and more than that, you won't even need talent.

Quentin Crisp wrote in a light, witty tone. There was a sense of polite, gentle humor in his work. His style had a relaxed eloquence. Much of what he enjoyed writing was commentary on social behavior (including his own). He told his sometimes-autobiographical stories in a narrative, anecdotal style, rarely acting out any of the characters. Mr. Crisp generally remained seated during his shows and talked directly to his audience, as if they were visiting him in his parlor.

Winfred from *Monster* by Dael Orlandersmith

I'm thinkin' of my girl Theresa. An I'm feelin' bad 'cause, you know, she ain't with me, right? I mean, you know what I'm talkin' about? Like when your woman ain't around, man. Dat's some hard shit. (beat) She write poetry and listen to classical and rock. You know 'bout that shit, right? Well, my girl, she like it too. (beat) You should see her, man, she got soft smooth skin. Yeah, an' she got much booty—I likes dat booty, man. In order for me to peep a broad she got to have some ass. Gots to. (beat) Man, ever since we wuz kids she wuz writin' poetry and stuff to me, thru the wall. Readin' thru da wall. See, the buildin' I lived in, right, her mother owned. Me, my sister Marsha, and my mother live there. And me, Theresa, an' Marsha wuz friends. Tight, like family, right? Like, I would look after dem, you know, 'cause it's rough. (beat) Like, I protect Theresa. Niggas round the way hated her 'cause she listened to rock and all that shit, and dressed different from them. But see, dey ain't know her like I did. Niggas wanted to get next to her, man—see, dat's what it wuz. And they wuz jealous, 'specially when I tole 'em how she would talk to me though the wall.

Dael Orlandersmith creates character monologues that reflect her experience as a black woman growing up in Harlem. Her language is rough and poetic. She's been called "a poetic sybarite, a black female Walt Whitman drunk with the power to pummel." Her choice of words and phrases reflects the neighborhood she grew up in. Her characters express the darker side of life. She does not attempt to make things nice. Her characters are blunt, raw. Yet there is a yearning, a need within all of her characters to be heard, to express themselves.

Craig from *Two Minutes and Under, Volume 3* by Glenn Alterman

(A loving inner monologue)

There are moments, just like this one, when your wife is fixing your tie, and you catch her eye, and she smiles. And you both look swell, all dressed up, ready to go out. You want to say, "Hey, honey, why don't we just stay home tonight? Let's forget about the party." But you don't; you let her continue fixing your tie as you smile at her like some adoring fan. And everything is perfect. And you think about your life with her. The kids, the house, the love. And you feel blessed. Feel like the luckiest guy on earth. It's at moments like this that I sometimes wonder, Why? Why, you know? Just—why? Why do I need Heidi, or Debby, or Dana? I mean, compared to this moment with her, they mean nothing. What, a quickie in a hallway, a hot time in a hotel? What's that about, really? Yeah, sure, it feels good, and the sex is great. But it's nothing, nothing compared to this moment. This is what's important in life. This, here, now. Not Nico, or Jose, or Juan. Why do I need those guys, those "hunting" weekends? Those weekends where she thinks I'm out with the guys shooting ducks. Well, I am sort of "out" with the guys. What she doesn't know is that we never leave the cabin. Yeah, sure, the sex is great. And there's things I can do with them I could never do with her. But sex isn't everything! And look at her, here, my beautiful wife. The rest, why do I need any of them? Bambi, Clint, Lacy, Walt? Why, what for?! You know, maybe, maybe, I should start cutting out some of the extracurriculars. Think of how much more quality time I'd have to spend here with her. I should stop all that stuff. I should. I will. Well . . . maybe . . . (sincerely) But for now, for now, there's just her, and me, and my tie, and this moment. And the way we're both smiling at each other. Perfect. And after she's finished, I'll kiss her, and let her know, by the look in my eye, how lucky we are, and how very, very much I love her.

This monologue is an example of an inner monologue. These monologues express a character's inner thoughts. Hamlet's "To be or not to be" speech is a famous example of a character inner monologue. One of the ways to work on the conflict in this type of monologue is to create a split in the personality within the character. The two sides then argue their points.

The style or attitude of this particular monologue is tongue-in-cheek humor. What he at first describes as the perfect marriage, we soon come to realize is nothing but a front to his self-gratifying, lustful escapades. The humor comes from how irresponsible and oblivious the character is about his infidelity.

From *An Evening with Shelly Mars* by Shelly Mars

I had a big strong jock dad. I was his girl-boy. His tomboy. I was like his girlfriend boy. I remember going by the drive-in and I said, "Dad, let's go to the drive-in and watch a movie." We always loved to sneak in places, get in free, being Jews and all. So he turned off the headlights, and we snuck through the exit. We were hanging out, and I remember a porno preview flashed on screen. It was a big blond babe getting banged from behind, by a black midget, and blondie kept screaming, "You're the best baby Daddy, baby Daddy, you're the best!" I was ten years old. Two years before Hermes. It was exciting. I remember turning into a boy. (Shelly acts this out.) My dad turned to me and said, "Ah, don't look!" I answered in a really deep voice, "Yeah, whatever."

Shelly Mars has been described as a self-styled transgender expert and drag king. Her writing is a combination of satire, reverence, and humor. Her stories are part autobiographical, part fantasy, and part sexual odyssey. She digs into her various closets and shares uncensored and provocative commentary on herself and the world around her. Her writing has a feeling of "I've been around the block, baby" and is filled with street savvy and wisdom. You can also notice a humorous, self-deprecating tone to her work. When referring to the drive-in, she says, "We always loved to sneak in places, get in free, being Jews and all." Shelly doesn't care about political correctness. Her humor is meant to constantly push the envelope.

From *Gray's Anatomy* by Spalding Gray

Ron was marrying us. He had joined the Universal Church of God in Fresno, California, for thirty-five dollars. We had written the ceremony together, and he spoke it beautifully, ending with, "May this couple be together for as long as they both shall love."

We run down to the sea together to look out, and then we went back to the house to celebrate.

I drink vodka and I drank white wine and I ate big fish.

I ate steamed vegetables and I ate wedding cake. I drank coffee and I smoked a cigar. I drank brandy.

And I ate and I drank and I smoked . . . everything that could make me blind. Thank you for coming.

Since the first edition of this book, Spalding Gray has passed away. Mr. Gray was a world-famous monologist and a personal friend of mine from our days at Emerson College in Boston. He directed me in a couple of shows there. Spalding was a unique, intelligent, extremely sensitive, and, unfortunately, tortured man. His monologue work was extremely cathartic for him, as it is for many artists.

Spalding Gray wrote autobiographically. He told his highly personal stories in what he called his "neurotic, ironic, nonathletic voice." His monologues were a way for him to confront his personal demons of neurosis, immaturity, and mistrust. You'd get the impression that he was sitting directly across from you at a table talking, which indeed is what he did when he performed his shows.

Gray was a storyteller, and his views about his life were the stories that he told. He didn't attempt to act out his characters, but let you get to know them through his very descriptive storytelling. He uses strong images and descriptive narrative phrases. His stories work on multiple levels, with seemingly unrelated stories coming together as a whole. Notice particularly his use of tense, both past and present (within the same sentence). It reveals how he saw that particular moment in his mind.

Cudjoe from *The Sun and the Moon Live in the Sky* by Ellen Lewis

Miss Money, she had these children and she name them all some sort of money, she had Little Money and Little Bit of Money, and Lotsa Money, the oldest name, Money.

She didn't always have these children. She was poor once.

But she know children will work hard, and she will be rich, but she didn't know nothing bout havin' children, so she went to Miss Story.

(Imitating MISS STORY)

Miss Money, what brings you here, you wish someone made away with, turned into, snake, frog, worm, something of that order?

(Imitating MISS MONEY)

Oh, nothing like that, Miss Story, I wish children.

(Imitating MISS STORY)

Children, oh, that's an easy one. I'll make you all the children you wan—he can do that, you know. Go home, you have children, but you must treat them right, or you lose them.

She says, "All right, Miss Story," and so went home. She gets home, and you should have seen, she had a whole house full of children, they all ran and hugged her and even called her Mommy.

(Imitating MISS MONEY)

There was More Money and Money Money Money—they were twins. A Whole Lotta Money, Money is the oldest, and Little Bit of Money, the youngest.

Oh, she enjoyed them children so . . .

(Imitating MISS MONEY)

I have More Money and Money, Money, Money—they are twins. A Whole Lotta Money, Money is the oldest, and Little Bit of Money, the youngest. I live on the most beautiful land of all. So we play. I throw them up in the air, toss them around, and have a good ole time. I get hungry but I don't pay that no mind. The land, it will give us food. I get too hungry to work the land, so I sell a piece to feed my children. Then I sell another, and we play, then I sell another piece of land, and we play. We play and play until no more land to sell. I know—Money, she's strong and I sell her off to another's land. "That will keep us," I said. Famine knocks on the doo'—all around, the whispers become dark. We ignore the knocks and go on playing some more. While we play, Famine shows up. I get scared. "What you want? Shoo, shoo, Famine, shoo," but Famine, she just stands there. I don't know what to do, so I give her More Money and Money Money Money, the twins. Famine takes Money Money Money and More Money away, but come back and just stand there some more. I give her Money Money; she's my favorite. "Here, take her," I say. That seems to satisfy Famine, 'cause she leave so's I could go on playing with my Little Bit of Money. I cry and play and cry and play and cry. A Little Bit of Money will take care of me, I know. Famine knocks again. This time I trick Famine and for sure get away. I say this to A Little Bit of Money. I look in the closet—I find a bottle of wine that I save for special occasions. I put music on the radio, I set the table nice, I bring out the bottle of wine, I toast, "to your health, to your health, to your health, and to your health again."

The bottle empties and Famine lay in a stupor across the table. I take A Little Bit of Money and run.

We walk up the road and down the road, up the road, down the road. I can't get away from the cries in the wind.

The Sun and the Moon Live in the Sky is a play about African American community, solidarity, traditions, cultural knowledge (its acceptance/denial), and most importantly, the healing power of memory and ritual. It captures a young girl's journey into the Sea Islands of South Carolina. This monologue is one of many fables told within the play. Heavy, stubborn, egotistical attachment to the material leads to famine of the soul. Cudjoe, who is experiencing his own transformation in the play, expresses his thoughts in this monologue.

From *Safe* by Taylor Mac

I'm safe. I'm not safe. I'm a New Yorker. I'm from California. This is my home. Home is where the heart is. My heart is here. Except in the winter. I hate it in New York in the winter. And the summer. It smells like cat piss in the summer. The spring, then? There is no spring here. Fall? Then the holidays are coming. I should move back to California. But the North Koreans. The North Koreans can reach California. I should go someplace safe. Someplace central. Someplace landlocked. Someplace where they like drag queens and gay rights and tranny rights. I'm a tranny. I'm a fag. I'm a boy. I'm a man. I'm an artist. I clean toilets. I love you. No I don't. I want to have sex with you. No you want to have sex with me. I want to make a life with you. You're too old, I'm too young, I'm too old, I'm overeducated, I'm undereducated, I AM HAVING A BAD DAY, it's such a beautiful day, MY ASS IS BLEEDING! I had beats. Call me, no don't call me I'll call you. Can we see each other again? I don't know, how should I know, I have to make oatmeal every morning in case my stomach lining should one day be diminished, DON'T YOU UNDERSTAND? We won the war! The war is over. It's still going on. It's a new enemy.

It's the old enemy. It's the old and the new enemy. We are the enemy. We are freedom. You can't make me sing that fucking anthem. What about the Kurds? What about the Palestinians? What about the Pakistanis? What about the Israelis, the Indians, the Mexicans, the grapes, there's too many pesticides on the grapes. CESAR CHAVEZ WAS A PEDOPHILIAC. GHANDI BEAT HIS WIFE. MARTIN LUTHER CHEATED. CLINTON CHEATED. I CHEATED. You can't go to work, I must go to work, you can't go to work, I must go to work. HOW MANY PEOPLE HAVE DIED WHILE YOU'VE BEEN TRYING TO GO TO WORK? I DON'T KNOW. HOW SHOULD I KNOW? I JUST WANT TO WASH GLITTER OUT OF MY ORIFICES. IS THAT TOO MUCH TO ASK FOR? IS IT? IS IT?

Taylor Mac's performance art work is primarily a response to and an exploration of homogony in western culture. Combining music, spoken word, and elaborate gender-bending costume designs, he creates full-length solo and collaborative productions that juxtapose stream-of-conscious images from such topics as the masculine "War on Terror," white appropriation of black culture, and patriarchy in romance. By showing the duality of human beings, Taylor provides a balance to our adoration of sameness. *Safe* is about fear and the conflicting mental acrobatics individuals go through when overcome by the "War on Terror." Simple daily stresses and issues of love are placed alongside thoughts of war because, the author believes, physical conflict stems from our fears of a life without love and happiness. The piece is a plea for joy.

Sam from *Jails, Hospitals & Hip-Hop* by Danny Hoch

(A corrections officer in his early thirties sits in the waiting room of an upstate New York psychologist.)

Hi, hello. How are you? . . . Who are you? Oh, you're Doctor Lemmings? Yeah, hi hello. Sam Knoll. Oh, I thought you were the secretary? Oh, that's cheap. I mean, that's smart, save money, I don't want to get into a whole thing. So you're the doctor? Great. . . . No, I mean, women doctors, they exist, I don't wanna, ya know . . . go there. . . . Oh, you're not finished? You're still with a patient? Well, I mean . . . I'm here! On time. I want you to mark down that I arrived for the session on time, because I went out of my way to be on time. . . . No, that's all right. I mean, what am I gonna do? You gotta do what you gotta do, I'll . . . I'll make a phone call. . . . No, that's all right. I got my own, thanks.

Danny Hoch writes character monologues. He has the rare ability to represent people as they really are. He gets inside of his characters' heads and shows their souls with compassion and humor. Many of his characters are angry, street-wise misfits. The dialogue in this piece is conversational, urban. This monologue concerns a corrections officer who is under psychiatric evaluation for roughing up a prisoner but is most worried about his child visitation rights following his broken marriage. Notice Hoch's use of dialogue. Notice the dialogue he uses to reveal things about this particular character. Lines like, "Yeah, hi hello. Sam Knoll." The dialogue is succinct, with no wasted words. Or, "I mean, what am I gonna do? You gotta do what you gotta do." You can sense the type of person who's speaking by the way that he speaks, his exact choice of words.

From *Time on Fire* by Evan Handler

One month after Dr. Nixon's diagnosis, I came walking down the hallway of Sloan-Kettering's twelfth floor. Earlier that day some bone marrow had been taken from the back of my hip to be examined and checked for any leukemia. If the marrow was clean, then I could go home, take a month off, before moving on to rounds two and three, known as "Consolidation Chemo."

In the room when I got there were Dr. Klaus and my parents. I tried my best to mask my awareness of what I was asking, and I faced Dr. Klaus and said, "Good news?"

"Yeah. Pretty good."

"What do you mean, 'Pretty good'? Is it in remission, or what?"

"Yeah, yeah, I'd say we have a very young, new, remission marrow. Don't get your hopes up too high, though. Still a long way to go." Then he added, "You know, that was one of the easiest inductions I've ever seen here."

I couldn't tell if he was congratulating me on a job well done, or telling me, "You just wait. We're gonna get you next time around."

Evan Handler's autobiographical monologue is a brutally frank and blisteringly angry account of his experience of having cancer and dealing with the medical establishment that treated him.

Mr. Handler has a novelist's eye for detail. Although he mainly writes in the narrative form, he pops in and out of present-tense dialogue, reen-acting short scenes, and then immediately returns to the narrative (which is the main form for his text). His use of the short-scene vignettes gives the piece an "in the moment" reality.

One thing that is just touched on in this short selection is Handler's sense of humor. His use of humor makes this harrowing tale of cancer and hospital bureaucracy a very real and life-affirming story.

From *Comedy You Can Dance To* by Kate Clinton

So I've been living in New York, which is a fine thing, except that my big concern is that the Ed McMahon's Publishers Clearing House people would not be able to find our house. I didn't know if they went to apartments.

This was an interesting thing I found out in couple's therapy. I'm now going to couples therapy, with my partner of course, because it would be silly otherwise. It's interesting because I'm now doing everything that I've always made fun of in my routines—except for guys, of course.

Our therapist is wonderful. She's a brilliant therapist, but the big problem is, and I'm not complaining, she has a wandering eye. One eye goes off to the side. Now, that is just not good in couple's therapy. We never know who she's really talking to. Our biggest fights are after therapy, when we say, "Oh, well, when she said that nice thing she was looking right at me." I have actually found myself in therapy, leaning way to the left, trying to get in her sight line. I found out in therapy that my partner actually fills out the map to our house so that Ed McMahon and the "prizemobile" could better find us on the great prize-rewarding day. I was shocked because she believes that statistically, at some point, Ed McMahon has to go to a gay household. Unless they're presorting by zip codes. You know, West Hollywood, no way! Provincetown, good-bye! I would love to see them open the door sometime on some square-bottom dyke, wouldn't you? Or open the door on some fabulous queen who's just, "Blaaaaah!!! Oh, God, we can redecorate!"

Kate Clinton writes about life in the gay and lesbian scene as well as poking fun at the rest of society as she sees it. There is a sunny subversiveness to her material. Much of it is personal and anecdotal, and includes one-liners and even some jokes. She writes in a seemingly free-associating style, using language with an admirable precision.

From *Full Gallop* by Mary Louise Wilson and Mark Hampton

(SHE CROSSES TO PHONE, CAREFULLY PICKS UP RECEIVER, AND LISTENS. THEN:)

Françoise!—I'll take this, Yvonne . . . Comment ça va? . . . Je suis arrivé!

Early this morning . . . Oh, it was glorious. Just glorious. London, Milano, Madrid, Paris . . . No trouble with customs, no, but I did have a bit of a set—to getting off the plane . . . Well, the stewardess attacked me with a Kleenex. "Here dearie, you've gone and got lipstick all over your ears!" Very efficient, these little steward . . . Oh, I'm tip-top! . . . Mmmm, really . . . I know, but I'm over it . . . It was ghastly. But I moved on . . . (SHE DISCOVERS A PACK OF LUCK-IES BEHIND THE CUSHION WITH TWO CIGARETTES IN IT)

Listen, you got my message? You're coming to dinner tonight? I realize it's short notice, but Va-Va Adlerberg will be here, and I've got a rather important party coming . . . Nubar Gulbenkian. You remember him?

Always wore a green orchid in his lapel. . . . Awful, yes . . . I'll tell you all about it when I see you, but right now I have to ring off. I have to keep the line clear. I'm expecting his call . . . the New York Post . . . about me? . . . . Really . . . Well I'm not terribly curious. Why, is it vile? . . . Well, I won't. I never read that rag. . . . Around eight. Yup. Can't wait to see you! (SHE HANGS UP, GOES TO INTERCOM.)

Demeyer! Baron Demeyer. That was the photographer I couldn't think of. Yvonne?

(VOICE OVER)

(Oui)

Where did you put that copy of the New York Post*?*

(VOICE OVER)

(Les Cigarettes)

Oh, the cigarettes, right. Now listen, the flowers have arrived, and . . . have you got ten dollars on you? (THERE IS A TINY PAUSE)

(VOICE OVER)

(Oui)

Give it to Lorenzo, he gave ten to the boy. (SILENCE.) *And I'll reimburse you later.* (SILENCE.) *Merci.*

There's no such thing as a slack French farce. Have you ever noticed this? I've given this a lot of thought, and I think it's because the French have to exercise their jaws so much and the insides of their mouth just to get the words OUT. Say "Bonjour" and see what your face does. (HOPEFULLY, THE AUDIENCE DOES) *Now. Try "Hi."*

The best thing about my life in London was Paris. I adored Paris. I adore it! I adore it! I was born in Paris. Did I tell you that? And you don't get born in Paris to forget about clothes for five minutes. I was always going there for my clothes. I was MAD about clothes, and makeup and everything.

In the case of *Full Gallop*, the actress Mary Louise Wilson collaborated with writer Mark Hampton on a one-character play based on a previously published book, *D.V.*, about the life of fashion legend Diana Vreeland.

Ms. Wilson and Mr. Hampton worked on this play for several years, workshopping it all over the country before bringing it to New York and later London (where it received rave reviews).

Diana Vreeland was a formidable force in the fashion world from the 1940s until the 1970s. Ms. Wilson's Vreeland speaks to the audience as if they were guests in her living room. What she and Mr. Hampton have caught in their dialogue (and in the play) is the essence of Diana Vreeland.

From *I'm Breathing the Water Now* by Bashore Halow

Because I'm lonely, Mr. Riley! I'm lonely! Do you understand that? You had a wife. You had a good long marriage to her. What do I have? I'm in my forties. My forties! And all I have to show for it is a tiny one-bedroom house, that I rent, that I don't even own, for God's sakes. You have children. Sure they're grown and gone now, but still they're there. They are someone to have Thanksgiving with, to have Christmas with, or maybe even to send you a card. I have a used car and lawn full of dandelions and what do you think it's like at Christmas time when all you get in the mail is a blank letter that every other blank person gets asking them for a donation to the Red Cross or to Easter Seals or whatever the hell you call it? So he's not Mr. Perfect. He is not a steady job holder. And yes, he doesn't cut his hair and he is not the best . . . or the better or even a good boyfriend, but he is all I have. What do you think I'm made out of? How do you think it is possible for me to hold, every day, the hands of people who die and stay strong through that, to watch that and then go home . . . to that home . . . to that life? You've seen one death. I've seen hundreds. I sit there. I don't even help because I'm not called until all hope is gone. I just watch. Just . . . referee the last little bit. Afterwards everyone cries. They are not tears of relief. It is not put on. It is genuine, rock-bottom sadness. It is living a horrible, answerless truth. And then you know what I do? I get my coat, five years old now, and my shoulder bag, and I get into my nine-year-old car and I drive home, where I turn the light switch on to the living room of my rented house; where I sit in front of the TV and figure out something to have for dinner.

Bashore Halow's naturalistic, touching monologue immediately brings us into the character's lonely and desperate world. We learn of her frustration, how she lives her life, the kind of woman she is, what she does for a living, and how she copes. The monologue begins as a poignant plea to her boss for his understanding about her situation.

From *The Finger Hole* by ty adams

I got out of town recently. Had to. I went up to the Catskills.

Had no idea where I was going . . . just pointed a finger at an ad in the newspaper, and went. But all I did when I got there was think about my life back in New York, my therapy, the unfulfilling home for my anger, the anxiety-driven energy of the city, an almost Dickensian bureaucratic inertia that hangs over the struggle . . . ya need a place to take this emotional weight and I didn't go to Crunch and bond with my sweat, so therapy was my place. With Dr. Nichols was my place. He was my Crunch and together we bonded with my sweat but on that day, a coupla months ago, THAT DAY he got off on my misery . . . well, it all changed. He might as well've trained a hot-white beam of light on a glass of milk and let it sit on the window sill for the afternoon. No glass of milk could take that. Ruined milk, that's what you get.

So I went up to the Catskills. Sunny Oaks. No sun. One oak. And it didn't take long for Sunny Oaks to turn into Rainy Oaks. Toward the end, the rain was so hard, it pelted the roof like baseballs. I'm sitting on the edge of my bed, crying, that wasted, self-pity crying. I was so pathetic in my effort to continue crying that I found myself trying to keep up with the rain . . . so silly, trying to cry at the pace of a hard, long mountain rain. I so much wanted to be amazing. Do something in life, amazing. Wouldn't it be amazing if I could keep up with the rain . . . well, I wasn't amazing.

I turned out to be an average crier. The rain turned out to be amazing.

It completely defeated me and without pause, soothed me, consoled me, and could've seduced me that night. The next day, the rain had stopped and I suddenly felt the courage to ask for a ride into town. The impossible had become possible. I was coming back.

In this monologue, Martha, a manic depressive, has returned to New York City from a three-month disappearance and explains her cathartic journey to an unsuspecting patient waiting to see his therapist. The way the dialogue unfolds, we immediately are drawn into the slightly off-kilter world of the character. The way she expresses herself, her description of things, the way she opens up to a stranger in a doctor's waiting room, all tell us about who she is. The piece is conversational, but the style has a certain elevated, poetic quality to it.

From *A Kiss to Build a Dream On* by Joe Pintauro

(Charlotte is Boomer's mistress)

I know he's using me. You think I don't know he's using me? But would you use me? No. What reason would you have to use me? But him, his wife is dying. The twenty-five-year love of his whole life is about to go off the cliffs into oblivion and you don't stop loving people who are gonna die. You love them more. But sex scares him with her, love scares him with her. That's why he runs to me. He's running from the biggest love of his life and the biggest grief of his life. He hides inside me. So I became Miss Sloppy Seconds on a 5 percent hope that he sees something in me I never saw in myself, couldn't see in myself even if it was there. Maybe it's nothing, just me being there, being there, being there. You know, he's not ashamed to cry in front of me. Is he gonna cry in front of her? I'm the one puts up with his narcissism, his whining, and for that alone he'll probably turn around and marry me, out of . . . I don't know, fear of living? You know, he's gorgeous. On the outside in spades, but his broken heart made him gorgeous in his chest, in here, and I'm the one who puts my head on that chest, so don't tell me he's using me. So don't even think I don't love him. It's glued to my insides, it burns in here, and I let it burn a hole right through me. There's nothing anywhere near like him ever gonna cross my path. If he takes off, what happens to an anybody like me? I stay what I am. An anybody who has nobody. And don't tell me I don't sound like myself anymore. I don't wanna sound like myself. Don't wanna be myself. I'm desecrating my innocence. You're absolutely right. It's so obscene and degrading, it's killing me, and I say, let it. You said I should love myself, like that's enough? You can get by on loving yourself? You tell me I should come first. That is bullshit. That doesn't work. You lose that way. You lose everything. Don't you know that? So it's no news that he's using me. You know what I say? Thank God he's using me. Okay? Thank God.

In this naturalistic monologue, we immediately get to understand the character's dilemma and how she feels about it. The passion of her feelings and upset are clearly expressed in the dialogue. Her pain at her predicament is made very clear by the playwright's words.

CHAPTER 8

using your acting technique to create character monologues

Since this book is a book for actors who wish to write their own material, I feel that it's necessary to explore certain acting approaches that can assist you. Generally actors are trained to work internally, that is, from the inside out, or externally, from the outside in. Either approach, or both of these approaches combined, can be helpful in developing fully realized characters for your monologues.

Working from the Outside in, as an Actor and Writer

Many actors, especially those who have studied the British technique for character development, work externally at first. Actors are informed about their characters by focusing on the character's age, speech mannerisms, appearance, and physicality. Actors gather information on these things from the dialogue in the play, the stage directions, and the action.

A CHARACTER'S AGE

A character's age quite often determines what he will think, feel, and do. It affects his behavior to some extent, perhaps what he'll be saying in the monologue and in his dialogue. The way the character views the world, his perceptions, are also based on his experiences in life. Younger characters will usually react differently to situations than older ones.

A CHARACTER'S VOCAL MANNERISMS

A character's vocal mannerisms can be very revealing. Characters who have a speech impediment, or who speak excessively slowly or quickly, or who hesitate while speaking, tell us quite a bit about who they are by the way they talk. Many of these vocal mannerisms can be indicated in your stage directions.

BODY LANGUAGE

A character's body language begins with the way the character holds himself. Look around and you'll notice how people in the real world walk and move. Their physicality tells you a great deal about them. If they walk stoop-shouldered, head down, eyes to the floor, it's a reliable indication of something about their personality. If someone holds his head high, chest out, looks straight ahead, with a warm smile on his face, that tells us something else about him, doesn't it? A character's physical attributes can be a great aid in helping to trigger the imagination. It's a useful tool that you shouldn't overlook in developing your character monologues.

THE CHARACTER'S APPEARANCE

A character's appearance tells us a great deal about him. A homeless person certainly looks different from a member of royalty. Does your character seem proud of the way he looks? Is he unkempt, a slob? Is he out of touch with how he looks? How does the way the character looks affect his behavior? Your character's outer appearance can be handled in your stage directions. Quite often in an evening of character monologues, the actor and director will choose not to change wardrobe during the play because of time restrictions. Sometimes something as simple as a hat, a scarf, or a jacket can suggest all that is needed. Eric Bogosian and Danny Hoch (see interview) dress in black pants and black T-shirts and don't change costumes during their shows. We learn about their characters by the way they move, their physicality, how they speak, and most importantly, what they say.

Working Internally as an Actor and Writer

Many actors in America are trained in internal or psychological acting techniques. The Actors Studio, using the famous "method technique," bases a great deal of the work on the actor's personal life and his inner responses to the character he is working on. Prior to having a character, writers can use some of these exercises to trigger their imagination to create one. This is, once again, like going to the other side of the mirror. Writers can use some of the method techniques and exercises, and then combine what they discover with some improvisation work and imagination. By working sensorially, using their own memories, and then adding their imagination to the stew, writers can create all sorts of characters from a very personal place. Writers working this way aren't working from their head, but from their inner experiences and memories.

THE CHARACTER'S ACTIONS

Continuing to work internally like this, the writer can imagine how the character he's developed would respond in different situations. *The character's actions can be created by deciding on an active present-tense verb.* Writers must decide when creating (as do actors while rehearsing) what the character is doing (specific actions) at particular moments in the piece.

THE CHARACTER'S INTENTIONS

The character's intentions reveal what motivates the character, what he wants. Active verbs such as "I cherish" or "I regret" can reveal what the character wants at different times during the monologue or during the course of your monologue play. As you may recall from some of your acting classes, knowing the characters' needs and knowing what motivates them is key to knowing how to play them. Knowing their needs is the first step to discovering what actions you must take to satisfy those needs. This idea holds true for creating the characters on paper. Deciding what your character wants and what his goals are is the driving force in creating a fully realized character.

THE CHARACTER'S BIOGRAPHY

A character's biography tells you about your character's history. It can also reveal some of the motivating forces underlying your character's behavior. Actors/writers create in-depth biographies of the characters they're working on to give them deeper, more detailed information. The more you know about the character you're creating, the more you can reveal in the dialogue that you're writing. The way to find out biographical information on a character is by asking yourself as many questions as you can concerning the character. For instance:

- Where and when was I born?
- Did I have a happy childhood? What was it like?
- What were my parents like?
- What kind of house and neighborhood did we live in?
- How old was I, and what was it like the first time I fell in love?
- When was the first time I had sex? What was it like?
- What dreams do I remember from my childhood?

One key question that can conjure up all kinds of possibilities for your work is, "What if . . .?" Perhaps you're familiar with working on this question as an actor. The great acting teacher Konstantin Stanislavski used to require that his acting students answer a series of "What if . . ." questions while working on a character for a play. It was a way of allowing actors to imagine themselves in their character's shoes.

For instance, for work on *Romeo and Juliet*, the actor might ask himself, "What if I were a prince who lived in Italy hundreds of years ago? And what if one day I fell in love with my father's worst enemy's daughter?" As you can see, these "What if . . ." questions are meant to fan the imagination. They allow you to wander away from your everyday world, into the imaginary world of the characters you're creating.

Asking yourself a series of "What if . . ." questions can help you develop themes for the monologue that you're working on. It can help you create deeper, more complex characters and give you ideas for situations that may be useful for your monologue. It's a form of theatrical role-playing that can get you into the situation that you're exploring. You'll find that you can jump-start a story, develop a character, or even create an entire monologue by using the "What if . . ." technique. Be adventurous and daring with your "What if . . ." questions. Don't censor or reject answers to your "What if . . ." questions because they momentarily might seem to have little value for the monologue you're working on. Let them take you as far as it can, and then, if necessary, later on, go back and rewrite.

Once your imagination has opened the door with "What if . . ." questions, continue your story by asking, "And then . . .?" As with the "What if . . ." technique, see where the "And then . . ." takes you. In the "What if . . ." phase, you set up an inquiry, an examination; you open up to an exploration. With "And then . . ." you continue on your imaginary road, following your own lead, taking yourself wherever your imagination wants to go. These two phrases, when used together, can be very helpful tools in triggering the imagination.

CHAPTER 9

starting
to write

Webster defines "inspiration" as "To breathe in; to arouse; communication of ideas from a supernatural source."

Two Scenarios

After you've done all the preparation and are ready to work, you may find yourself experiencing one of the two following scenarios.

SCENARIO 1: FREE FLOW, OUT IT COMES, I'M OFF, WHEEEE!!!

Some of you, from the very get-go, will find yourself filling yellow pads or tapes with exciting material. You may be shocked at how much you have to say, how the material is just flowing out of you. You have suddenly discovered a floodgate opening, dialogue pouring out, characters emerging that you never even knew existed.

To some degree, that was my experience when I first started writing character monologues about twelve years ago. Each morning when I sat down to write, I was amazed at how much came out. It was a nonstop roller-coaster ride for many months. What amazed me at the time was that I was an actor; I thought of myself only as an actor. I'd never really written anything before, certainly not creatively. Where was all of this coming from? Who was this person sitting on my couch, writing in such a frenzy? That writing spree went on day after day for nearly six months. During that time I developed dozens of character monologues, which eventually led to the publication of my first book, *Street Talk: Character Monologues for Actors*.

If that happens to you when you first start out, my only advice is: Work every day for as long as you can. *Don't stop!* Keep going, every day! Also, don't throw anything away; file everything. If you're working on a computer, store everything. Congratulations, you've won the creative lottery. Enjoy it for as long as it lasts.

SCENARIO 2: HELP, I'M BLOCKED! THIS WRITING THING ISN'T WORKING!

Unfortunately, this second scenario also occurs to some just starting out (as well as experienced writers). Nothing seems to be happening. Nothing. Getting started feels futile. You're frustrated, bored, restless. You begin questioning your talent, your capability. You wonder why you're even bothering. You have all the symptoms of writer's block. It's a feeling that nothing is happening or probably ever will happen. It can happen to anyone, at any time, but probably is most unsettling to those just starting out, who don't quite know the lay of the land yet. It's nothing to be alarmed about. Don't give up! It's not fatal, you won't die, don't panic. It's just a temporary condition. This too shall pass.

Understanding Writer's Block

Sometimes, to get to the really good creative stuff, or even get started, you have to clean out the exhaust pipe. Think of how, in a car, the exhaust pipe needs to be free to allow smoke and fumes out. It should never be blocked. Well, sometimes our creativity feels like a blocked exhaust pipe. And the harder we try to force the smoke out, the worse it seems to get. We are plagued with doubts and negative thoughts, such as: Who's going to care about this, anyway? Am I really good enough? All artists deal with doubts like these all the time. I'm sure that you've dealt with them as an actor. Eventually you will learn to live with your doubts, and you will realize that self-censoring and insecurities are all part of the creative process.

One solution to the problem of writer's block is to realize that to get "there" (wherever it is you're hoping to go, creatively) you have to start with "here." And "here" is the room that you're in, with nothing on that paper, nothing on that tape, and no energy. You have to allow and accept the present moment. You have to live with the frustration that, indeed, nothing is happening. Just acknowledge it, try to live with it, and, when you're ready, move on.

An image that's been used to describe being creatively blocked is "rocks in front of a cave." It may seem like there are some huge boulders blocking some magical creative cave. If only I could get behind those rocks, you think, I just know, *just know* there's some good creative stuff inside that cave. If only . . . if only . . .!

One of the great creative jokes is that sometimes the rocks that seem to be blocking the creative entranceway are, themselves, pure creative gold, the very stuff you've been looking for. But with all the effort to create, you didn't realize, couldn't see their value. They are the starting point! What I'm saying is that you have to start where you are. Start in the exact moment/place of your frustration or anger. What does that feeling do to you? What does it look like? How does it sound? Put it into words, write it down, put it into the character you're trying to create.

It all boils down to this: Don't work too hard and try to be easy on yourself, especially in the beginning. Once you get started the momentum will pick up, and soon you'll be on your way. Remember, whatever you go through, it's all part of the creative process, your creative process. When creating, trying to create, nothing's ever wasted.

Techniques for Dealing with Writer's Block

- Some writers say that just writing anything, even copying a page word for word out of a book or magazine, is one way that they get back into the groove of writing.
- Some monologists will go see another monologist's or playwright's work. They say that just being in a theater and seeing good material can be quite inspiring.
- Keeping a pad around to jot down a thought or line of dialogue can also be a helpful aid during writer's block. One strong thought or image or some great line of dialogue can be just the trigger to get started.
- When working on a piece, some monologists purposely end each day's work in the middle of a sentence or thought. When they return the next day, they can pick up the thread of where they left off and not have to look at an empty page.

Nothing, a Whole Lot of Nothing

And if all else fails and you find yourself sitting with writer's block, enjoy it. There's absolutely nothing wrong with just staring at the ceiling for a while. Yes, you read correctly. Stare at the ceiling, or perhaps move those books around on the bookshelf (for the twelfth time), or give in to any slight diversion from doing your work. Meander, let your mind go, mentally wander. Yes, go ahead and avoid writing. Let yourself off the hook, obligation-wise. While sitting there, perhaps feeling frustrated, let your mind go wherever it wants. Give yourself permission to daydream, fantasize. This is one of the few times in life that it's not only okay, but perfectly appropriate. Remember back when you were in school and were bored? Back then you'd daydream all the time. What I'm talking about here is volitional daydreaming. Back in school, no one ever had to give you permission to let your mind wander, right? It was an escape from the boredom. If you're feeling blocked, there's nothing wrong with some creative avoidance.

There's something very freeing about doing nothing, experiencing nothingness. Samuel Beckett wrote brilliant existential plays about nothingness. Larry David, the creator of the TV show *Seinfeld*, proved that something about nothing could become very popular (and lucrative). Perhaps, just perhaps, in the middle of your daydreaming, you may find a thought, a word, or a memory that stirs you to action; perhaps not. Let yourself off the hook and go fishing mentally.

Writing about Painful Events

One form of writer's block occurs when writers try to write about painful events from their lives that are still affecting them. You can't force yourself to write about something that is still too painful. Sometimes you have to wait until you have a manageable distance from the event to be able to exorcise it artistically. As with acting, writing should be organic. There must be a willingness and readiness to deal with the things that you want to express. Sometimes you just have to put those traumatic experiences on the back burner until you can find the right perspective.

Free-Writing: An Invaluable Exercise

Free-writing is probably the best way I know to start out on a new project. It can also be helpful in curing that writer's block. Free-writing is a method by which you put your pen to paper and write nonstop for at least ten minutes. It's a method for generating new ideas. With this method, you allow ideas to lead you (rather than the other way around). When it's working well, one idea will ignite another. You'll be amazed at what and how much you have to say. This method is about quantity, not quality. This exercise is about first thoughts, impulses, anything that comes to mind. Quite often we squelch our impulses. This exercise helps you free yourself from that tendency. The only purpose of this exercise is to *keep writing nonstop for ten minutes*!

RULES TO FREE-WRITING

- Write as quickly as you can.
- Allow yourself to totally lose control while working.
- Don't stop to censor or revise anything.
- Don't stop to figure out what you've written; don't analyze it. Don't attempt to think or get logical about the words you've written.
- Pay no attention to spelling, grammar, or punctuation.
- Write all over the page; don't be concerned about margins or even the lines on the page.
- If you can't think of anything to write, then write about that.
- Don't cross out anything you've written.
- If something comes up that is embarrassing, painful, or frightening, quickly write it down.
- Take a sentence from what you've written, put it on the top of a page, then write for ten minutes about that sentence, using it as a topic sentence.

TAPE-RECORDER USERS

Those of you working with tape recorders, adjust the exercise to nonstop talking (riffing). You can do this either standing or sitting, but most actors I know say they like to move around. The energy of working like this can take you all over the room. Just go with any impulse that you have. You're not allowed to revise or censor anything.

BENEFITS OF FREE-WRITING

Free-writing instills discipline. It's a productive way to work through fears and anxieties about creating new material. Some writers use this method as a daily warm-up exercise before starting work on their piece. When you're working under pressure, it can jump-start you into your day's work. Free-writing is also a useful tool that can give you ideas, help you learn to write effortlessly, more spontaneously. It can help to turn off that self-censoring device that can be destructive, especially in the early stages of creating. By using free-writing, you can train yourself to set deadlines and learn how to access that special energy that you need to meet them. It helps you learn to trust yourself as a creative artist and is a great way to view your stream of consciousness. The wonderful thing about this technique is that it not only helps with writer's block, but can also reveal organized patterns of thought that are right below the surface.

AFTER A FREE-WRITING SESSION

Remember, this exercise is about process, not product. After you've done your free-writing session, look through the material to see if there is anything that you can use (a word, a phrase, some dialogue) for the project that you're presently working on. If there is, take it out. Then, immediately get rid of rest of the free-writing work that you've done. The reason you do this is that sometimes there's a tendency to want to revise what you have on the page, using it as a first draft. As I've mentioned, that's not the idea of this exercise. It's not a first draft.

Here is a sample of one writer's free-writing work:

Here this is ridiculous. I can't . . . don't. What a waste. . . . I hope that I'm . . . Ridiculous. Crazy, I'm hoping, hopping, he held her at the dawn of light in the kitchen by the alcove under the kitchen sink with the plumber trying to fix the faucet. It wasn't broke, but it was her heart on her sleeve that really bothered the mailman on Monday after the cat came into the latrine. I'm not making any Look at them they know, they know what the story is really. Ridiculous is an absurd catch of the day by the fisherman on a Friday night because they're not allowed . . . Can't eat fish under the sink in retrospect my mother never made anything but pasta with sausage and lots of seasoning and my poodle named Sam would get up and eat it off the table and mama would cry at the sight of good food . . . is this ever going to end Probably on Tuesday in the mechanics shop, the car Anything. ANYTHING! Try to keep my mind I don't know. Keep it under your hat, loose lips sink cowboy hats under, a thunder at the door with a key in the open doorway . . . Tightly charged little men in the basement of the house without any warrant to arrest in the best behalf of some small characters in a novel by DeGaulle of the Parisian guard at the door to her hallway on a summer night where the breeze is nothing but a sty in the eye of anyone watching.

—by Patrice Jeston

As you can see in this section of Patrice's free-writing sample, she let her sentences start and stop, didn't attempt to make sense of things, and let her thoughts unfold in any fashion. If you'll notice, she expresses her frustration about the exercise in some of the words she uses (and then moves on). As I've mentioned repeatedly, the main purpose of this exercise is to keep going no matter what. Later on, Patrice may discover a word or a line in her free-writing that evokes something that will give her an idea for a monologue. She may sift through the material and find something that conjures up a character that she may want to develop. I suggest that you try free-writing at least once a day as a warm-up before you start your day's writing work.

OPEN-IMPROVISING

Just to give some equal time to the improvisers, I'd like to mention the value of open-improvising (the improv version of free-writing) to warm up. Depending on how comfortable and adept you are at improvisation, it can be an extremely useful tool. You can work either with or without a tape recorder. Some actors find the tape recorder intimidating, saying it makes them feel like someone is watching them, judging them. Others say it frees them up to totally let go, knowing that they can play back the recording later to perhaps find tidbits that they can use in their work. Open-improvising is different from regular improvisation in that regular improv work is specifically focused on material, characters, or dialogue that you're working on. This is more free flowing, open ended.

Reread the above section on free-writing and wherever possible apply it to your open-improv riffing sessions. Don't forget to work for at least ten minutes. Let yourself go wherever you want in the room. Just start, say, and do anything that comes to mind. Let your body become involved. Try not to become confined to any scenario or character. As one actor told me, "I just totally let myself lose my mind for a while. It's a great warm-up, really energizing and freeing."

Clustering (or Webbing): Finding the Initial Core of Your Work

Once you have prepared yourself and perhaps done the free-writing exercise, unless you're very clear about what you want to do and how you want to do it (and more specifically, about what you want to say), I suggest starting out with an excellent exercise called "clustering."

Clustering is a very popular writing method that was created by Gabrielle Lusser Rico and discussed in her book *Writing the Natural Way,* an excellent book for writers. Her technique helps you focus on what you're trying to say in your work. It utilizes the left side of the brain's ability to organize information. Sometimes, when we start out on a new piece, we may be overly enthusiastic, and we can't seem to find the root, the starting point, of where we want to go. And sometimes, even if we do know the starting point, it may be difficult to determine which areas of our work we need to focus on. Clustering helps you to find the through-line to your work. It helps you to zero in when too many thoughts and ideas seem to blur your creative landscape. Ironically, it's also useful when there's a lack of ideas.

Like free-writing, which it has similarities to, this technique helps you to bypass your conscious mind and get to your unconscious—perhaps the most creative part. The best way to describe clustering is "total free-association" or "brainstorming."

HOW TO CLUSTER

Start this exercise with a fresh sheet of paper. Write a word that is somehow connected to the monologue that you're about to start work on. Don't be concerned about which word you choose; whatever word comes to mind will do just fine. If you don't have a particular monologue in mind, or even have any ideas for one, just let any word that comes to mind be the one you choose.

Place the word in the middle of the page. Circle the word. Look at it for a moment. This *core word,* or *nucleus,* is the jumping-off point for the exercise.

Now, as quickly as you can, allow yourself to free-associate around your nucleus word, writing down as many words, images, short phrases, and bits of dialogue as you can. Each new word or phrase that you write down should radiate out from the nucleus word.

Draw circles around each new word or phrase. Link and connect similar ideas, phrases, bits of dialogue, etc. You can add arrows indicating direction if you wish.

If nothing spills out, doodle, putting arrows on your existing cluster. The doodling allows your hand to keep moving and may allow for possible associations to come to you.

Don't waste time trying to analyze anything; just go with your gut feelings. Don't stop until you have exhausted all possibilities. Keep going until you feel the need to write something. This shift will come in a thought like, "I've got it! I know what I want to write!"

Generally, most writers work with clusters for up to a few minutes. When you feel compelled to write, start immediately! Don't give yourself time to get back in your head. Start writing as fast as you can.

If nothing particular inspires you to write, then look at the words or phrases in the cluster and select any one of them. Start writing about that word or phrase. As you start writing, you'll probably notice a connection of ideas stemming from the word. Keep writing for at least ten minutes if you can. You can refer back to the cluster if you wish.

Remember, there is no right or wrong here. This should just be thought of as an exercise. Between five and ten minutes into this speed-writing there should be some effort to reach closure. Don't force it.

Here is an example of a cluster group exercise I did that eventually led to the creating of a monologue.

I began with the core word "Mars." I circled the word and let my mind free-associate. I kept going for almost three minutes. Here is just a sampling of some of the many words that I came up with. I circled, linked, and connected them.

> *yellow, tea, coffee! Help . . . fight . . . ugly . . . creepy! America . . . wired . . . scared . . . kill . . . run . . . fight, flag, kill, God . . . man . . . day . . . go . . . beat . . . proud . . . See . . . Everyone . . . Told ya. Out . . . get out!! . . . Zoom! . . . Smile . . . . Yes . . . Yes!!*

After looking at the group of circled and linked words for just a moment, I began what turned out to be the first draft of a monologue, which eventually became the following piece.

Sal from *Street Talk: Character Monologues for Actors* by Glenn Alterman

He wanted home-fried potatoes, that's all. I don't know, I remember, he came in here lookin' like anybody else. Short guy, sat at the counter. Right over there. I asked him, "Yeah, what'll it be?" And he said, "Home-fried potatoes." Nothing unusual, no big deal. So I ordered up with Sam, my short-order cook. And I turn around and this guy's like smiling. Not unusual. But . . . there's like this green glow comin' offa him. Yeah. That's the best way I can put it. Right then and there I knew somethin' strange was happenin'. Now listen, we get all kinds comin' in here. Two, three in the morning, we get truckers, drag queens, hookers, but none of 'em, none of 'em ever glows with green rays comin' out of 'em.

> *So, I kept it together, said, "Excuse me . . . um, is there somethin' else I can get'cha . . . besides the potatoes? And he stopped smilin'. He was like starin'. Intense. Like he was studying me or something. He looked at me like . . . like I was some kina insect. Creepy. Very creepy! If I wasn't the only one behind*

the counter, shit, I woulda jumped and ran. But the boss woulda killed me for leavin' the register.

Now there were a couple of regulars at the counter, drinkin' their coffee, oblivious to the whole thing. Whereas I was freaked! I never seen anybody glow. Ever! And it kept gettin' brighter and brighter.

I was trying to keep my composure, but I was fallin' apart.

Then, we get like into this starin' match. Him and me. And even though he's not sayin' anything I can hear his thoughts. Yeah. An' he was sayin' some weird shit. Stuff like a computer. Yeah. Like, "The population of New York is . . . The size of the city . . . Elected officials are . . ." All this data shit.

And I'm getting' so scared I think I'm gonna shit in my pants. I don't know what to do. Should I call 911? My wife? My mother? The army?

An' this guy's glow is gettin' brighter and brighter. Takin' over the whole diner! This green shit's coverin' everything!

Finally I say, "Hey mister, your fries should be ready in a minute. You want something to drink, like coffee or somethin'?"

Then he screams in this high-pitched tone, "Coffee?! Cof-feee?! You mean caffeine? Caf-feeine?!"

I said, "Uh, . . . uh we got decaffeinated if you like, or tea . . . or somethin'. I don't know."

Then his green shit gets brighter, and floods the place! Guys at the counter, they fell over backwards. I figured they was dead.

I lost it, screamed, "Mama mia, what are you doin', mister?! Ya food'll be ready in a minute. Please stop, please!"

Then the whole diner starts to shake. Yeah. Like it was an earthquake. Dishes flyin' all over the fuckin' place. Sam comes runnin' out of the kitchen, screamin', "What the hell . . . !," but when he sees this guy, he turns and runs back in, leavin' me alone, face to face with it! Whatever it was.

And then, then his face starts contorting in these weird ways, like it's made of rubber. Its mouth opens wide, and out comes this long, pointy yellow tongue. And this tongue starts comin' at me. Long and pointy and sharp. And the place is shakin' like crazy. . . .

Finally, I totally freaked! I said, "Enough! Enough! Get that fuckin' tongue back in your mouth and get the hell out of here! Now! Who the hell you think you are?!" I felt so strong. Like I wanted to wave a flag or somethin'. At first, nothin' happened. But then the place stopped shakin' and calmed down. My heart was racin' like crazy, but I stood there locked, with my fists like clenched. Then I pointed to the door and said, very softly, "Get out."

And the green rays zapped back into his body. An' he pulled that tongue of his back in. His face stopped contortin', and he looked like anybody else.

But then he kina slumped over in his seat, looked dejected or somethin'. He put a buck on the counter for the home fries, which he never got, an' said, almost in a whisper, "Thank you. Thank you very much, sir." And he started to leave.

I stood there, still shakin', an' said, "Sure. You're welcome. You're welcome." An then . . . he left.

CHAPTER 10

creating your monologue: structure and process

Before you actually start working on your monologue, I suggest that you create an outline, perhaps based on some information learned during the free-writing or clustering sessions. This outline should be much more detailed than the preliminary one that you did earlier. The purpose of this outline is to serve as a road map for your work.

Write out, in as much detail as possible, the story that you plan on telling. If it's a short character monologue, describe the character physically, listing personality traits, desires, quirks, etc. If it's a character that's speaking conversationally, either to someone else or to the audience directly, you might want to write out the story of the piece in narrative form first.

If it's an autobiographical monologue, pinpoint important moments, dates, details, and a rough outline of the storyline. You should begin with a general sense of how you want the piece to go—that is, where it'll start and where it will end. It's better at this point to have an abundance of information, much of which you may not use.

If it's a reality-based monologue, line up your facts, dates, and characters. Since this material is factual in nature, accuracy and specifics are very important. You may need to arrange tape-recorded interviews. You should start thinking about the tone and form that you want the piece to take. Anna Deavere Smith's *Fires in the Mirror* has a documentary-style feel to it. She recreated the people that she interviewed, using their exact words to tell her story.

If it's a performance art piece, list some of the ideas that you have in mind for the presentation. What form do you see it having? What audiovisual material will you need? Will you be using dance, songs? Will you need to secure the rights for any materials? Describe the piece as you see it in your mind. What is it that you're hoping your piece will say to an audience? You don't need to intellectually explain it; just tell why you are writing it. What's your point?

Write down any ideas or suggestions that you feel eventually may be helpful in creating your monologue. List all the potential characters that might be a part of your story. Give some thought to how you would like to develop them. List any scenes or locations that you might include.

Outline the journey (where you want to take your audience) of your piece as you now see it. Write the story out in a narrative form.

Remember, this is still just a preliminary overview, and things will probably change (maybe even substantially) as you go along. You're not married to any of the ideas, images, or characters.

How We'll Be Working from Now On

Because we are dealing with so many different types of monologues, I'll mainly be discussing the work in process terms. I'm sure that you'll be able to see where your particular piece fits in as we go along. Since each solo artist progresses at a different pace, I'll discuss the work in small increments.

Now that you've done all the preliminary "head" work—thinking, structuring, perking, and planning—the only thing that remains is the actual doing, the writing, the creating of your monologue.

Comparing the Actor's and the Writer's Processes of Starting Out

During that first read of a new play, you, the actor, (hopefully) have no preconceived ideas of what your character will be about or how you will go about creating him. It's a very vulnerable, open time in an actor's creative process. It's a time of taking in, reading the script, digesting the information, and then preparing to respond creatively to what you've read.

After that initial reading of the play, you have feelings and ideas about the character you are about to take on. Creative juices are flowing; the imagination is at work. Starting with some initial impulses, you begin thinking about how you will create your new character.

At the beginning of a new monologue or monologue play, you, the writer, are opening a door for yourself. From the very first lines you write, you are taking yourself somewhere, although you may not be quite sure where yet. The more spontaneous you can allow yourself to be, the more personal and original your work will be.

The outline that you've created can serve as a sort of skeletal script, giving you a sense of direction as to where you might want to go on this journey. The more you can *surprise yourself,* especially here at the beginning, the more exciting the ride will be, both for you and for the audience.

Both actors and writers begin at a similar point: a place of vulnerability, openness, potential. Anything can happen; the sky's the limit!

The Importance of the Narrator

In many monologues, there is a narrator who takes us through the journey of the piece. In autobiographical material, it can be the character representing the author; in an evening of character monologues, it may be the person who ties all the characters and/or the story (or stories) together.

In performance art pieces, it can be the performance artist himself, telling the story as he wants to tell it. We (the audience) should like or identify with the narrator in some way. At the very least, we should be interested in listening to what he has to say.

If the narrator is written as an unlikable character—a villain, like Salieri in *Amadeus* or the emcee in *Cabaret*—the audience must find something that is intriguing or fascinating about him. It's helpful if you can find some captivating detail of his personality that allows us to see the world through his (perhaps) distorted point of view. We have to trust or be intrigued by the narrator, or at the very least, believe that what he is telling us is true (or at least true to him). If we don't believe him, or can't follow his thinking, we'll lose interest early on in the monologue.

THE ROLE OF THE NARRATOR IN MONOLOGUES

As I've mentioned, generally the narrator is at the core of certain monologues or monologue plays. It's important to decide, early on, what role you want the narrator to have in your piece. Here are just a few suggestions.

- Does he represent the neutral, calm voice of reason?
- Is he the protagonist?
- Is he that cynical voice that we all have at one time or another?
- Is he the patient teacher, educating the audience?
- Is he the injured party, the victim?
- Is he an everyman most people will relate to?

Your Opening Section: The First Paragraphs

The opening section of your monologue is quite important. It's your diving-off point. It's your welcome mat to your audience. It's the "once upon a time" element that invites your audience to sit down with you for a while and listen to what you have to say. Your monologue should begin where it needs to begin—for you. It should start where your story has to start—for you. The beginning of your monologue is your foundation, the base that the rest of the piece will stem from. It should hint at, if not actually state, where you're going to be going for the rest of the piece.

While working on the beginning, it's especially important not to censor or stifle any images or ideas. Your monologue starts anywhere it needs to start. Don't become too preoccupied with how effective your opening is.

You'll find that openings and closings of monologues are the parts that generally receive the most rewrites. Once you've completed the entire monologue and know what it's about, then you can go back and see if the beginning and ending need further rewrites.

GIMMICKY OPENINGS

Try not to manipulate the opening section of your monologue "for effect," to get a rise from your audience. Gimmicky beginnings, unless honestly organic to the story, usually come off as desperate ploys by insecure writers to get an audience's attention. If your opening needs to start out with something shocking, something that's germane to your story, then by all means do so. But that's very different from just arbitrarily opening your piece with some obvious attention-getting device like loud noises or flashing lights, just for effect.

Here are some examples of opening sections of monologues.

From *Charlotte* by Penny Arcade (from *True Stories*)

I'm wearing a wig! I have to. I had a face-lift. Well, I had to. Well, I had to work. See, I figured I could work four or five years if I got my face done. You know my friend Sandra, the big blonde? Well, she had her eyes done up here in New York, and that cost her twenty-five hundred dollars. Well, I did not have that kind of money. But I know this gal, she used to be a madam up here in New York, but she retired to Caracas. She's real well-connected down there, you know, diplomats and all. Now, she told me I could go down there, stay at her house, and use her doctor. She has a beautiful home there. They call that a villa. Now, the only thing that she did not tell me was that her doctor worked at a teaching hospital. They gave me the face-lift of an eighty-year-old woman!

From the opening lines, we get a sense of who this character is (or may be). By the author's use of an exclamation point at the end of the first sentence, we can feel an energy, an immediacy to Charlotte's character. What she has to say seems very important to her and therefore engages us.

As she continues to speak, we learn of her situation, a bit of where she's at in her life, her style of speaking, even what's important to her at this time, and why. That's a lot of information in under twenty lines. Ms. Arcade chose a conversational style for her character's dialogue. You feel like the character is talking directly to you. Using this conversational form in monologue writing is one way to engage an audience.

Bernice from *Two Minutes and Under, Volume 2* by Glenn Alterman

(An angry tirade)
Don't! Don't tell me what I just said, Fred! I know exactly what I . . .! You asked me where the ketchup was; the ketchup! And I clearly said,

"The ketchup's in the kitchen on the counter." Clear, simple English. Never said fridge. I-never-said-fridge, Fred! Those word didn't came out of my mouth. If ya keep ketchup in the fridge, Fred, it can freeze. Everyone, everyone knows that!

This playful monologue starts off as an angry tirade. These kinds of monologues have a built-in start-up energy. The use of short, exclamation-pointed sentences ("Don't!") gets you off to a running start, like jumping off a diving board. The character's harsh choice of words, sentences, and thoughts immediately inform of us of the type of woman she is. We get a sense of her volatile relationship with her henpecked husband. We get her right from the start, and have a good sense of their relationship by the end of the first paragraph.

From *Swimming to Cambodia* by Spalding Gray

It was the first day off in a long time, and all of us were trying to get a little rest and relaxation out by the pool at this big, modern hotel that looked something like a prison. If I had to call it anything, I would call it a "pleasure prison." It was the kind of place you might come to on a package tour out of Bangkok. You'd come down on a chartered bus—and you'd probably not wander off the grounds because of the high barbed-wire fence they have to keep you in and the bandits out. And every so often you would hear shotguns going off as the hotel guards fired at rabid dogs down along the beach on the Gulf of Siam.

Gray opens his autobiographical monologue with a description of the hotel in Cambodia that he stayed at during the shooting of the film *The Killing Fields*. He is setting the scene, recalling his impressions of the place. He uses the narrative form. We learn quite a bit about Gray from the descriptive words he uses, his feelings about where he was. Calling his hotel a "prison" and then a "pleasure prison" gives you an insight as to how he viewed his surroundings. By mentioning "barbed wire fences" and "guns going off in the distance," Gray chooses images that begin to take us into the world he was living in.

From *Pretty Fire* by Charlayne Woodard

One day, when Allie and I were watching old black-and-white movies, Mommy walked into the living room and turned off the TV. She said, "Ladies, tell me what would you like to be when you grow up."

(Raising her hand) "Me first, Mommy, me first! (Standing) I want to be . . . Lassie. Yes, Mommy, I want to run through the field and jump over the fence, and see . . . the little girl . . . trapped in the mine . . . and I will call for help!" (Barking) Arf, arf, arf, arf, arf arf! And evening will come and they will save that little girl trapped in the mine. Then they'll say, 'Good girl, Lassie. (Reacting to her neck being petted as if she's a dog) Good girl, Lassie . . .' And Mommy, they will love me!"

The opening words, "One day, when Allie and I were watching old . . .," are similar in effect to the "Once upon a time"–style opener for many stories we've all heard growing up. Its friendliness and informality immediately invite you to come inside and enjoy listening to the story. Ms. Woodard's autobiographical character monologue begins with a reminiscence about an event in her childhood. There is a friendly, warm tone to the piece. Notice that she doesn't say "my mother," but rather uses the word "Mommy." See how that affects the tone of her storytelling.

By "present tensing" the dialogue in her story, the event takes on an immediacy. We get a sense that the past is momentarily occurring in the present. Present tensing can be very effective when you're repeating dialogue from the past.

Ms. Woodard's monologues are written in well-drawn vignettes. She brings to life not only assorted incarnations of herself, but also other family members and people from the neighborhood. Her stories are funny, poignant, and tragic. She has the ability to crawl into the skin of her many characters without letting us see her tracks.

Blanka from *Some People* by Danny Hoch

(Blanka, a young, twenty-ish office worker, stops by her friend's house to borrow shoes.)

Listen Linette, lemme borrow your shoes? The short black ones. No because Manny gets off Footlocker in twenty minutes and I have to take the bus. But I can't be looking ugly in the bus. So find them! Don't stress me more all right? My life is already stressed enough, can I tell you? The other day right? I was at Manny's house, and we was fooling around, and like you know how guys be getting all shy like when they wanna say something really important but they don't say it? Or like they say it, but like their voices be getting all low so you can't hear what they saying? So he was doing that right, and I don't like playing that. I was like, hello-excuse-me-I-can't-hear-you-what-you-saying-right?

Danny Hoch writes mainly urban character monologues. The form of writing Hoch uses is conversational dialogue. He opens this particular monologue with the character Blanka engaged in a conversation with her friend Linette. We become eavesdroppers listening to Blanka speaking. We quickly learn personal information about Blanka by her choice of words and her unique manner of speaking. We learn about her sense of herself and how she feels about Manny, her boyfriend.

Jo from *Eternal Pyramid* by Anastasia Traina

I wanted to tell her a story, a story . . . of a sunny day when I took my socks and shoes off and sat near Indian Pond, watching the crayfish jump as

I threw them some bread. I liked it there, sitting under that tree, near the water. It had motion . . . I wanted to say . . . Life was good and terrible at the same time . . . I mean, with all the fighting going on at home . . . I use to like to watch TV . . . I loved the cowboy stories, John Wayne, Roy Rogers, and the Cisco Kid . . . Oh and Tarzan and Superman too . . . Both my parents started taking sleeping pills . . . I was very overweight and awkward looking as a child. I went to school sometimes in the same outfit, it was a very soft pink shift dress and it had a little red bow that you could tie on the side, I loved that dress . . . yes, the fights would go on and on . . . We had the police at our house quite often. One time Mama took the car and aimed it right at Papa, she meant to run him over. I think he got out of the way. So it didn't happen. I don't remember a lot of things . . . sponged out.

Anastasia Traina's character opens this monologue with a narrative, poetic memory sequence. This type of opening feels personal and invites the audience into the character's private world. We also get a sense of location, where the piece is taking place. We get to know Jo, feel we can trust her. For the duration of the piece, she will be our guide.

Master of the Stale from the play *The Dark String* by ty adams

(Harvey Rothchild is on the phone talking to an old friend.)

Well, it's essential isn't it? It's my job. As a photographer's agent, it's my job to match the artist with my clients. It's about chemistry. And a photographer may have an original, fresh, honest portfolio. But one brilliant, honest shot will not even get you windows at Marty's Diner on Lex. So . . . how do I do it? I go mad . . . Take, for instance, Lizbeth at Bergdorf's. Ad Manager Extraordinaire. She calls, says, "Harvey, I need a photographer. To do Windows. I need smooth. I need fresh. I need Now." So I get them smooth. I get them fresh. I get them Franko. Why Franko? Because his photos are brilliant? Because his photos are honest? No. Because Franko is smooth and fresh and can play the game.

In this monologue by ty adams, the character is talking on the phone. We learn a great deal about the character in this opening sequence. The conversation opens us up to the character's world of fashion. Phone monologues can be tricky. Because the character is "responding" to the unseen other voice on the phone, the writer of the piece must give us basic information without telling too much in the part of the phone conversation that we are hearing. The artistry in these kinds of monologues is how you let the audience follow the story without telling the whole story. If the phone monologue is going to go on for a while, you might want to give the character activities to do, such as making a drink, cleaning up, etc. Standing there for a long period of time just talking on a phone is not always very theatrical.

CHAPTER 11

developing your monologue

Let's assume at this point that you're satisfied with the opening section of your monologue. Allow yourself to move on, using the outline and opening section as a springboard for new ideas, images, and dialogue. Once again, it's not necessary to always know exactly where you're going to go with the monologue. Now it's really just a matter of trusting your instincts and impulses and allowing them to propel you forward, letting your imagination guide you. At this point, the most important thing is to just keep going.

Developing Your Role (as an Actor)

This early stage of developing your monologue can be compared to a similar stage in an actor's process. In rehearsal, you start saying the lines in the script to the other actors. One line of dialogue leads to the next; you go from action to action. The other actor responds to you, and you respond to him, and so it goes. You know where the play ends, but now you have to explore, to see where your character fits into each scene. At this point in the actor's process, you're not (or shouldn't be) limiting yourself in any way. It's a time to *fly and try*.

Developing Your Monologue (as a Writer)

Similarly, as a writer, this also is a time when you should allow impulses and ideas to lead you. Let yourself be both the leader and the follower. If what you're writing makes you smile or laugh, assume that it's funny, and that an audience will also laugh. If it makes you cry, trust that it will have the same effect on an audience.

Don't try to second-guess or manipulate anything. This is also not the time to over-analyze or revise anything you've written so far. It's a time of moving forward at your own pace, letting each section unfold into the next section, each creative segment melt into the next one. Remember, any rewrites can always be done later on.

The Ongoing Day-to-Day Work

Your work continues until you've completely told the story that you wanted to tell. You shouldn't be too concerned at this time about particular sections along the way that may not quite be there yet. At this point, it's really more important to get the story down. That doesn't mean that you should be rushing to get to the end of a first draft. Take your time; enjoy yourself.

If you feel an impulse to travel off course, away from the outline you created, go there, try it; see where it takes you. You can always backtrack later and return to your original ideas. Sometimes those great surprises that you come up with while traveling off course become the unusual twists and turns that make a monologue most memorable. This should be a time of experimenting, writing impulsively, wandering wherever you want to go.

It's important to try to work every day, even if it's just for a half hour. When you're not working on your piece, it's usually a good idea to have a pad and pen around to jot down ideas or dialogue that may suddenly come to you during the day. One thing you'll start to realize is that your subconscious mind is always working on your monologue, even when you're not consciously thinking about it. Some of the most inspired moments and best lines of dialogue occur when you're sitting on a bus going uptown or watching TV. If an idea comes to you, simply take out your pad and pen and write it down. I'm sure that as an actor, while working on a role, these inspired insights also occurred when you weren't actually rehearsing.

While working on short character monologues, audition pieces, etc., don't be concerned about how long the piece is running. Even if it's running pages longer than you originally intended, keep going. Later on, in rewrites, you can always trim the piece down.

With larger pieces such as monologue plays, performance art pieces, etc., some writers prefer working in chunks or sections of the play, dividing it into acts. When they feel they have a substantial amount of material, they'll revise what they have, then go on to the next chunk of material, etc.

Other writers (most of the ones I spoke to) prefer to go the whole route, continuing until they finish a complete first draft of the entire play. Then they'll backtrack, doing rewrites on various sections as needed. Once again, whatever works best for you is the best way.

When working on an evening of character monologues, each monologue can be thought of as a separate block and should be worked individually. Naturally, you need to keep in mind the thread that ties all the pieces together. This may be a group of neighbors, a common theme, a storyline, etc. But don't let that device restrict you in any way. You don't want an evening of individual character monologues where all the characters are too similar.

Working on Performance Art Pieces

Performance art pieces, as I've mentioned previously, don't follow many of the same rules as other monologues. They allow for a freer creative style. However, certain things that you should keep in mind when working on performance art monologues are:

- How do you plan on telling your story? What form do you think it will take? Do you plan on using dance? Visuals? Music? Lighting? Poetry?
- What ideas are you trying to express? What are you trying to say?
- Describe, in as much detail as you can, the theatrical journey that you hope to take your audience on.

Some performance artists I spoke with prefer not to use an outline of any kind. They feel that they are too constricting. When they begin work on a new piece, they may have just an idea or image in mind. They develop the piece in sections, working moment to moment, allowing their ideas or images to lead them into the form that the piece eventually takes.

A Word about Songs, Music, and Dance in Monologue Plays

Some monologists like to incorporate songs and music and dance into their monologue plays. This is especially true in performance art pieces. If used well, music and dance can certainly enhance written material and showcase an actor's musical ability. I suggest, though, that you only use song and dance if you feel they will add something not already said in your text. They should be thought of as a sort of seasoning, and shouldn't overpower the text (unless that's your specific intention).

Another matter to take into consideration is their legality. If you write your own songs or music, obviously there's no problem. If, however, you want to use someone else's copyrighted material, you'll need to get their permission first (and perhaps pay royalties). The same is true of using text from other sources. For example, Mary Louise Wilson had to get the rights to the book *D.V.* before she could begin work on her play *Full Gallop*.

Mixed Media

To visually enhance their performances, many monologists use slide projections, artwork, and so on, as an aid in expressing what they're trying to say. If using visuals is something that you wish to explore in your work, fine. Just one word of caution: Be careful; don't overdo. Always keep in mind that you're just one person alone on a stage performing. The more visuals you use, the more the audience's focus will be divided. If that's your intention, then go ahead. But in general, in monologue plays, less is more. Sometimes, out of insecurity, the monologist (or his director) overdoes the visuals, lessening the effect of the monologue itself.

That Old Devil, the Self-Censor

One interfering monster you may come up against is the self-censor. The self-censor is that judging, criticizing spoiler inside our heads who stops the rhythm of what we're doing by making negative comments. It happens at different times to all artists. There is no way to avoid it; it comes with the territory. Some writers have the ability to ignore it; others are temporarily stymied by it. How you learn to deal with your own self-judging and self-criticizing is a valuable part of your creative process. I'm sure that as an actor, from time to time, that same judging voice interfered with your work on developing or performing a role. The only thing that you can do is acknowledge what it is and keep working, trying not to let it interfere or overwhelm you. The more confident you become as a writer, the less it will affect you.

Taking Mini-Breaks, Breathers

Write or improvise for as long as your energy and stamina hold up. Some monologists can only work for about twenty or thirty minutes before they feel they need a break. Others can work for many hours nonstop. You'll know instinctively when it's time for you to break.

While working on material, occasionally you go through dry patches, or what seems like a temporary stop in the creative flow. It feels like you've run out of ideas. This is generally one of those times to take a breather. Relax, stop what you're doing, and temporarily do something else.

During a break I'll get up, leave the work area, perhaps go into another room. I try to get my mind momentarily off what I'm doing. Sometimes you just need a good stretch, perhaps a brief walk outside in the fresh air. I'll listen to music for a few minutes, have a light snack (preferably a healthy one), or fix myself a cup of coffee. Any short distraction will work, as long as you keep your mind off the monologue.

You may find that while you're recouping, fresh ideas related to the material start coming to you. If that occurs, fine; simply jot down whatever insight or dialogue came to you, and continue on with what you're doing. Don't give these new ideas too much thought at this point. When you feel refreshed, go back to the work area and pick up where you left off. Hopefully you'll feel recharged, ready to continue work.

Looking Over What You've Written So Far

After the break, I usually browse over what I've written so far. My main purpose in reviewing material is to get me back into the groove of where I was before the break. It's important not to judge or censor what you've written so far. If you can, resist revising anything. Revising puts your mind in an analytical mode, something that we're not up to yet. The idea at this point is to continue onward, not to backtrack or clean up roads you've already passed through.

After the Break: Two Scenarios

After the break you continue working in the same way that you were prior to your break. You may notice that you suddenly have fresh ideas, have a new outlook, are able to look at the material from a new point of view. If that's the case, the break was successful.

If, however, you're still creatively dry, you have two options. You can either take another break, or—this is more advisable—work through the dry patch. Periods of mental lethargy can be frustrating, I know. But many times they come out of a psychological avoidance of something within the material. If you can, push through, try to find out what's on the other side of the resistance. Once you get there, things will flow a lot smoother.

Working Till the End of the First Draft

Continue working on your monologue until there is nothing more to say, until you feel you've completely told your story. In the case of character monologues, you should feel that each of the monologues has a workable beginning, middle, and end. You should have a feeling of completion, accomplishment. That's not to say that there won't be sections, lines of dialogue, and even characters that you know still need further work. But that should not short-change your feeling of accomplishment after completing the first draft of your monologue. Enjoy the moment and then give yourself a well-deserved break.

CHAPTER 12

developing your monologue II (the ongoing work)

At this point we're about to begin the craft part of the work. You're about to shift from the creative mode of inspiration and creation to the more analytical one. To begin this process, you have to reread the entire first draft with a different mindset from when you were creating it.

The "Who Wrote This Monologue and What's It About?" Exercise

One way to approach the first read-through of your material is called the "Who Wrote This and What's It About" exercise. It's a way of separating yourself from your work and reading the manuscript with a fresh perspective. Rather than just picking up the script and reading it straight out, try playing this little game with yourself. When you sit down to look at the manuscript, pretend that you didn't write it. Pretend that you're seeing those words on the pages for the very first time. If you're listening to a tape-recorded first draft, pretend that you've never heard those words before. Pretend that you don't know anything about the author of the piece. As you're reading, jot down *anything* that seems unclear to you. If you have any questions about any specific section, character, or idea, just jot them down as you go along. The idea is to pretend that you're a member of the audience, a critic, a person with a very discerning, critical mind.

I know that at first it may feel a little strange trying to pretend you've never seen this script that you've been working on for however long. But this exercise can be very helpful. The more objective you can be during the first read-through, the more efficient the rewrite process may be later on. You'll also find this to be an interesting (if not unusual) acting task.

Questions to Ask Yourself While Reading through Your Script

Whether or not you decide to use the "Who Wrote This . . .?" exercise, here are some important questions you should try to keep in mind while reading through your monologue (play). You should refer to these questions periodically, also using them as guidelines during subsequent read-throughs:

- Does the script engage you? The moment you feel disengaged, just mark the passages, then continue reading. Don't analyze or try to fix anything at this point.
- Do you find the story interesting, easy to follow? If not, where does it become convoluted or confusing? Mark those sections. Again, don't try to fix anything.
- About the characters: Do you believe them? Do all the characters seem fully realized? If not, at which point do you feel they lose you? Be as specific as you can and underline the line or moment.
- Does the way each character speaks sound authentic? Mark the words or passages that sound false.
- If there are multiple characters in the piece, do you feel that all the characters are interesting? Necessary? Do any of them seem too similar to other characters? Can any of the characters be combined?
- Do you care about these characters? Do they offend you, annoy you, seem too abrasive, seem too sentimental?
- Do you feel at any point that there's too much narrative or exposition? Always keep in mind that this monologue will be performed, not read.
- Do you notice any repetition in the dialogue, the same words or phrases being overused? Keep in mind that in everyday use, there are certain colloquial expressions that people do use repeatedly. Does the repetition make your dialogue sound authentic and specific, or does it just sound like sloppy writing?
- Do you feel that there is a repetition in the ideas being expressed? Are some characters expressing the same ideas repeatedly?
- Is it clear what the writer is trying to say in this piece?
- How do you feel after finishing the piece? Did you find it satisfying? Do you wish there was more? Do you feel that there was too much of any one element, character, scene, and so on?

At What Point Should You Have Someone Else Read What You've Written?

This is a very tricky question. Many writers want to get feedback on their monologue as soon as they've finished working on the first draft. Getting it to someone for a response at the right time can be very helpful. But getting it to a reader prematurely can be damaging to your process, your future work on the piece. Once you let others into the stew, so to speak, they become a part of your relationship with your own material. Their input, comments, and suggestions will have an impact on your future rewrites. You may want to wait until the second or third draft before handing it over to someone else for input. There is no rule on this; only you will know when the time is right. The best rule of thumb here is to give it to someone else to look at when you honestly feel that you've done as much work on it as you possibly can for the time being.

Selecting the Right Person to Read Your Monologue

Deciding whom you ask to read your manuscript is very important. You should trust and respect the opinion of the person you're asking to read your material. You should feel that he can intelligently articulate any problems that he sees in your text. It's a very vulnerable time for you as the writer of the script. You need to make sure that the person you've asked to criticize your piece is someone who will be honest with you, but also supportive. And always remember, no matter whom you choose, he is just one person, with his own subjective point of view. He's not God. At the end of the day, it's always your opinion that carries the most weight.

I personally feel that writers should hold off as long as they can before handing their work over to someone else for criticism. Try to give yourself as much time as you need, live with your script for as long as you can. Only give it to someone else when you honestly feel that you can no longer be objective about it or feel that there are large problems that you just can't get a handle on. Do not expect or ever allow the reader you've selected to give you solutions to problems that he sees or suggestions as to how you should rewrite your monologue. The best readers are the ones that can pose the right questions to you, not give you answers.

Performing the First Draft for a Director

As to whether you should perform the first draft of your monologue for a director for feedback, again, that's your call. If it's the director whom you've selected to direct your play, it can certainly be helpful to have him included early on in the process. (See "Selecting a Director" in chapter 14.) As I have previously mentioned, quite often one of the functions of directors of solo shows is that of dramaturge. It's also an opportunity for you both to see how comfortable you feel working with each other. If you have a particular director whom you're thinking of developing the piece with, discuss with him which way he feels would work best for the two of you.

Performing the First Draft as a "Work in Progress" for an Audience

Some monologists prefer to develop material in front of an audience early on. After the first draft or two, they begin performing it for small groups as a work in progress, making their revisions based on the audiences' nightly responses to their work. The audience may be a few friends in a living room or a paying audience in a small club or theater. Letting the audience know in advance that this is a still work in progress lowers the audience's level of expectation. Some audiences enjoy seeing works in progress because they feel that they're contributing to the monologist's process. After each performance, there's a question-and-answer session where the audience can make comments about the work they've seen. Their comments can be very helpful to the monologist and the director of the piece.

Making Repairs: Rewriting

Successful monologue writing (actually, all writing) relies heavily on rewriting. That first inspired batch of material may feel complete, but always be ready and willing, at any time, to revise, rewrite, perfect. That's not to say that sometimes you can't get it right that first time out. That does happen, but generally, most writers, playwrights, and performance artists I've spoken to think of their early work, that first draft, as "fodder, raw material." You should look forward to chiseling away at your work until it expresses exactly what you're trying to say at every given moment. Never settle, never rush, never compromise.

Revising and Reshaping

One of the most important aspects of the rewriting process is revising and reshaping your text. The more you understand what you've written, and more specifically, what you're trying to say (at any given moment), the more you'll know precisely what needs editing or further developing. The first stage of revising is similar to cleaning out your closet. As you look through it, you realize that some things are unnecessary and can be thrown out. Eventually new clothes will be bought and added to your wardrobe, filling up your closet again. Only you can decide what remains and what goes. And only you can decide what new clothes you want to buy.

The Three Golden Rules of Revising

1. Eliminate any *words* that don't relate to the *main idea* of the sentence
2. Eliminate those *sentences* that don't relate to the *main idea* of the paragraph
3. Eliminate the *paragraphs* that don't relate to the *main idea* of your monologue

What follows is a question-and-answer section pertaining to techniques for revising and reshaping monologues.

Are there sections that seem extraneous to the story?
Part of the job in writing monologues is learning how to best tell your story. Unfortunately, sometimes monologue writers fall in love with their own dialogue or refuse to cut a beautiful phrase or a colorful word because they like the sound of it or the image it evokes. To make your story clear, you sometimes have to sacrifice. Monologues are meant to be performed. Extraneous dialogue can weigh your story down and bore your audience. Be succinct in your storytelling. Get to the point and then move on.

Are there any sections that need to be opened up, further developed?
On the other end of the storytelling spectrum is not giving your audience enough information. This usually happens when there is more going on in the writer's head than he has put down on the page. The writer's thoughts are not yet being fully expressed, the story is not being completely told. The bottom line on this is that if it's not on the page, it's not on the stage. It's always easier to write the material and cut back if it turns out that you are over-explaining.

When you become aware (either by your own reading or through feedback from other readers) that a particular section needs further development, try to trace your steps back to where the confusion began. At that juncture, pick up where you left off, working to reveal, to open up, what's missing in that moment (through the use of dialogue or narrative). Continue working that way until you've opened it up as much as you can. Then, later on, perhaps during subsequent read-throughs, return to the section and see if it needs to be pared down, if perhaps you've overwritten it.

It's the constant back-and-forth revisions to the section that will reveal the clearest truth of what you're trying to say. The rule of thumb here is to only say what must be said, nothing more and nothing less.

Here are some questions that you can ask yourself to find out if a particular section of your monologue needs further development:

- Have I referred to places, people, or events in my monologue that the audience may not be aware of?
- In general, does my audience have enough background information on the story that I'm trying to tell them? Could I give them some more exposition?
- Have I made a strong enough case for the idea that I'm trying to get across to the audience?
- Have I taken into account possible arguments or problems that members of the audience may have with my ideas? If so, what is the best way for me to answer their objections in advance?

Are there too many characters in the monologue?
Always keep in mind that your monologue will only be performed by one actor: you. Having unnecessary characters in your piece will only add to your creative burden as an actor and, ultimately, to the audience's confusion. Certain characters may be too similar; combining them will make your story sharper, clearer. Also, multiple characters revealing the same information tend to "bloat" the monologue. Try combining them into a single character who can more effectively be the messenger of the story you're trying to tell.

Are there too many stories in my monologue (monologue play)?
Any of the longer monologue plays (autobiographical, narrative, etc.) can handle several intermeshing subsidiary stories. But try to avoid having too many complex stories with unnecessary characters. If you do so, your audience will lose the impact of the main story and/or the ideas that you're trying to express. If possible, try to somehow connect or funnel the subsidiary stories, having them relate to or resonate with your main story or idea(s).

As for an evening of character monologues, try not to hamper the individual monologues with too many stories or overfill them with too many characters. That's not saying that the monologues taken together can't spin a complex and layered yarn; just try to tell each part of the story with clarity and simplicity.

Does my monologue go off on tangents? Does my story meander? Am I repeating myself?
As I have mentioned earlier, keeping your story focused and succinct are two of the most important aspects of successful monologue writing. Long-winded and unyielding stretches of dialogue or narrative don't play well in performance. A character or narrator who talks endlessly on the same subject quickly wears out his welcome. As you read through your monologue, look to see if you're repeating yourself too often. It may be a word, phrase, or idea that is being irritatingly overused.

One way to avoid meandering is to build your story methodically, block by block. Be precise in your storytelling. It's almost as if you're telling a story to a little child. In effect, you're saying, "And what happened next was...And then the next thing was . . . And then . . ." And so on, and so on, step by step by step.

Be careful about any of your characters proselytizing. Nothing is more boring than being in an audience and feeling that you're being endlessly lectured or preached at. If you want to get a message across to your audience, be creative. Find a way to make it intrinsic to the action of the monologue.

What is the best way to shape and develop your material?
This is where the fine-tuning of the monologue comes in. It requires that you have an overview of the entire piece as well as the ability to pay

attention to specific moments and details. It's a constant giving and taking, adding and subtracting, rewriting and refining. Basically, it all comes down to your taste and your personal sensibility to the story you're trying to tell.

Too much of this can make it too humorous, too much of that can weigh it down dramatically. Too much exposition here, too much dialogue there. Is that character really necessary? Does he serve any purpose at that point? It goes on and on—questions that only you can pose to yourself and then answer. Be tough on yourself in rewrites.

The Subconscious and Rewrites

Sometimes, when working on a piece, writers become frustrated with a problem that they're trying to work out in a particular section. No matter how hard they try, they just can't seem to get it right. Finally, exasperated, they give up on the project for a while, shelve it. This is a good thing to do sometimes, rather than beating your head against a wall.

When the writer returns to the work (with its previously unsolvable problem), he's amazed to find that his creative dilemma is now somehow easily resolved. Having stopped all the agonizing to make it work, the writer has allowed his subconscious mind to help him out. When you find yourself working too hard on a section for too long, with minimal, diminishing results, perhaps it's time to let it go for a while. Put it in a drawer and just forget about it. When you come back to it with a fresh, open mind, you may find the problem easily resolved.

CHAPTER 13

completing work on your monologue

The monologue ends when you have completely told the story you set out to tell. Like the opening section, the closing section has a significant effect on an audience. It is the last thing they'll hear from you. Because of their impact, opening and closing sections generally receive the most rewrites in a manuscript.

Things to Keep in Mind in Your Closing

You want to be certain that the closing section has a feeling of completion to it. That doesn't necessarily mean that everything needs to be neatly tied together in the last sentence or two. There are some monologues where the endings seem to just drift off gently. This is usually in keeping with the story that came before and works organically with the rest of the monologue.

The ending should always be in the same style as the monologue that has preceded it. If you've written a monologue that has a naturalistic feel throughout, you don't want to finish it in the last line or two with a bizarre or surreal ending. The jarring quality that an ending like that has will totally confuse and disorient your audience at a very important moment.

You also don't want to end a monologue too abruptly (unless that's in keeping with the monologue's style). If you do, you'll be hearing members of the audience saying, "That's it? It's over? That's the end?" They'll be confused and probably annoyed, and they'll feel cheated that the piece didn't pay off.

And finally, you don't want the ending to go on for too long, having your monologue outstay its welcome. If you dawdle endlessly at the end, you'll notice people in the audience yawning, coughing, and looking at their watches. Say what you have to say, put the period at the end of the sentence, lights down, and then come out for your well-deserved curtain call.

Knowing When the Monologue Is Ready to Be Performed

Only you will know when your monologue is finished. There are several ways to gauge if it still needs some fine-tuning. First, read it as objectively as you can. You should feel absolutely satisfied that you've accomplished everything that you set out to do. Don't be too easy on yourself at this point. Next, if you have yet to locate a director, find one you would want to work with, and ask for his comments. (See the sections on selecting and working with a director in the next chapter.) Start performing your monologue as a work in progress for small, select audiences, perhaps in your living room. After each performance, ask the audience members for any comments. If you're hearing the same criticism from several different sources, it might be something that you should look at. Always think of your work as an ongoing process. Even after you've opened and had a run, always look for new things: nuances, moments, etc. Some monologists say that they discover such things a year or two later.

A Checklist to Decide Whether Your Monologue Is Ready to Be Performed

Here are some general points to help you decide whether your monologue is complete and ready to be performed. Many of these items have been discussed earlier in the book, but bear repeating at this point:

- Have you told the entire story that you want to tell?
- If you're doing an evening of character monologues, does each one of the individual monologues tell the complete story that you wish to tell?
- Are you satisfied that you have made all the points (arguments) that you set out to make? That doesn't mean that you're responsible for resolving them.
- Does your piece have a clear beginning, middle, and end?
- Is there an arc? Is there a turning point?
- When you rehearse the monologue, are there lines of dialogue that feel awkward, unnatural, or uncomfortable?
- Is there any past-tense dialogue that might be more effective if you brought it into the present?
- Are there sections that stand out, that don't seem to fit with the rest of the monologue? Sometimes an idea in a particular section may work, but the way that your character's expressing it doesn't.
- Are there any sections that could be condensed? Are you embellishing where it's not necessary?
- On the other side of the coin, are you sure you've given your audience enough information? Do they need to know more about a character's background, about some plot point, etc?

- Do you feel that the characters you've created are ones you're able to get inside of? If not, what do you think the problem is? Is it the dialogue, the character, the situation, etc.?
- Are there too many characters? Can several similar characters, or characters making the same point, be eliminated?
- Are there too many locations, too many scenes? Will the audience know where they are at any given moment?
- If you've repeatedly been hearing the same type of comments from your director and audience members, have you been able to make the necessary changes? If you don't agree with their comments, ask yourself why.

You may have to go through several (or many) drafts of your monologue before you feel that it's ready to be seen by a paying audience.

For those of you who have written short character monologues, the best places to try them out are at acting classes or for friends. I wouldn't recommend trying out new audition material immediately at auditions. Give yourself a few test runs before placing yourself on the line like that. Remember: You won't receive any constructive feedback from the auditioners (even if you do get the job). As to whether you should tell them that you've written the material, that's your call. My experience has been that it's not helpful for them to know, and can possibly be held against you.

CHAPTER 14

preparing to perform

Much of what I'll be discussing here is for those monologists who are looking for a director for their monologue plays. For those of you who would like a director to work with on your (shorter) audition monologue, I think you'll still find the following information to be of use. But you should be aware that many directors aren't that interested in working on audition monologues with actors. What you might actually be looking for are acting coaches who specialize in this type of work.

Selecting a Director

Finding the right director for your piece can be very difficult. Here are some things to consider before committing yourself and your monologue to a particular director. Many monologists find their directors through recommendations from other actors who have worked with those directors. Another way to select a director is by seeing his work, especially if it's a one-person show. If he has a play in town, try to catch a performance. If you like what you see, give him a call and set up a meeting. If he presently doesn't have any of his work on display, and the recommendation was strong enough, you should also give him a call. You certainly have nothing to lose.

When meeting with potential directors, always look for directors who are articulate and seem to know what they're talking about. Look for directors who are supportive. You need to find someone who understands and appreciates your work. You certainly don't want a "yes" director, nor do you want to work with someone who is too negative. If, prior to your meeting, you've gotten your monologue to him for him to read in advance, ask him to *tell you the story of the monologue as he sees it. Ask him how he sees the piece as a theater piece. Ask him how he likes to work on one-person shows.*

The relationship between monologists and their directors is usually a very intense one. As opposed to a regular play with other actors involved, there's just you and your director. You'll want someone you feel you can get along with, whom you feel comfortable with. If, early into the collaboration, you notice a personality conflict between you and your director (and it can't be worked out), you may want to start looking for a new director as soon as possible.

Working with the Director in Rehearsal

I personally feel that it is always advantageous to rehearse your monologue with a director. Some of you may be planning on directing yourselves. If you honestly feel that you can do it, fine. But remember, having that second set of eyes—other input—can be very helpful, especially in the pressure-filled final phase of development. If you're determined to direct yourself, at least allow directors you trust to drop in on occasion and see a rehearsal or two, and get their response.

When you've found a director you like, you should both set up informal ground rules for how you'd like to work together in rehearsal. You don't want to be too rigid in setting up any rules because you'll notice that how you work will evolve as you get to know each other better.

You and your director should both be of the same mind concerning the meaning and interpretation of your piece. You don't have to agree on all aspects of it, but certainly on all the major points. It's sometimes helpful to read through the piece together, then follow with discussion.

Many monologists divide their monologues into small sections, or *beats*. Slowly and methodically, they rehearse each beat. By working this way, two things are accomplished at the same time. First, you'll attain a better understanding of the material you're working on. And second, just by the repetition, you'll learn the text quicker than if you sat down and tried to memorize it by rote.

Once you are in rehearsal, you should be willing to try things that your director suggests, even if they sometimes seem a bit far-fetched. This is a trust issue. You should also feel comfortable enough to fall flat on your face in rehearsal and know that he will still be supportive.

You may notice, from time to time, that you'll be encountering some of the same problems and frustrations that you experienced when you worked on other writers' texts. Even though you wrote the material yourself, you'll come to a word or section that seems difficult to say or realize. It's hard to know what you were originally thinking when you wrote that section, but if you feel it doesn't work now, fix it.

During the rehearsal phase there'll probably be a lot of rewriting. As you become more familiar with the monologue, you'll discover which sections are extraneous to the story you're trying to tell, and which sections still need further development. Because you're working at this point both as an actor and as a writer, you may at times feel somewhat conflicted. It's at these times that you should rely more on your director's feedback to help with some of the decision-making. If your director suggests rewrites on specific sections, listen to what he has to say and feel free to question why he feels any particular rewrite is necessary. Many directors' greatest contribution to the collaboration on your piece will be their contribution as dramaturge. You'll find that some directors can be very helpful with the structuring and order of your piece. If however, you really feel that a suggestion the director makes is not at all what you had in mind, it is your obligation to discuss this with him. Never make any change that you absolutely don't agree with just to appease a director.

It's important that you and your director develop a sincere trust and respect for each other's work during the rehearsal process. Originally, you, the actor/writer, had total control of your project. You must be willing to relinquish some of that power to your director. As you get closer to performance, you may need to rely more heavily on him for his feedback. It's not a time to be questioning his intentions, perceptions, or motives. On the other hand, some actors have a tendency to rely too heavily on their director, making him into a parent figure. Try to maintain your integrity and self-sufficiency, especially when the pressure builds toward performance.

Rehearsing the Audition Monologue

For those of you who are dealing with audition monologues, I suggest also rehearsing the piece in beats. Quite often an audition monologue that's rehearsed and memorized by rote sounds like it. It may feel a bit strange to be memorizing your own words, but by and large, it's usually easier than memorizing someone else's. And you'll notice that when you audition with your own piece, if you should happen to go up on lines, it's far easier to ad-lib until you come back to the actual text.

Many actors like to use improvisation while rehearsing their audition monologue. Find an improv situation that can connect you to your material. You may notice that when using improv in rehearsal, new lines of dialogue will come out of your mouth. It's never too late to do rewrites.

One word of caution: Don't get too married to your own words. What I mean is, when I used to use some of my own monologues for auditions, there was always a part of me (the writer part) that wanted to make sure that the auditors heard every one of my terrific words. By keeping this as your intention, you can lose the focus of what you're really trying to say in your monologue. They'll hear all your fabulous words, but they won't be getting the deeper meaning, the *character's* intention. In rehearsal, try working more with images, thoughts, and intentions, rather than just on memorizing the words themselves.

Performing the Piece

Deciding when the monologue is ready to be performed is a decision that you and your director should make together. The director can give you a sense of how it looks out there to an audience. And you can let him know how it feels to you, from inside. At this point, many actors are dealing with their nerves and insecurities. Having a director reassure you that the piece is ready can be very helpful at this last phase.

The show will continue to grow after you begin to perform it. Every audience will teach you something about your show. The audience is the last ingredient in the process. Once you start performing the monologue, *everyone* will offer his opinion and comments. Don't allow all these "helpful comments" to sabotage what you and your director have worked out together. Outsiders don't understand the creative process that has gone on during rehearsal. If someone makes a comment that you feel may be useful, mention it to your director, see what he thinks.

Prior to an actual theatrical engagement, it's always smart to have friends and supporters see a few final dress rehearsals. Once again, you and your director should agree as to when and if this is necessary.

CHAPTER 15

marketing your solo show

Only you can decide when your monologues are ready for public performances. (See "A Checklist to Decide Whether Your Monologue Is Ready to
Be Performed" in chapter 13.) If you live in a city that has a small theater
where solo material is performed, contact the theater staff and see if they'll
allow you to perform and further develop your piece in front of an audience. Sometimes theaters allow this on their dark nights. Generally, actors
are required to do their own publicity and provide an audience for such
performances.

If you do find a theater that will allow you to perform your work, it's in
your best interest to do everything in your power to get literary and/or
talent agents to come down to see the show (see Appendix F, Literary
Agencies). They can be very helpful later on in moving your piece to other
venues.

Another way to promote your work is to send it out to theaters that are
looking for new solo material (see Appendix B, Theaters That Accept
Solo Material). To save time and energy, *do not* send material to theaters
unsolicited, unless they permit it.

There are also contests (see Appendix D, Playwriting Competitions
That Accept Solo Material) where you can enter your monologue and perhaps receive a prize and/or a production of your work.

Preparing Your Marketing Package

Your solo-show package should consist of:

- The manuscript of your play
- A videotape of you performing it (if possible)
- A cover letter
- Your résumé
- A synopsis of your monologue

These are only to be sent to theaters, agents, or organizations that accept unsolicited material or that have requested that you send them your material. *Do not send this package unsolicited to anyone else!* You'll be wasting your time and money.

THE MANUSCRIPT

The monologue should be neatly typed on white 8.5" x 11" paper. The manuscript should have one and a half spaces between lines. Any stage directions should be indented and single-spaced. Make sure the script is neat looking and well typed, with no typos. Remember: This script is your calling card; it represents you. I personally check all the pages of every script I send out. It takes a bit of time, but sometimes the photocopy machines screw up. Sections may be put in the wrong order or, even worse, not copied at all. Make sure the script is well bound, with no loose papers. Always make sure the manuscript has a title page that includes the name of your play, your name, address, phone number (or your agent's), and an e-mail address. If they request that you send a SASE (self-addressed stamped envelope), send one or you can kiss that material good-bye.

THE VIDEOTAPE OF YOU PERFORMING THE SHOW

If you can arrange to have a professional videotape made of you performing your show, by all means do so. Try to videotape your show in front of a live audience. You'll want a lot of close-ups of you performing the piece on the videotape. You'll also want some shots cutting back and forth from your face to your body. Just so you're forewarned, many of the people that you'll be sending your videotapes to never return them, so be sure to make multiple copies. Generally, many of the festivals to which you'll be sending the tape want it to be under an hour; try to keep to that rule. Many viewers of the videotapes watch about the first five minutes of each tape, so the best advice is to cue the tape up to what you consider a strong section in your show.

YOUR RÉSUMÉ

Your résumé should include all pertinent information, such as your name and address, your telephone, fax, and e-mail address, your theatrical background (including, for example, names of shows and theaters you've performed in), academic and theatrical training that you've had, any theatrical unions that you belong to, and theatrical groups that you're a member of. If your work has been published, make sure to include that on your résumé as well.

I suggest that the résumé you send with your manuscript should not be your regular acting résumé. Rather, it should be a résumé focused more on your one-person show. It should feature any and all information pertaining to your show, placed in strategic areas on the résumé. It should also, however, include all of your other acting credits.

YOUR COVER LETTER

Your cover letter should be addressed to an individual (if possible), rather than to just "literary manager." Let the person know why you are contacting him. Introduce the monologue and give some basic information about it. Explain why you think your monologue might be right for that specific theater. If you've performed the show at other theaters, include that information. You can mention that the show was well received or got good reviews, but don't get into too much detail about it. If you've performed the play in many theaters, there's no reason to list them all; just list the main ones. (The others are listed on your résumé.) Tell the theater personnel a bit about who you are. Let them know that you look forward to hearing from them. If they requested a copy of your monologue prior to this letter, let them know that you're looking forward to hearing from them with their response. End the letter with an expression like "With warm regards" or "Sincerely."

THE SYNOPSIS OF YOUR MONOLOGUE

Many writers find it very difficult to summarize the story of their monologue. Unfortunately, in some cases (not too many), the theater or producer requires this summary. Here are some things to keep in mind regarding the synopsis: Without going into too much detail, briefly summarize the basic features of the plot of your monologue. What is the story you're trying to tell? Your synopsis should include a basic description of the theme and the style of the monologue. Avoid clichéd statements to describe any aspect of the work. Be original, honest, and personal in describing your work. Your synopsis should be a page or less.

Management/Booking Agencies
That Handle Solo Artists

The following are just a few management/booking agencies that work with solo artists. This list is just a starting point; there are many others.

Washington Square Arts & Films
310 Bowery, Second Floor
New York, NY 10012
Tel: (212) 253-0333
Fax: (212) 253-0330
Web site: *www.washingtonsquarearts.com*
Contact: Kathleen Russo

This agency is dedicated to artists who are "unique, challenging, powerful, and fun, artists whose work is designed for diverse and wide-ranging audiences." They are a relatively small agency handling a select, handpicked group of artists. Their present roster includes: Danny Hoch, Hazelle Goodman, Holly Hughes, Marga Gomez, Bob Holman, and others.

Columbia Artists Management, Inc. (CAMI)
165 West Fifty-seventh Street
New York, NY 10019
Tel: (212) 841-9500

This company was formed in 1930 when Arthur Judson, a cofounder of the Columbia Broadcast System, merged seven independent concert managers to pool their musical knowledge, commercial know-how, and booking facilities. The corporation consisted of managers whose lists represented the most famous artists of the day and whose activities covered all of North America. Today, aside from solo artists, they also handle ensembles, orchestras, dance companies, and popular and theatrical attractions.

CAMI is a diversified artist management company offering personal direction for solo artists and performing arts organizations. The company has taken a strong role in finding and developing the careers of solo artists.

CSTAR (Creative Stage Artists Management)
50 Baywood Avenue
San Anselmo, CA 94960
Tel: (415) 453-3883
Fax: (415) 456-3883
E-mail: *greg@cstartists.com*
Web site: *www.cstartists.com*
Contact: Greg Phillips or Cathy Pruzan

This relatively small management company handles a select group of artists. Some of their clientele include Kate Clinton, Sherry Glaser, Debby Gravite, and the New Century Chamber Orchestra.

PART II

interviews with monologue writers and performers

CHAPTER 16

lanie robertson

To begin this section, I wanted to include a segment on Lanie Robertson's play, *Lady Day at Emerson's Bar and Grill,* the first solo show I ever saw. I remember how impressed I was that one person (with a back-up band) on a stage could hold an audience's attention just as powerfully as a play with full cast of actors.

Lady Day at Emerson's Bar and Grill has had legendary success in the solo play world. There have been countless productions over the last twenty years or so. There are still many productions each year, all around the world.

Lanie Robertson is a playwright, not a performer, who wrote this material first and found an actress to perform it once it was completed. Other interviews are with performers, who either shaped material for themselves or created it in collaboration with a co-writer or director. The questions I put to Robertson were somewhat different from the ones I asked the performers; therefore, the format of this interview is somewhat different from the format used in the chapters that follow.

© *Martha Swope*

Lanie Robertson began his playwriting career in Philadelphia with his first play, *The Insanity of Mary Girard.* His plays have been performed at many regional theaters through out the United States and the world. His New York City productions include *Back County Crimes* at Playwrights Horizons, *Nasty Little Secrets* at Primary Stages, *Lady Day at Emerson's Bar and Grill* at both the Vineyard Theatre and the West Side Arts Theater, and *Bringing Mother Down* and *Cannibal's Waltz* at the Abingdon Theatre.

In 1987 he won the Outer Critics Circle Award for his off-Broadway hit, *Lady Day at Emerson's Bar and Grill,* which starred

Lonette McKee as Billie Holiday, a role later assumed by Eartha Kitt, S. Epatha Merkerson, Loretta Divine, and Jackee Harry. He was awarded the prestigious Kleban Award as best librettist for *Stringbean*. His play *A Penny for the Guy* has been produced by the Virginia Stage Co., the Geva Theatre, Buffalo's Studio Arena Theatre, and the Manitoba Theatre Centre. His play *Alfred Stieglitz Loves O'Keeffe* toured with Stacey Keach and Margot Kidder in the title roles. It was later produced in Paris and Warsaw.

For television, Mr. Robertson wrote the Diana Ross special *Red Hot 'n' Blue* for ABC, and *Journey Into Genius*, which aired on PBS's *American Playhouse* and starred Matthew Modine.

His latest solo play, *Woman Before a Glass*, starring Mercedes Ruehl as Peggy Guggenheim, recently opened in New York.

GA: What prompted you to start writing your *Lady Day at Emerson's Bar and Grill?*

LR: The inspiration for the play came from someone else's personal experience. A lover of mine had seen Billie Holiday at a dive in North Philly. He said there were only five or six others there. She had come in "high as a kite," carrying her little dog, tripped on the wire to the mike, and sang. He said there was a water glass of booze atop the upright piano, but she never touched it. She sang thirteen or fourteen songs, then staggered out.

The incongruity of a major American artist performing for so few at the end of her magnificent career haunted me. How could this have happened? What in our society causes us to so undervalue the artist?

The figure of her standing there, performing in a dump, remained a strongly vibrating dramatic symbol on many levels. I couldn't forget what he'd described. But it was totally static, i.e., a nondramatic image.

GA: How and when did you first start?

LR: A few years later I saw a play on Broadway about Edith Piaf. The only part of that play that interested me was a moment when the character learns of the death of her lover, crosses to a mike, and sings "Mon Homme." At that moment, I knew that if I could find a way to make Billie's songs an extension of an internal monologue, rather than a stop/start songfest, I would have a play. It was then I decided to try to write *Lady Day at Emerson's Bar and Grill.*

GA: When starting out, did you have any specific things that you wanted to say or did you just allow yourself to explore freely on the subject?

LR: When I began the actual writing, I knew Billie Holiday's bio so well that I thought the most important stories needed to be told. But the reason I wanted to write the play didn't really have anything to do with those events or experiences. I wanted to deal with something elusive, something I wasn't aware of consciously. So though I had a sense of where I wanted to go, the ground I wanted to cover, there was a sense or feeling that was somewhere between triumph and tragedy, failure and enormous success, that I hoped to find. I only felt I'd done so once "the voice" spoke to me.

GA: How did you technically begin working on the piece (notes, yellow pads, etc.)?

LR: I wrote everything out in longhand at first. I plotted the "stories" she would recount and I was clear about their order because I felt the selection of the songs determined (through lyrics or sound) the mood swings necessary for the play. I did much research, listening to her recordings, reading everything I could, and speaking with people who'd known her. Once I'd done that, however, I had to await the "arrival" of the text. Then I rapidly typed, typing as fast as I could without thought, just feeling to guide me. I tried to be the character so I could work it through my own consciousness.

GA: As you developed the play, how did you shape it?

LR: At the beginning, I thought the character herself would be haunted by the question I myself couldn't resolve. How did she wind up a few months before her death performing for a handful of patrons in a down-and-out dive in a city she hated, a city that had sent her cold turkey to prison? From research about her, I knew the stories, the events in her life I wanted her to tell, important segments of the "Rosebud" question, and so I listened endlessly to her recordings in order to find the songs that would provide the structural basis of the play. I shaped its structure by means of those songs because they were to function as extensions of the "inner" monologue.

GA: Did you have readings of segments of the play as you were writing it?

LR: No. The major problem for me was a failure to find the voice of the character. I'm not an African American, and the "voice" remained mine no matter what I did. After listening for eighteen months to a tape recording I'd made of her songs, I dreamt I was hearing Billie Holiday speaking to me. I also dreamt that I was at my typewriter (remember those?), typing what she said. I awoke enough to realize I was in bed. I ran to my typewriter and began writing . . . somewhere in the middle of the play, but it didn't matter. What mattered was I'd found the voice. I couldn't prove it was her, but the important thing for me is that it was!

GA: How did you know when the piece was ready for a first complete read-through?

LR: When I finished the first draft, I knew the play was "done." I'd lived with it for so long that I just knew. It was all I'd wanted to do in terms of dealing with the artistic struggle of the singer on stage. For me, she was Casey at the bat, desperately trying not to strike out. I couldn't do any more.

GA: How did those early readings go and how did that affect your rewrites?

LR: The readings went well, but mainly as a confirmation of what I'd done, not as a reason to do otherwise. Usually I gain greatly from asking actors to participate in readings or simply to read for me alone. But in this case it was all too immediate, too personal for me to gain much from the objective experience of hearing it read. I didn't rewrite.

GA: How did you find the actor for the original production (workshop, showcase)?

LR: The theater held auditions, and it came down to someone who could do the workshop but not move should the production go on, and someone who was free to do both. Fortunately, we went for the latter. The *hit* that resulted from that production provides about half my income twenty years later.

GA: Did the play evolve much from the showcase (workshop, readings) to the actual first production?

LR: No. It was one of those seldom-in-a-lifetime experiences where . . . once it happened . . . it was as finished as I was able to make it once the words "Curtain, end of play" were reached.

GA: Describe your relationship with the director of the first major production. Where was he or she most helpful?

LR: The director was a European whose approach to directing was to prefer a dead playwright. I was persona non grata, and he wasn't at all interested in my ideas about the play. He threatened to quit when I asked if I could give him my comments.

The actor was an African American from Detroit who rehearsed the play in a British accent. My one success was my appeal to the producer to convince the director to allow the actor to try performing the play in her native Detroitese. The producer, who also hadn't wanted to hear from me, heard the difference, and the play was allowed to come alive for the first time.

Any playwright knows dialogue is like music. It has its own rhythm, tone, and mood. An actor "singing" out of key can ruin a play. Happily for me and my play, this was avoided—barely so, but it was.

GA: How did those first performance(s) go?

LR: Excellently. The first performances were in a showcase theater with fewer than ninety seats, but the *New York Times* came, saw, and gave it two rave reviews on the same day: one for the play and one for the jazz. The showcase production was sold out within two hours. Almost immediately, plans were made to move the production for a longer run.

GA: How is writing a one-person play different from writing a regular play?

LR: Not at all different. The conflict consists simply of pitting one part of the character against another part of that character. Or it may be pitting the character against his/her world. The answer is always conflict, conflict, conflict. Character is the embodiment of that conflict.

GA: What advice do you have for other actors/playwrights just starting out who want to develop one-person shows?

LR: Know the character well enough to look for the point in his/her life that is the key or can be used as the key to unlock the demons within. We all have them—we all try our best to avoid acknowledging them. In writing a play, those demons must be made manifest both visually and verbally in order for an audience to glimpse their own.

The interviews in the following chapters were with solo show writers/performers. These were the general questions asked:

- What prompted you to start writing your own show?
- How and when did you first start?
- Did you have any specific goals or things that you wanted to say, or did you just allow yourself to explore freely?
- How did you begin working? What kinds of things did you do those first times?
- As you developed your piece, how did you shape it or do rewrites to illuminate things?
- How did you deal with self-censoring, doubts, etc.?
- How did you know when the piece was ready?
- How did you rehearse the piece?
- Describe your relationship with your director. Where was he most helpful?
- What was it like performing the piece that first time up? How do you feel the performances have changed?
- What's it like for you to perform your own work every night in front of an audience?
- As you've worked on new material, how would you say your work process has changed?
- What advice do you have for other actors just starting out who want to develop their own one-person shows?

CHAPTER 17

sarah jones

© *Stella Magloire*

Sarah Jones is an Obie Award–winning playwright, actor, and poet. She attended Bryn Mawr College, where she was the recipient of the Mellon Minority Fellowship, then returned to her native New York and began writing and performing. Called "a master of the genre" by the *New York Times*, Jones and her solo shows—*Surface Transit*, *Women Can't Wait*, and *Bridge and Tunnel* (this show was produced by Meryl Streep)—have garnered numerous honors, including a Helen Hayes Award, an award at HBO's Comedy Arts Festival for best one-person show, and two Drama Desk nominations.

Jones's plays have enjoyed sold-out runs at the Kennedy Center, the Berkeley Repertory Theatre, and the American Place Theatre, among others, and have been presented for such audiences as the United Nations, the Supreme Court of Nepal, and members of the U.S. Congress. She has received grants and commissions from Lincoln Center, the Ford Foundation, the W.K. Kellogg Foundation, and many others. Jones recently made history by suing the FCC for its ban of her celebrated poem/song "Your Revolution," and eventually forced reversal of the censorship.

Margo Jefferson in the New York Times *says, "The humor and compassion that come from paying real attention to people who are not like you have been pitifully rare in mainstream theater. Humor, compassion, and daring have more often found a place in solo performance. This form frees gifted artists to change sex, race, age, body type and personality in an instant. It takes great craft and generosity. Sarah Jones has both. You see this in every moment of her new show,* Bridge and Tunnel.*"*

Michael Kuchwara, drama critic for the Associated Press, said, "Don't believe reports that Bridge and Tunnel *is a one-woman show. There is a whole parade of real people on stage at Off-Broadway's 45 Bleecker Theater, where*

Sarah Jones is holding forth in what is the most satisfying solo show since Mike Nichols unveiled Whoopi Goldberg and Lily Tomlin searched for signs of intelligent life in the universe nearly twenty years ago."

Writing as an Antidote

The dearth of material that affirmed voices like mine, or even acknowledged the existence of the kinds of characters and experiences that were part of my daily life, was plenty of motivation. According to most of the mainstream arts and entertainment establishment, New York life in the late 1990s looked something like *Friends* on TV. Of course, nothing could have been further from my reality, and the absence of any accurate, nuanced representations of the diverse, complex cast of characters that made up my world was enough to make me sick. I wrote and performed my own work as an antidote.

Validation

I became interested in the competitive performance poetry slam scene emanating from the Nuyorican Poets Café in New York in 1996 as an audience member. It wasn't long before I had read at my first open mic there, and I continued developing my writing and performance style, eventually winning the coveted "Grand Slam" Championship in 1997. The validation gave me the permission I needed to begin shifting my focus from poems to monologues, and from one kind of "spoken word"—performative voice—to the multicultural range of voices and personae I wanted to bring to life on stage. I wrote and first performed *Surface Transit*, a series of interconnected monologues, at the Nuyorican Poets Café in 1998.

I think everyone who commits to the process of writing has a goal of some sort in mind, even if that goal is to "not say anything in particular" or to explore "freely" in defiance of or in opposition to the notion of being constrained by a certain purpose or message. As a woman, a black American, and a person of multiethnic heritage from working-class roots, I don't feel I have the luxury of abstract "freedom," creative or otherwise, as long as the majority of the voices that inspire me are relegated to the margins of literature, performance, the arts in general, and the world at large.

My Unconventional Route

Looking back, I realize my unconventional, almost accidental route to performance helped engender in me a kind of fearlessness. To perform work that had not been vetted by anyone, had not been honed through techniques learned in any writing course or acting school, had never even read aloud except in front of my bedroom mirror, seems pretty insane to me now. But my total lack of experience meant I had few expectations and little sense of the risks of performing untested material or improvising wildly if the spirit possessed me. I had the basic structure of *Surface Transit* in my mind, but I performed a different version of it nearly every night for the first few weeks of my initial run, changing a character's biographical information, altering a monologue to reflect a current event, even killing off a character one evening only to resurrect her/him the next. My director, Gloria Feliciano, joked about how excruciating it was for her to watch my eyes flicker in the seconds before I'd literally begin to rewrite a whole scene on stage, feeling my way for whatever felt true for the character.

This problematic style of performance grew in part out of my belief that I was incapable of memorization, and my obsession with capturing whatever the character would *really* feel and say in a given moment, such that I couldn't commit to a final script. Gloria wasn't thrilled with my unpredictable meanderings, and the process was often unnerving for me, too, but at the same time always exhilarating. I liken the feeling to dancing along a narrow beam, very gradually coming into a sense of my own balance, but being mostly unaware and unconcerned that I was actually a mile up in the air with no net below me.

Eventually, I discovered the joys of writing *before* I took the stage, as well as the joys of editing and adhering to a script. I also began to watch and listen to tapes of my performances to improve the physical and vocal characteristics of each role, from the shaking hands and raspy "Noo-Yawk-ese" of one character to the limping gait and Georgia drawl of another. The more fully human each character became, the better I was able to construct and animate the reality of each scene, the layers of every relationship, the syntax of every line.

I thought (and still think) of all my characters as real people, so I let them take the fall for everything.

Rehearsing in Front of the Audience

I hadn't really thought about it before exposing the work to audiences, and fortunately their responses were encouraging enough that I didn't worry too much about my readiness or lack thereof. However, in retrospect, I don't know if I'd be writing and performing today if I'd waited until I was "ready" by my own standards, or anyone else's, for that matter.

My rigorous rehearsal regimen consisted of performances in front of audiences. The concept of performing full-time, just being in the theater, was so new to me, that I didn't have much discipline where rehearsals were concerned, so the shows themselves provided my only focused "rehearsal time." I also listened to and/or watched tapes of the performances as a form of rehearsal, and to incorporate any improvised lines I wanted to add to the script.

Gloria Feliciano taught me to trust my own ears, to believe in my own body, and how not to over-think my characters. Rather, she helped me to allow them to continue developing naturally, through observation of real people over time. She convinced me never to underestimate my writer's intelligence simply because I found the various ethnic dialects and work-a-day experiences of my characters to be richer material than the impenetrable dialogue and bourgeois themes that constitute many "well-made" plays.

Every night it is different, but there are a few constants: I always slip out of my body at some point during the performance to give the characters space to stretch out and commune with the audience; I always have one "perfect" moment—sometimes more than one, but always one at least—in which I have disappeared and the audience has disappeared because for that instant the character's life is fully realized and being lived onstage; I always feel an intense surge of emotion, two parts gratitude, one part exhaustion, during my bow.

I now have a set of routines I know work well for my character development and writing. I know how many days it takes for me to filter an accent or vocal quality through my ears before my mouth can have comfortable control over it. I know how much information I need about a character and her/his world before I can believe in her/him enough to write. And since I alleviated the anxiety of my former tight-rope walk, improv-in-front-of-paying-audiences approach, I enjoy the process much more.

Advice to Other Actors

Study the work of other solo performers you admire greatly (and even those you don't care to emulate—there's plenty to learn from them, too). Watch them work live if you can; get video recordings of their plays, films, and interviews; read pieces they've performed. I hadn't done much of what I'm advising when I began (in fact, I had only seen Lily Tomlin, Whoopi Goldberg, and Tracey Ullman on TV), but if I had, I would have had a clearer context for my own work, in spite of my lack of formal training. Take in as much of what's out there in the way of one-person shows as you can. Then make sure what you have to contribute to that teeming sea has some set of unique qualities, compelling perspectives, voices seldom heard, that will make your work a buoyant example of the genre at its best.

CHAPTER 18

spalding gray

© Paula Cort

Spalding Gray created fifteen monologues that were performed throughout the United States, Europe, and Australia, including *Sex and Death to the Age 14; Booze, Cars and College Girls; A Personal History of the American Theater; India and After (America); Monster in a Box; Gray's Anatomy*; and *Swimming to Cambodia*. Appearances on Broadway and off-Broadway include the portrayal of the Stage Manager in *Our Town*, directed by Gregory Mosher, and the Performance Group's New York premiere of Sam Shepard's *The Tooth of Crime*. He cofounded the Wooster Group, and he wrote and performed the autobiographical trilogy *Three Places in Rhode Island*.

Film credits include Roland Joffé's *The Killing Fields*, Jonathan Demme's *Swimming to Cambodia*, and David Byrne's *True Stories*, as well as *Clara's Heart, Beaches*, and *The Paper*. Publications include a collection of monologues, *Sex and Death to the Age 14* (Random House), *Swimming to Cambodia* (Theater Communications Group), *In Search of the Monkey Girl* (Aperture Press), *Gray's Anatomy* (Vintage), and the novel *Impossible Vacation* (Knopf). *It's a Slippery Slope* was published by Farrar, Straus & Giroux and was released on compact disc (Mercury Records). Mr. Gray received a Guggenheim Fellowship and grants from the National Endowment for the Arts and The Rockefeller Foundation. His *Swimming to Cambodia* won the Obie Award.

Peter Marks, in the New York Times, *called Gray "the grand master of the first-person singular . . ." and went on to say, "It's a Slippery Slope* is a clear-eyed and life-affirming performance piece."

Reviewing It's a Slippery Slope, *Mark Wasburn of the* Village Voice *wrote, "Spalding Gray's brilliant life-monologue is in another league. Funny and touching, Gray slides down the slopes of his uncertainties, creating a theatrical landscape of remarkable internal dimension."*

Aural Autobiography

First of all, it's important to say that I don't start off writing material, although I like to consider myself a writer. I'm definitely an aural composer.

I was working with the Wooster Group in 1976 and 1977; I was evolving with the group theater pieces that involved stories of my life. One of the seminal pieces was *Rumstick Road*, which was about my mother's suicide. In that I'd do little direct addresses to the audience. I'd be saying, "This is me, I'm Spalding Gray, and this is what happened to me." Those little stories, when printed up, read like writing. I saw that I was doing a form of autobiographic writing. But it was theatricalized, made into theatrical metaphors by Elizabeth LeCompte (the director).

Once I split from the Wooster Group (1979), I wanted to go solo. But what I wanted to do was tell my story. So I sat at a little desk in the Performing Garage in September of 1979 and started telling my story, beginning with the first monologue, *Sex and Death at the Age 14* (later performed at the Performing Garage).

I sat down with an outline to guide me through the narrative of memories, but then I tape-recorded it and listened to what I had said. It was that way of working that gave me my structure. The next evening, I went back after listening to it and tied it all together. So in that sense, you might say I was working structurally from the original memory. I wasn't sitting down and saying, "How would this go better?" If I had any goals in mind, it was just to tell the audience the stories, my stories. I'd see how it sat with the audience.

I don't like to rehearse. My first rehearsal is with and in front of an audience. I say that I work improvisationally, but the way it's different from most improv people is that eventually I want it to be set. Most improv people want it to stay open and keep on opening up. When I was a traditional actor, I had to memorize lines and then pretend that I didn't know them. Now I don't memorize lines because there are no lines. It's like bushwhacking.

In a way I'm corralling memories and trying to find the right words for them each time. And that's what gives it its freshness. And that's what makes the audience think that I'm saying it for the first time. Because what they're witnessing is something that's in the moment. And what that is, is a recollection each evening of a text that is only in the memory.

Rewriting

The way I rewrite is by doing the next performance. So, in a sense, I get paid to rewrite. I tape each performance for sometimes up to thirty shows. Each tape is new and helpful, filled with insights. I think better in front of an audience. Between the first show and the thirtieth show, I believe the detail of the story changes, as does the structure.

As the shows progress, I get more cinematographic and do quicker cuts. I have a photographic memory, and at the beginning I tend to remember too much; there's just too much information. It's like a kid telling his dream. As I go along, I cut to the chase and get better and better. As far as clarity, let's think about water going down a mountain. It runs all the different trails until it finds that one trail. In my work, once it finds that one trail, the piece suddenly becomes clearer, a condensed stream of thought. But that one comes through many flows, believe me. That's what it is for me. It takes many performances to lead to that absolute, heightened language that is no longer just chatting to the audience. So when I sit down and perform my *It's a Slippery Slope* piece, which I really know, having performed it for four years, I can go right into it. I immediately find all the rhythms.

I think each piece goes through at least three clear delineations. The first is the actual public memory with the audience, where I'm speaking it and trying to figure it out for myself with them. My early audiences get to see me discovering things. I'm doing it with them. There's an enormous amount of dialogue there at the beginning.

The audience began, quite a while ago, to teach me and give me my sense of humor. I've developed it with them. I had been more of an existentially dark, tortured New Englander. I think by coming to New York, I came to the right place to find dialectic. I really think of my work as a dialogue with the audience.

My Sense of Reality

I remember when I was an actor playing roles, I always felt a bit removed. I would think things like, "This isn't really me. This isn't really real, and this didn't really happen." I've personally always felt that life is such a dream, such a fiction, so ephemeral. It only comes around once. It has nothing to compare it to. So I think that that my monologues are a form of coming round twice. First of all, of reincarnation, by retelling the story. And also of grounding myself, by saying, "I'm Spalding Gray and this happened to me."

I don't make up fictitious stories; it's not my way of working. My son Forrest, who is now five, will sometimes ask me to tell him a scary story. And nothing ever comes to mind, no story. And finally, exhausted, I'll say, "Forrest, this is the scary story; just look around."

When my self-censors come in, which only occurs minimally, I welcome them. Otherwise, I tend to get too self-indulgent. By the way, my definition of "self-indulgence" is "lack of awareness." What is narcissism? A narcissist is someone who doesn't know he's a narcissist. As long as I'm aware (through hearing the tape) of what I'm saying, then I can at least make conscious choices and accept it or not accept it.

The Dance of Dialogue

I'm always testing out my stories on the people that I live with because I'm a storyteller. I'll start talking at the end of the day, incessantly. I make outline journals in my head of, say, some thing or things that happened yesterday. And then I'll tell the stories to Kathy (the woman I live with), or my therapist, or whomever. I'll say certain keywords that remind me of the event. At some point in my process of developing a piece, I'll call in what I call a "creative consultant," to help me, just be a mirror to what I'm saying. I'll say to him, "Here's what I'm hearing. What could go better?"

What I do with an audience is transference. That's where the dance is, where the dialogue is, where they affect me. A year or so after performing a piece, I will call a director in, because sometimes the piece has become unwieldy or too long. It can use some minor tuning. When we did the CD of *It's a Slippery Slope,* James Taylor was the producer. It was James's ear and fresh take on the material that enabled me to go through the whole process of recording it. He was hearing it fresh and was excited by it.

CHAPTER 19

mary louise wilson

© *Ron Rinaldi*

Mary Louise Wilson's one-woman show, *Full Gallop*, was performed at the Bay Street Theatre, the Manhattan Theatre Club, at the Westside Arts Theater off-Broadway, and in London. On Broadway, she has appeared in *Showboat* (Harold Prince, director), *Prelude to a Kiss* (Norman Rene, director), Neil Simon's *Fools* (Mike Nichols, director), *Alice in Wonderland* (Eva LaGallienne, director), *The Philadelphia Story* (Ellis Rabb, director), *Gypsy* (Arthur Laurents, director), and *The Royal Family*. Off-Broadway, she appeared in *Baby with the Bathwater* (Playwrights Horizons, Jerry Zaks, director), *Sister Mary Ignatius Explains It All for You* (Playwrights Horizons, Jerry Zaks, director), and *Buried Child* (Theatre de Lys, Robert Woodruff, director).

She has worked in film with directors such as Woody Allen (*Zelig*), Alan J. Pakula (*Klute*), Susan Seidelman (*She-Devil*), Peter Weir (*Green Card*), Chris Columbus (*Stepmom*), and Colin Higgins (*Best Little Whorehouse in Texas*). *Full Gallop* won the Drama Desk Award and the Obie Award, and received an Outer Critics Circle Award nomination. Her performance in *Cabaret* (1998 Broadway revival) garnered her a Tony Award nomination. She recently appeared on Broadway in the revival of *The Women*, and as Queen Elizabeth in the highly acclaimed New York Theatre Workshop production of *The Beard of Avon*.

Vincent Canby, in his New York Times *review of* Full Gallop, *wrote, "In addition to Vreeland's invigorating buccaneer personality,* Full Gallop *calls attention to the evolution of the one-character play as an unexpectedly rewarding, freewheeling source of entertainment in the contemporary theater. . . . [T]he play effortlessly unfolds as a high-flying, idiosyncratic memoir, a history of a marriage, a family, and a gaudy career."*

Inspiration

When I was a child, I was fascinated with Ruth Draper, so I thought about monologues, but it didn't seem like something someone did in modern times. I hated the idea of a one-woman show. A one-person show just seemed like something that couldn't be done. You needed two actors for a play to happen. The only one-woman show I ever saw that I liked was Pat Carroll's *Gertrude Stein*. I liked that show very much, was very impressed with it. It was an inspiration to me.

To be honest with you, I decided to do my show because I was so fed up with where I was in the business, the work I was getting. I thought, "What the hell have I got to lose?" I'd spent years playing nurses and maids and secretaries, really boring and unnourishing stuff.

A friend of mine, Mark Hampton [co-writer of *Full Gallop*], was as fascinated as I was with Diana Vreeland. When she died, I realized that I must get the rights to the book *D.V.* I thought, If I don't get the rights to it, someone else will, and then I'd kick myself for the rest of my life. I was amazed that they actually entertained the idea of Mark and me possibly doing this. It seemed that each step of the way, the door would actually open.

I've always been fascinated by people in power and what happens to them when they lose their power. Also, I understand what it's like to be out of work. But mostly, the woman [Vreeland] is so different from me. She was such an up, such a survivor. She had a joy in living that was pretty irresistible. She was a combination of what I always wanted to be as a kid—funny and glamorous at the same time. I remember as a child thinking that Carmen Miranda was someone else who "had it."

Lists, Linkage, and Index Cards

Mark and I sat around for days, talking and taking notes. Then we took the book *D.V.* and indexed it into sections. We whittled it down to our favorite stories. We also had access to audiotapes of her talking, so we also had the advantage of learning how she told a story. We also read other things about her, what other people said, interviews, etc. At first she was hilarious, just that; then we began to find her very moving. I found her gallant, no bitchiness about her, not interested in going on about something she hated.

Something else that fascinated me while working on this piece was the amount of minutiae that you unearth about a person's life. I would explore how she would get ready in the morning, the objects she touched, her life.

Getting back to those first steps, I filled legal pads with notes that we took from all our research. There were index cards that had various stories laid out. We played with the arrangement of things. We were trying to build it, give it a climax. We decided to only use stories that were germane to moving the play forward. It really was heartbreaking, because there were a lot of great stories that we couldn't use.

I found the index cards to be a very valuable tool. The cards can be placed on the floor and can assist you in finding the play's arc. You can rearrange them over and over until you have the best sequence, the best arrangement.

As far as shaping the piece, I used *Gertrude Stein* as a model. The things that were most important to me were the following questions:

1. Where are we?
2. Who are we?
3. Who are we talking to?
4. Where is the character in her life?

Answering those questions is, I believe, crucial to a successful one-person show. I find that so often they are not addressed in one-person shows. I spent months answering them.

So what we had were these wonderful stories. What we needed was a linkage, something that could hold them together. Basically, what we needed to supply now was a dramatic line.

Originally we had a maid in the piece, another character. She would come on and say "Oui" or "Non." We thought this was great. But eventually, as the piece developed, we let her go. You must realize that we took six years to write the play. We did readings and workshops during that time. And after each reading or workshop we would take another leap forward in the development of the script.

Since this was collaboration, you should understand the relationship that I had with my co-writer, Mark Hampton. We both intuitively understood the woman. But I, as an actor, was trying to make everything real and not campy, based in emotional things. Mark wanted to put in jokes. We both would give in to each other, depending on how it went in the reading.

From the very beginning, I knew that there had to be one set, and it had to be where she would talk. It seemed inevitable that it should be her living room.

Development

The readings would be done all over. Once we did one at Playwrights Horizons, and Andre Bishop invited us to do a reading at a ladies' club. At that reading, we met Sybil Burton. She arranged for us to do full-out productions for two weekends at Bay Street (in Sag Harbor). We did readings at Juilliard (a fundraiser), at nightclubs, wherever. After one reading, in this nightclub, a friend of mine saw it and mentioned it the next day to Jack O'Brien. It was at that nightclub fundraiser that we got a director and a literary agent.

I took on her manner and voice in rehearsals. I'd walk on the road near where I live in the country, and memorize it. Mark would be my outside eye. We continued to rewrite even after we did it at the Old Globe, right up until we opened at the Manhattan Theatre Club. One of the lessons that I learned while working on her was to intuit the way she would say things.

When the director came into the picture, the whole piece took on more of a physical life. Mark stopped coming to rehearsals after the piece was finally down on paper. The director took over at that point.

I did find it somewhat difficult going from being the writer to just being the actor. I remember, time and again, looking at a line and saying, "Who wrote this? I can't say this!" It was a bit conflicting.

In order to write what you want to say, you have to write badly. It's the biggest lesson that I've learned. Say I wanted Diana to be really witty. I'd write the first thing that comes into my head. Quite often it would be terrible the first time. That wouldn't be discouraging, it just meant I'd have to improve on what I just wrote. You have to learn to say, "No, that isn't what I want to say. This is what I want to say!" When you're stuck, you can't wait for inspiration; you just have to sit down and write!

We got the name *Full Gallop* after a lunch that I had with Vreeland's son. (I had to be approved of.) He told me that she always had visitors over, even when she was ill. If she didn't feel well enough to come out of her bedroom, the maid would serve the guests a meal, and they would talk to her through the door. He said, "Mom never liked to appear unless she was at full gallop."

Collaborations

I think that it's great to work with someone. It's a huge help. When the two of you show up, then you have to do something. There is the responsibility to your partner. There were, however, days of staring contests, where nothing happened. It would be terrible. Fortunately, they were rare. Also, working with someone may not be for everyone. It really is a marriage.

Another piece of advice: You have to connect with the audience. It's imperative in this type of theater. You must feel them and be open to them. In a sense, they are your scene partner. I have found that doing a one-person play is very empowering for actors. I hope that other actors don't wait as long as I did to get started. There is so much pleasure in this type of theater.

CHAPTER 20

charlayne woodard

© Helen K. Garber

Charlayne Woodard's first play, *Pretty Fire*, which she wrote and performed, enjoyed successful engagements at the Manhattan Theatre Club and at the Seattle Repertory Company. It was published by Penguin Press. Her second play, *Neat*, also enjoyed sold-out runs at the Manhattan Theatre Club, Seattle Repertory Theater, and the Mark Taper Forum in Los Angeles.

As an actress, Ms. Woodard performed in the original cast of *Ain't Misbehavin'* on Broadway. Off-Broadway, she performed in such shows as *Hang On to the Good Times* at the Manhattan Theatre Club, George C. Wolfe's production of *The Caucasian Chalk Circle*, and opposite Michelle Pfeiffer in *Twelfth Night* at the New York Shakespeare Festival. Regionally she has worked at the La Jolla Playhouse in Tony Kushner's adaptation of *The Good Person of Setzuan* (with Lou Diamond Phillips). Film credits include: *The Crucible* with Winona Ryder, John Schlesinger's *Eye for an Eye*, with Sally Field, and *One Good Cop* with Michael Keaton. Television credits include: *Run for the Dream: The Gail Devers Story* (playing Gail Devers), Oprah Winfrey's *The Wedding*, and *Buffalo Girls* with Melanie Griffith and Angelica Huston. *Pretty Fire* won a Los Angeles Drama Critics Circle Award and the NAACP Theater Award for Best Play and Best Playwright. *Neat* was nominated for an Outer Critics Circle Award and an Ovation Award (Los Angeles) for Best Play and Best Actress. It won the prestigious Blanche and Irving Laurie Foundation Theater Visions Fund Award. Acting awards include: Tony and Drama Desk nominations for *Ain't Misbehavin'* and a second Drama Desk nomination for *Hang On to the Good Times*. Ms. Woodard received an AUDELCO nomination for her performance in George C. Wolfe's production of *The Caucasian Chalk Circle*.

Charlayne Woodard's latest theater piece, *Flight*, recently opened at the new Kirk Douglas Theatre in Los Angeles. It was commissioned and developed as part of the Center Theatre Group's P.L.A.Y. (Performing for Los Angeles Youth) program, which targets young people and their families.

David Richard, in the New York Times, *called* Pretty Fire *"one of the most positive pictures of the Black-American experience I've seen on stage."*

Howard Waxman in Variety *said of her second play,* Neat, *". . . a frequently funny, often frightening, and ultimately very moving series of vignettes. . . . With just a few carefully nuanced gestures and vocal changes, Ms. Woodard offers a spectacular gallery of family portraits."*

Keeping My Chops

I had moved to Los Angeles. I believe that if I'd stayed in New York, I'd never have written anything. I was too busy working all the time. When I moved to Los Angeles, I thought I'd be just as busy tackling new stuff. That's not how it worked out, though. I was getting guest spots on TV shows with like three lines or something. And even though I'd be on the set all week, I had a lot more time. Between guest-spot gigs, you might have like two weeks of nothing. And I was so used to working. So I'd come back home just to do a play. I kept feeling, I've got to keep my chops, I've got to keep my chops.

So I decided [that] since I'm a member of the Actors Studio, to work on a piece. I wanted to work on something just for myself. I felt if I kept working on something, it would keep my chops up. At the same time, I was meeting with lots of people, and I'm talking a lot, because basically I'm a storyteller. I found myself telling people about my life. People out here in L.A., it seemed to me, had never met anyone like me. In some sense, L.A. is a very segregated town. I felt that I had to explain myself when I was around people who weren't black. I'd tell them about where I came from, my family, [stuff] like that.

I had this friend Shirley, who's an artist. And she said she hadn't had a black model in over fifty years. She asked me if I'd sit for her. Now what can you say to that? Of course I said yes. So as I sat there posing for her, I told her about my life. And she said, "You must write this down." My husband had also been prompting me to write my stories down. But prior to this time in L.A., I never had time to before. I was reluctant to start writing. I thought I was an actor only.

Cut to when my bishop's wife had asked me to sing at this women's retreat. I said, "No way." I mean, everyone there sings like Jennifer Holiday. She said, "Look, I'll give you twenty minutes to do anything you want. It doesn't have to be singing." That's when I wrote my first story. It was about what turned me into being an actor. It's called "Joy." It's the last piece of my first show, *Pretty Fire.*

First You Talk, Then You Write

My process is to talk. I must have a person to talk to. I'd been telling the story of "Joy" for a year. Many of the stories in *Pretty Fire,* I'd been telling around for over a year. At dinner parties, lunches, wherever. When you have a person listening to your stories, you can see his reactions immediately. If he looks confused, you realize you have to clarify. Next time you tell that same story, you won't have that same confused moment. People's emotional reactions are very helpful to me. When they say, "Oh my God, I'm having goosebumps!" Or, "Oh my God, I'm crying," I know I've hit a nerve.

Then I'll tell that same story three or four more times over maybe a year. Then I'll write it down. I'm constantly refining it. When I finally get to the point where I write the thing down, that's basically what you're going to see. I start off with a script that's really fat; then, slowly, I begin making cuts. I don't just want a lot of monologues; I want a night of theater. It's after I'm on my feet with the piece that I start really rewriting, living the piece. Basically, I create from the doing. Once you are on your feet, you no longer tell your story; you start to live it. You'll find that you can cut a lot of expositional material now because you're doing them.

I live every minute sensorially. In my plays, sensory things are everywhere just so I can hook in. The sensory informs my emotions. That's what makes it exciting for me. I try to tell as little of the story as possible. My rehearsal period is about: How can I stop just telling this, and show it?

In *Neat*, I talk about how my aunt had an epileptic seizure. And I wrote a beautiful thing about how she jerked around and how her body followed, and how she banged into a chinaberry tree, bounced around, etc. In rehearsal, I decided to try actually doing it rather than just talking about it. It really upset me. But that was a good thing. I said, Okay, that's real, we keep it.

I was doing *Pretty Fire* in Seattle. During a break, I told Dan Sullivan a story about my aunt. He loved the story and said, "Charlayne, create a play about it and we'll workshop it next year." So, for a whole year, I told stories about that phase of my life. Then we workshopped the piece at Seattle.

Rehearsal

The way I rehearse is, I enter the room, the director's there, and I stand up and just start reading what I wrote, just like that. It's usually kind of not happening at that moment. It feels stilted. I change the words as I talk in rehearsal. Then I start moving around, writing down the changes. The director will remember the stuff that you came up with.

The script is just an outline with the main points. Sometimes I go off to a whole other thing that I'm reminded of, and then that new thing becomes part of the play. My workshop process is where I actually write it.

A play is not complete until I have the workshop audience. They tell me what is and isn't working. They are my scene partners. I never feel alone on the stage except for the first ten seconds. It's at that point that I look out and see what I call "my anchors." I find two anchors out in the audience, two people who are just waiting and ready. I start off just telling those two people my story. Then I open it up to the whole audience. My intention is, "Let me tell you something." Pretty soon, the whole stage gets crowded with all my characters. I don't feel alone anymore. All of their reactions make you feel good, goose you.

Living It, Breathing It

In the workshop production I read the play off the page. When I'm in an actual production, I have the piece in my soul. Ideally, by the last performance of a run I'm living and breathing every minute of it. I let it take me on a ride. Early on in workshop and early previews, you can't expect to be taken on a ride. It feels strange and it can sometimes be difficult. All through previews, I'm constantly changing it. You just have to roll with it through those tough times. The way it finally becomes part of your soul is when you've connected with audiences. Once we open, however, I freeze the show. But I don't ever freeze my life in it.

CHAPTER 21

tim miller

© Dona Ann McAdams

Tim Miller is an internationally acclaimed performance artist. His creative work as a performer and writer explores the artistic, spiritual, and political topography of his identity as a gay man. Hailed for his humor and passion, he has tackled this challenge in such pieces as *Live Boys* (1981, created with John Bernd), *Postwar* (1982), *Cost Of Living* (1983), *Democracy in America* (1984), *Buddy Systems* (1985, created with Doug Sadownick), *Some Golden States* (1987), *Stretch Marks* (1989), *Sex/Love/Stories* (1991), *My Queer Body* (1992), *Naked Breath* (1994), *Fruit Cocktail* (1996), *Shirts & Skin* (1997), *Glory Box* (1999), *Body Blows* (2002), and *Us* (2003).

His performances have been presented all over North America and Europe in such prestigious venues as the Yale Repertory Theatre, the Institute of Contemporary Art (London), the Walker Art Center (Minneapolis), and the Brooklyn Academy of Music. He is the author of the books *Shirts & Skin* and *Body Blows*. His solo theater works have been published in the play collections *O Solo Homo* and *Sharing the Delirium*.

Since 1990, Mr. Miller has taught performance in the theater department at UCLA and the dance program at California State University, Los Angeles. He is a cofounder of the two most influential performance spaces in the United States: Performance Space 122 on Manhattan's Lower East Side and the Highways Performance Space in Santa Monica, California.

Mr. Miller has received numerous grants from the National Endowment for the Arts. In 1990, he was awarded an NEA Solo Performer Fellowship, which was overturned under political pressure from the Bush White House because of the gay themes of his work. Mr. Miller and three other artists, the so-called NEA 4, successfully sued the federal government with the help of the ACLU for violation of their

First Amendment rights, and won a settlement in which the government paid them the amount of the defunded grants and all court costs. Though the Supreme Court of the United States decided in 1998 to overturn part of his case and determined that "standards of decency" are constitutional criteria for federal funding of the arts, Mr. Miller vows "to continue fighting for freedom of expression for fierce, diverse voices."

He can be reached at MillerTale@aol.com or through his Web site, *http://hometown.aol.com/millertale/timmiller.html.*

> *Tony Kushner, author of* Angels in America, *has said, "Tim Miller has been at the heart of things, giving voice to what matters most, for the entirety of his career. His work is an extraordinary fusion of history, observation, politics, and a kind of shamanism."*
>
> *Michael Feingold of the* Village Voice *has said of Tim Miller's work, "The [title* Glory Box *is] the Australian equivalent of 'hope chest,' but if you think it contains a double entendre, you're probably right, since this glory box is Tim Miller's latest solo piece and the writer-performer isn't likely to let such implications pass unnoted. The subject—immigration rights for same-sex partners—is a thorny one, but Miller has a gift for letting one topic open surprising doors onto a multitude of others; his works are as canny and complex as they are charming."*

Starting Out, Being Out

I have made about twenty full-evening solo performances over the last twenty years. When I arrived in New York City as a nineteen-year-old queer performer, I felt that if I wanted to see a fierce and lively queer performance and thriving theater, I would just need to make it myself. I believe my mission—should I decide to accept it—as an artist and a gay man is to give witness to this challenging time, to live out loud and give that voice to my community.

When I was practically still a kid, I cofounded Performance Space 122 in 1980 in Manhattan, and began using that space as a lively tree-house stage for my performing, teaching, and programming.

I got such inspiration from performances I saw as a high-school kid growing up in Los Angeles. These performances—especially the wild performance art pieces I was seeing at the Women's Building in downtown L.A.—really encouraged me to take chances and raise my voice. My hope in my performances is that any time we witness one person raise his voice and tell his story—as well as bring our focus to systems of injustice—that it can encourage any of us to find that truth within ourselves too. I have received that encouragement in my life from other theater artists and social movements, and I hope my performances have emboldened people as well!

Performance-Making

I suck up inspiration wherever I can! When I was a nineteen-year-old starting to make work in New York City, my primary influences were Allen Ginsberg, Walt Whitman, Vladimir Mayakovsky, and feminist performance art practice that was bringing personal life into creative work in such a direct way. Those sources all were trying to figure out the relation of self to society, and they continue to embolden and challenge me. Those sources were on fire within me and fueled my crazed, Artaudian early performance works about queer sex, the horrors of Ronald Reagan, and my growing up in California.

I teach performance-making a lot. Often I first locate the terrain of a piece by improvising something I want to explore within a workshop setting, where I am there as the teacher, but also as an artist making material. That improvised piece—in the oral tradition, as it were—then finds it way onto the computer and is honed into a full-evening performance.

Acknowledge those feelings of doubt. Look them in the eye. Push through and kick ass in the performance you make. I say this as someone who has regularly been messed with by the U.S. government for the content of my work. In 1990—during George Bush the First—I, a wandering queer performance artist, had been awarded a NEA Solo Theater Fellowship, which was promptly overturned under political pressure from the Bush White House because of the lush, wall-to-wall homo themes of my creative work. We so-called NEA 4 (me, Karen Finley, John Fleck, and Holly Hughes) then successfully sued the federal government with the help of the ACLU— if you're not a card-carrying member, become one!—for violation of our First Amendment rights and won a settlement where the government paid us the amount of the defunded grants and all court costs. The last little driblet of this case was the "decency" clause, which Congress had added to the NEA appropriation under the cattle prod of Jesse Helms. This "decency clause" is what we would later lose over at the U.S. Supreme Court.

My many performance works live and breathe in workshop settings for awhile. Then on mixed bills with other artists. Finally, they connect with an audience as a full-evening solo show. I tour all over the country every year, so my audiences end up playing a big part in my understanding of the shows. I have never worked with a director. But I keep threatening to! I am such a giant Virgo control queen. When opening night has arrived, [the show] is ready for that night. Or it better be!

The first full performance is a stressful high-wire act. I keep learning from each and every performance, and the pieces keep evolving. I end up doing probably at least two hundred performances of each of my full-evening shows, so there is a lot of room for growth and change over those many shows.

Over the years, I have trusted my intuition more and more to guide me and challenge me as I create a new work. Often the show ends up being about something quite different from I thought it was going to be.

Taking the Audience on a Journey

I love performing! The full buzz of the audience connecting with the humor, politics, and erotics in my performances. I trust humor a lot to make this connection with the audience happen. To be queer—or a queer artist—in America means that your identity and sexuality is constantly under the microscope (on a good day) or under attack (on a bad day). My recent shows about the battle over gay marriage are simultaneously my most personal pieces and my most political—my funniest shows and the most intense. The subject matter really looks at that harsh reality of the fact that our most intimate and sacred love relationships and sexuality are treated like shit in America. By necessity, these charged feelings bring forward more "accessible" humor/narrative as a way of dealing with the situation and reaching my audience. In my pieces, I cleverly manage to get people laughing about butt-plugs and spanking, etc. This lets people relax, see the fun and joy in our bodies and desires. And hopefully just relax with the journey I will take them on!

Advice to Actors Starting Out

Claim your voice. Take power over your creative destiny as a performer. Know why you *must* create the piece. Then do it!

CHAPTER 22

danny hoch

© Dona Ann McAdams

Danny Hoch performed his solo show *Some People* at P.S. 122 and at the Joseph Papp Public Theater in 1994 (directed by Jo Bonney). The show toured over twenty U.S. cities as well as Austria, Cuba, and Scotland. It also aired on HBO. Mr. Hoch has written and acted for television and several films, including HBO's *Subway Stories*, Terrence Malick's *The Thin Red Line*, and Fox Searchlight's *Whiteboys*. His writings have appeared in *Harper's Magazine* and the *New Theater Review*. *Out of Character; Jails, Hospitals & Hip-Hop*; and *Some People* were published by Villard Books, a division of Random House.

After a forty-city tour in 2000, *Jails, Hospitals & Hip-Hop* was made into a film and a spoken-word CD. Mr. Hoch won an Obie and a Fringe First Award (Edinburgh Festival) for his solo show *Some People*. The show was nominated for a Cable Ace Award for the HBO production. He is the recipient of a Solo Theater Fellowship from the National Endowment for the Arts, and a CalArts/Alpert Award, as well as a Sundance Writers Fellow and a Tennessee Williams Fellow. At Berkeley Repertory Theatre, *Jails, Hospitals & Hip-Hop* received a Bay Area Theater Critics Circle Award for Outstanding Solo Performance and a Drama Desk Award nomination.

Mr. Hoch is the founder of the NYC Hip-Hop Theater Festival, which has presented over fifty hip-hop-generation plays in four years. He is a founding member of the Active Element Foundation, which builds relationships between grassroots youth activists, professionals, donors, and artists through grant-making, technical assistance, and hip-hop culture. He works with the International Hip-Hop Exchange, which fosters pan-hip-hop arts cultural exchanges between the United States and four continents. He directed Will Power's *Flow* and his play *Till the Break of Dawn*, premiered at Baltimore's Centerstage.

The New York Times *called Hoch "a remarkable young performer who finds crusted layers of cultural contradictions . . . part sociologist, part moralist, and part super-chameleon."*

James Hannaham, in the Village Voice, *said, "[Hoch's] characters are beautifully developed, in an honest and virtuosic style . . . [His] strength lies in his ability to represent people as they are rather than as political discourse would dictate."*

I Never Wanted to Be a Writer

I never wanted to be a writer; I only wanted to act. But there was no theater, film, or TV that reflected my generation or responded to my community. So why be an actor if you're going to act about nothing that has to do with your community? I developed my work, orally, in front of an audience. I've forced myself to become a writer, but that's certainly not how it started out.

My first show was a piece called *Pot Melting* at a place called the Gas Station on the Lower East Side. It was about ninety minutes long.

I had graduated from the Performing Arts High School and went on to the North Carolina School for the Arts. I ultimately dropped out because the goal was to go back to New York after four years and audition for the same agents, casting directors, and producers I had auditioned for when I was at Performing Arts. I stopped looking through *Back Stage* and returning calls from the agents who were calling me for work that I just couldn't relate to, or didn't connect to. The material that was around just seemed ridiculous to me.

So I just started creating these monologues. I did them in front of audiences that I had invited either to my house, or at some performance evening somewhere. I'd work on ten or twenty minutes' worth of new material, and just start riffing, in character, in front of the audience. I knew who the characters were, where they were, and why they were there. But the dialogue, the language could go anywhere, anyplace. The goal was to let the character live and breathe. Eventually, after doing the characters many times, I got rid of what didn't work, kept what did. I worked totally from memory.

Eventually I had ninety minutes and about fourteen characters (two were eventually cut out). Initially I had a four-night run at the Gas Station, but that short run turned into a four-month run, based on pure word of mouth.

Later, as I toured the show, the characters kept evolving. They were living, breathing characters, not confined to a page. As time went on and issues changed, so did the characters. I worked mostly on structure and improvisation. I guess you can say that's how I work. Some characters in subsequent shows were offshoots of those original characters.

Some People

My next show, *Some People*, evolved a lot because I toured with it and did it so often. It was constantly changing. For instance, there was one character whose dialogue had completely changed from when I first did him, totally! I mean, he was talking about totally different things because time had changed.

By the time I got to the Public Theater I was writing things down, because I was working with a director, Jo Bonney. She forced me to write down everything I was saying. Initially, I was very reluctant because I thought, We're getting into literary dramatics here, and I don't want to be a playwright. I told her, "I don't write stories. I work with pure characters and oral language." It's the most organic and visceral way for me to work. If I'm sitting in front of a computer and trying to write dialogue, it's very unorganic for me. I'd feel detached, very intellectual, working like that. But Jo said, "If you look at what you've said on the page, you'll be able to dramaturge your own work, and see what the flow of it is."

See, when I'm on stage, I'm in a relationship with the audience. It's just them and me. So at those times, obviously, it's impossible for me to have a third eye. That's the work of the director, to be that third eye.

What I'm Trying to Say, How I'm Trying to Say It

The goal, for me, is the telling of the story. In the United Sates, most of us are not indigenous to this place. We come from many cultures and histories and languages. The idea that we're supposed to get along and understand each other is preposterous. The idea of one government and one president just doesn't make sense to me. So how do we wind up communicating? How do we communicate across cultures that claim us, even though we don't belong to it?

Everything is language. My mother is a speech pathologist, constantly working with all sorts of speech problems. As a kid, I was a mime. Actually, I was a street mime for many years. I think it's a combination of the knowledge I have of my mother's work and my mime experience that informed a lot of what I do.

Some of my characters took three years to evolve; some took just four days. I think Jo Bonney was a major catalyst to my work. She brought in a critical development. What she brought was an understanding of the dramatic experience. I was coming from a place that was way inside the character.

As an actor, I was concerned with what the audience was thinking at different times. As a playwright, however, I could have cared less. I wasn't concerned about having a story with a through-line. My only concern was, Is this character living and breathing? Jo Bonney came into the picture as a dramaturge-director.

To me, theater must be functional. Theater, for me, must be the most powerful form of communication; otherwise, it's not functional.

I used to create with wild abandon, until there were critical eyes on me, then I thought about self-censoring. But really, I think I still walk the edge.

I think a piece is never really finished: it's always ongoing. I notice that the longer I work on a show, tour with it, etc., the more it seems to evolve.

Writing and Rehearsal

It's interesting that one of the best monologues I have is one that I wrote first—something, as I said, I never do. It's a wonderful piece. Ironically, when I got up to perform it, I didn't do it. I mean I couldn't physically perform it in front of the audience. When Jo asked me why I couldn't do it, I told her it's because I wrote it first. The difference was that there was a story I wanted to tell, rather than a voice that I wanted to hear.

There are important questions to keep in mind when writing solo shows: What is the drama? What is universal about your show? It's not enough for an actor to get up on a stage and tell his life story.

I don't rehearse like most actors do. When I meet with Jo, we do a lot of sitting and talking. The majority of our rehearsal time is dramaturging, not physically rehearsing. We practically wait until tech before deciding if I'll go, say, to stage left or right to do a moment. The real rehearsing is in front of an audience.

My process really hasn't changed much since I started. It's really only accelerated and has become fine tuned. I do, however, write things down now. I work in front of an audience, do my shows, and then write it down, rather than just remembering it from show to show. But I don't actually put it on paper until after doing it maybe eight or ten times in front of the audience. I don't write it down to memorize it. That's not the purpose. I rarely even look at it. I give it to Jo, and she discusses it dramaturgically with me. Then I try to remember the structural changes.

Who's Your Audience?

My sense of performing in front of an audience is, on the one hand, lonely because you're the only one up there. There's no one else to share the energy with. On the other level, it is very fulfilling because you're sharing that energy with the audience, and you don't have to share it with anybody else.

Every audience is different, depending on who's dominating the audience. If the audience is dominated by the *New York Times*–reading people from the suburbs, I don't feel so great. Many of these people are coming purely to be just entertained. There's a sense that they deserve to be there more than other people. And we get into this "deservement" kind of thing.

You know, "I deserve to be here, I paid for my ticket"–type situation. When I'm in a university theater situation, say, in Kansas, chances are, my show will be a lot better.

I constantly ask people who want to do solo shows, "Who is your audience, and who do you want your audience to be?" My personal dream audience is between sixteen and twenty-five years old, and diverse economically, racially, linguistically.

It's Not about the Money

The important thing for your readers to ask themselves is, "What is your purpose in doing a one-person show?" If it's just for commercial success, you'll find yourself very disappointed, especially after putting all that work into the show. I've seen it happen to a dozen people.

CHAPTER 23

dael orlandersmith

© Alan Kirschen

Dael has toured extensively with the Nuyorican Poets Café throughout the United States, Europe, and Australia. She has appeared in productions of *Macbeth, Romeo and Juliet,* and *A Raisin in the Sun.* She can be seen in an offbeat role in Hal Hartley's *Amateur.* She premiered her one-person show, *Monster,* at the prestigious New York Theatre Workshop as part of the Solo Mio festival. Her solo show, *The Gimmick,* was performed as a work in progress at the Sundance Film Festival. It later ran as a commissioned work by the McCarter Theatre and then at the Long Wharf Theatre and at the New York Theatre Workshop. Other solo pieces are *Liar, Liar* (American Place Theatre) and *Leftover Life to Kill* (MCC Theater). Dael won an Obie Award for her solo show *Beauty's Daughter.* She was recently a finalist for the Pulitzer Prize in Drama and the Susan Smith Blackburn Award for her solo play *Yellowman,* and is the recipient of a New York Foundation for the Arts Fellowship and the Helen Merrill Award for Emerging Playwrights.

In the New York Times, *Peter Marks said,* "Monster *is a courageous performance piece. . . . There is no hint of pretension, not the slightest trace of sentimentality, in [Orlandersmith's] funny, dead-on impressions of her relatives, friends and neighbors. . . . "*

Wilborn Hampton, in the New York Times, *said of* Beauty's Daughter: *"First and foremost, Ms. Orlandersmith is a poet possessed of an exciting new voice. . . . The language of Ms. Orlandersmith's poetry is like an electric charge, living in imagination and illuminating in its insights, at once full of anger and compassion. "*

Why I Started

I began to do this, quite frankly, because there wasn't any work for me as a black actor. When I walked in to audition, they'd say things like, "Either gain fifty pounds or lose fifty pounds, or go get your jaw broken or something." They were not very encouraging with accepting me the way I was.

It seems like as black women, we graduated from playing heroine prostitutes to crackhead prostitutes, or playing welfare mothers. The opposite end of that was total conservative stuff like *The Cosby Show*. I didn't fit into any of those molds. I'd think, "I'm an actor, I can do all kinds of work. Just give me a chance." But no one was giving me the work. The kinds of things people would say was, "I can't wait for the day when everybody can do every role, regardless of color." Those were what I called "POPs"—people of power. They're the ones who could do this. They have the ducats. But they were waiting for someone else to do it; then they'd just jump on the bandwagon. So I was being stereotyped left, right, and center. Obviously I got pretty disgusted with the way things were.

When I'd look for monologues, the only things that appealed to me were things like from *Colored Girls*, or *A Raisin in the Sun*, stuff like that. So I began to write my own stuff back in like '87 to '88. I got accepted into the Actors Studio by contacting Estelle Parsons, letting her see my work. She said, "You should be writing every day." It was then, at that time, that the writing really began to happen.

Bringing the Darkness to Light

My favorite playwright is Eugene O'Neill; my favorite poet is Rimbaud. I'm heavily influenced by like poetry and stuff. I loved Rimbaud's process of the disorganization of the senses. I wanted to do that with language. I wanted to attack the senses, and show and delineate the human condition, no matter how dark it is. I want to bring it to a light. And that's what I think that people like Eugene O'Neill and Rimbaud do—they show us the darkness, the morbidity of the human condition. Because we all have it. It's what's hidden, what we hide. It's the thing that makes us afraid. I like the kind of theater that keeps me on a certain edge, forces me to look in myself in certain ways, forces me to think.

I was talking about this piece I'm writing, and this guy said, "Your piece bothered me because there was no redemption, no hope." I told him I wasn't interested in redemption or hope just for the sake of redemption or hope. I'm interested in what is real. The truth is that sometimes some people just don't make it. It's very easy to sugarcoat something. But the truth of the matter is, in some situations there's just no hope. I'm not writing the way I do just so that people will perceive my work as morbid, or dark, or deep. It's just what interests me.

My favorite painter is Francis Bacon. My thing is, what we perceive as normal is false. The nine-to-five thing, the coffee break, hour off for lunch thing is a joke. The average lifespan is seventy-five. You do this until you're sixty-five years old and then wonder, "How come I'm not happy?" How could you be happy? You bought into it, you've never questioned. That stuff makes me angry.

Dreams and Alchemy

In my plays there's a beginning, middle, and end. There is the story, the conflict, and the resolution of that conflict. Back when I started, a story would just come to me. I was living in a room in Harlem. Like most people's work, my work is autobiographical. I was really poor. All I could afford at the time was to buy books because I read voraciously. I would read about my dreams. I'd look up what my dreams meant, what they signified. I read guys like Freud and Toni Morrison. So it's from the dream state where I begin to write. I'd try to write the way Francis Bacon painted and the way Jimi Hendrix played. What was I feeling at the time I wrote this? I'd remember my dreams pretty well. I'd ask myself what was I feeling in the dream and then take it from there. Then I'd apply it to where I am now. I can't type; I do all my work longhand. When I first started, I was dreaming about being poor; a lot of the colors were very dark colors. Where I used to live were two crack houses and a house of prostitution right across the street. You'd watch chicks in the back alley perform.

So I'd put some words down, some thoughts down, and I'd try to figure out, How do I put all of this together? Let's go beyond the dream state; I'd just write what I'm interested in and apply it to that. And that's how it comes about. Names and characters come to me very quickly. The first thing I do is write the monologue, then take it from there. Then I ask myself, What is the story within this monologue? I write an outline from the monologue.

I've been a liar and thief and a hypocrite and that's what I tell people. I don't try to make anything, including myself, all nicey. The director is the one who helps me to decide when the piece is ready. The director is the alchemist. I'd bring the director [Peter Askin] what I've written. I'd show him my monologues; I'd say, This is the story I want to tell. He helps me to shape it. When I'm reading him the piece, an idea will come to me. He'll say, "Put it in the piece." Peter might say there's too much of this or that. He keeps getting me back to, "What is the story? What is the story?! What is this piece about?" That's kind of it in a nutshell. He'll make me work on what the story is truly about.

We'll look for the event of the piece. Then I'll write toward the event. The process of development is a back and forth, chipping away, as to how the story has to be told. I can be very expositional; we cut a lot of that away.

Processless Process

I'm not sure when a piece is really ready until I just know. It's something that I feel inside. And that feeling can sometimes occur a month into the show. It's just a gut feeling that it's now happening, really happening.

My process changes all the time. It still starts off initially with my having an idea; something will haunt me. You might say my process is, I don't have a specific process. It really depends on where I am in my life and all that stuff. I only know that when I'm working, I don't want anyone near me. I can spend extended periods of time alone; I mean days or weeks.

I don't talk directly to an audience. I'm very aware that they're there. I tell a story and I just hope that they're open enough to hear what I have to say. In a sense I'm saying, Here's my vision, my story, my play. I care that you [the audience] hear it. But I'm not going to write something or eliminate something from my story because you may find it offensive or it doesn't apply to your history.

CHAPTER 24

quentin crisp

© Greg Gorman

Quentin Crisp was a famous wit and celebrated author whose autobiography, *The Naked Civil Servant*, has become a literary classic, as well as an award-winning play and film starring John Hurt. He played Queen Elizabeth in Sally Potter's 1993 film *Orlando*. Other films include *The Bride, Philadelphia*, and *To Wong Foo, Thanks for Everything! Julie Newmar*. He contributed "The Diary of Quentin Crisp," a column about New York and American culture, to the *New York Native*. He appeared in television commercials for Levi Strauss jeans, Calvin Klein's CK One fragrance, and for Reebok sportswear.

Other books include *Resident Alien: The New York Diaries; Quentin Crisp's Book of Quotations: 1000 Observations on Life and Love by, for, and about Gay Men and Women; How to Become a Virgin; How to Have a Lifestyle; Manners from Heaven: A Divine Guide to Good Behavior*; and *Love Made Easy*. His articles appeared in the *London Times, Newsday, New York* magazine, the *New York Times*, the *Washington Post, The Advocate*, and the *Los Angeles Times*. On television, Mr. Crisp appeared on the shows of David Letterman, Dick Cavett, Jay Leno, Phil Donahue, and Tom Snyder. Mr. Crisp was named one of the "leading thinkers and visionaries" of our time by *Utne Reader*.

Richard Eder, in the New York Times, *said, "Mr. Crisp has a valiant and original mind and a lovely way with words. . . . Both in words and in his fussy, faintly self-mocking gestures, he asserts his identity. But what he draws out is universal: gaiety—in the original sense of the word, for once—and themes common to all of us: the need for courage and individuality, and the ground of tragedy on which they are exercised."*

Clive Barnes wrote in the New York Post: *"[Crisp] is an unexpected and endearing mixture of an off-form Oscar Wilde, an off-beat Dear Abby, and an off-center Will Rogers."*

Since the first printing of this book, Quentin Crisp passed away. I knew Quentin. I met him through a mutual friend, Jack Eric Williams. The three of us went out for dinner on a regular basis for years. During that time I learned a great deal about this fascinating man. His life, which he wrote about in his book (and later movie) *The Naked Civil Servant,* was filled with challenges and extraordinary adventures. He was a very funny, self-deprecating, and somewhat modest man. Wherever we'd go for dinner, people would often come over to our table and tell him how *The Naked Civil Servant* had affected their lives. In his memory, I'd like to share some of his thoughts in this, one of his very last interviews.

Talking to People

My first show was never actually written down. My agent in England had taken a theater behind a public house in Islington. In those days there were opening hours—that is to say, from about half past eleven in the morning until half past one or two in the afternoon. And then they shut up for a few hours. Well, my agent took a room behind the public house in order to put on a show for one of his clients. But he didn't want to waste the lunchtime hours. The stage was small and there was a flimsy curtain. And I agreed to go on for lunchtime. When I asked what I'd do on the stage, he said, "You could talk to people." So there was no script, just impromptu talking. He said, You needn't say the same thing each day; just say whatever you want.

At that original show, there were about three people in the audience. But everything changed when they showed the story of my life, *The Naked Civil Servant,* on the television. After that was televised, you couldn't get into the theater, it was so crowded.

Before that televising, I spoke about anything—it was always different. After, I started to make it the same speech. But nothing was ever written down. It was a show with no script, no direction, and no rehearsal.

What I spoke about was happiness, because happiness is the only thing that I understand. Whatever we say we're talking about, we're really talking about happiness. Whether we're talking about religion or politics or anything else, we're really talking about happiness. I told people how to be happy, which of course consists of never doing any work. I explained that happiness was never out there, it was always in here. I also spoke about style, about being yourself. I never spoke about myself at all.

Developing the Show

So I built up, developed this show, so that it had a beginning, middle, and end. The way the show changed was that I altered it in areas where I felt people didn't understand me, what I was talking about. If people didn't laugh at certain jokes, I'd leave them out the next show. I was learning by doing.

The entire show was about an hour. The rehearsal, you might say, was the night before's performance. It greatly developed, changed. I always remembered what I did the night before. I'd discuss what it was they could do in their lives to be happy. I don't think they believed me, but they listened.

After I spoke there would be an interval, and the audience would then ask questions. Naturally, that part of the show changed from night to night. By their questions, I learned what they understood me to say. That was also a way that I changed the show: by their questions each night.

When Mr. Elkins [Hilard Elkins] came to London to see me, I was performing at the Duke of York's Theatre, which is a real theater [a West End theater]. I was performing five nights a week there. The members of the audience who had questions would write them down on cards, and I'd answer them in the second half. Mr. Elkins prepared the way for me to do my show in America.

Other than in Australia, where I was asked about my sex life, I was never asked embarrassing questions. But I always, even in Australia, answered them as best I could. I tried to make myself infinitely available to the audience.

Now my show does have a script. It was Mr. Elkins' idea. We recorded one of the shows, and the script was typed up from that show. I memorized the script from that recorded show, and that is the show that I now perform, word for word. The second act, however, is still questions from the audience. The reason that the show is now better [with a script] is that I don't pause or stop; I continue right through.

Getting the Audience to Like You

The way to get an audience to like you is to get them to feel sorry for you. That's what Judy Garland did. When I went to see her perform, that's what impressed me—how she got people to feel sorry for her. I believe that my need is sincere; that is, I *do* need them to feel sorry for me, just like Ms. Garland.

CHAPTER 25

marilyn sokol

Marilyn Sokol starred on Broadway as Miss Lynch in *Grease*; in Herb Gardner's *Conversations with My Father*; in *Welcome to the Club* by Cy Coleman and A.E. Hotchner; in O'Neill's *The Great God Brown*, directed by Harold Prince; and in Moliere's *Don Juan*, directed by Stephen Porter with the Phoenix Rep. Her regional theater credits include: *The Sisters Rosensweig*, *Gypsy*, and *Fiddler on the Roof*. Her films include: Milos Foreman's *Man on the Moon*, *The Goodbye Girl*, *Basketball Diaries*, and *Foul Play*. TV credits include: *Law & Order*, *All My Children*, and *Sesame Street*. Ms. Sokol is an Emmy, Obie, and Bistro Award–winning actress, singer, comedienne, and writer.

Stephen Holden, in the New York Times, *wrote, "[Sokol] keeps the audience perpetually off balance as she whizzes between comedy routines and torch songs, trying on different dialects, characters, and confessional shticks."*

Nick Popp of Show Business *said Sokol's one-woman show* Guilt Without Sex *"serves up a . . . theatrical smorgasbord consisting of torchy, tongue-in-cheek song stylings, comedic childhood reminiscences, and a pastiche of incisive and insightful observations about the social, sexual, and psychological culture in which we live. 'The world according to Marilyn' is very much her own original."*

Different Incarnations

When I started auditioning after college, I'd go into the auditions, shake the auditors' hands, and say hello, and they'd quite often say, "Do you have an act?" I suppose they knew I was a comedienne and assumed that I had an act. At that point, I didn't. But what was bothering me at that time was that I couldn't get to the next rung in my career. I couldn't get the kind of parts that I wanted.

Also at that time I was singing around a lot at clubs, and I wanted a record deal. But how do you do it? The solution: You create your own act. I put three songs together and went into Reno Sweeney's nightclub, and got a two-week gig. So I had to quickly put a show together. I couldn't just sing; I had to fill it with stuff, spoken material. So what I did was fill it with characters that I had developed earlier, when I was with the improvisational group The Ace Trucking Company.

I got together with a friend of mine, Seth Allen, and I would just go over stuff with him. The material was mostly anecdotal, autobiographical. I had a very funny mother. When in doubt, I'd slip into my imitation of her. So all the ideas were mine and then I'd bring in writer friends and actor friends and work with them on the material. Their role was just to bounce the material off them, maybe give me some feedback.

Another friend of mine, Ken Friedman, was a wonderful comic writer; he'd write some punch lines for me. I'd come up with the character and some basic material, and he'd help me to punch it up with punch lines.

To go back a bit, I was always writing, even in college, even when I was a little girl. I was always writing for the page, for the written page. I was prolific in school. It was habitual, part of schoolwork. In college I did a lot of creative writing, some autobiographical.

Improvisational Way of Working

Since I was so improvisational, I found it almost sacrilegious to write down material, to be that scripted. Since I am innately silly, I relied on that rather than some script.

Of course, as the act developed, some nights were funnier than other nights. I would just remember and retain what I did from night to night. There were hardly ever any recordings to rely on. I'd be talking about necking and petting and the first boy I ever did it with, that kind of stuff and much, much more.

I got a gig at the New Ballroom in SoHo; I think it was 1976. It was a twelve-week gig. In preparation for that I got some gorgeous new songs, and I developed some set comic material. That show was more scripted. The words were the glue in that act.

Another exercise that I did was every day I would just lie down on the couch and let my mind just drift. Whatever came into my mind was fine. No censoring. In the early 1980s, I went through a very difficult period in my life. After working a lot of things out, I came out of that period with a stronger sense of self-confidence about my work. I no longer felt the need to have my writer friends come into my rehearsals for their feedback.

Guilt Without Sex was an unpublished book that I wrote with my friend Ken Friedman. So what I did was I exhumed parts of the book and that was the essence of a new show that I was developing.

This show was entirely scripted. This show also had songs. Some of these songs were originals, some of which I wrote the lyrics for. That show ran on and off for about a year and a half at the Kaufman and the Houseman on Theatre Row in New York. I started working with Sue Lawless, a fabulous director. She helped me make it funnier, more entertaining. She also helped me with editing. She helped me with the nipping and tucking of the piece.

There is an incredible value of [artistic] accidents. Always use your accidents as an actor. I learned how to repeat them. They can become the funniest parts of your show. An accident is something that you hadn't planned on happening, that happens on stage and ignites something, sometimes a moment, sometimes a lot more. It can be invaluable to an actor. The next show I did was less scripted and, once again, more improvisational.

Using Therapy As a Tool

One thing I really feel is that it's very difficult to use autobiographical material like I did without the help of some kind of introspective discipline. In my case, that has been psychotherapy. To loosen unconscious material, deep and understated. The emotional stuff is essentially unusable until some perspective is gained.

Though it's sometimes arduous, this road to self-knowledge is invaluable for an actor or performer, not to mention for life. The stronger the inner connection with yourself, the stronger the connection with the audience. I feel that you need the therapy to loosen it up. Even Uta Hagen says you can't use an emotion, such as something tragic, until you've understood it. You need to work it through. If any actors want to do material from their life, I highly recommend psychotherapy to assist them in their process.

CHAPTER 26

evan handler

© Chia Messina

Evan Handler is an actor, author, and screenwriter. He has played leading roles in Ron Howard's film *Ransom* and in *Taps, Sweet Lorraine*, and *Dear Mr. Wonderful*, as well as featured roles in Oliver Stone's *Natural Born Killers* and *The Chosen*. Evan has worked on two network television half-hour comedies, *Sibs* and *Woops!*. He is also a veteran of seven Broadway productions, including *Six Degrees of Separation, I Hate Hamlet, Broadway Bound, Brighton Beach Memoirs*, and the national touring company of *Master Harold . . . and the Boys*. His numerous off-Broadway performances include *Big Al*, at Ensemble Studio Theatre (and at the American Jewish Theatre); Donald Margulies's *Found a Peanut*, at the Public Theater; and *What's Wrong With This Picture?* at the Manhattan Theatre Club.

His writing credits include assignments for the *New Yorker, Elle* magazine, *Mirabella*, and *USA Weekend*. His first book, *Time on Fire: My Comedy of Terrors*, an expanded telling of his onstage memoir, was published to overwhelmingly positive critical response. The book has been optioned for a film version, for which Evan has written the screenplay. *Time on Fire*, his critically acclaimed one-man show, played to sold-out audiences in New York, Los Angeles, Boston, and Baltimore in venues ranging from a ballroom at Caesar's Palace to the grand stage at Carnegie Hall.

Most recently, he played Kristin Davis' divorce attorney turned lover—and later, husband—on the HBO series *Sex and the City*.

Variety called Time on Fire *"a powerful punch . . . intelligent and uncompromising . . . direct, unsentimental, and thoroughly engaging. . . . Handler's unswerving recounting always rings true. His conclusion is as rich and contradictory as all that's come before, and one is left hoping that this actor-turned-playwright continues with both endeavors."*

The L.A. Times *said, "Filled with humor and impressively surrealistic detail, this one-man show is a revelation. Handler is a charming young actor with a wicked sense of humor. The great accomplishment of* Time on Fire *is that he not only survived the ride, but also transformed it into a life-affirming act."*

Disclosing the Self

My reason for writing my show was emotionally based. I had been through this jarring experience that was not shared by many people in my age group. I felt like I had a certain amount of isolation that I felt from those involved and attached to the mundanity of their lives. I thought by telling the story of where I had been, this kind of covert war that I felt I had fought, that it might actually breach some of the distance between me and the folks that I used to feel close to. At one point I had thought of doing a show where all the doctors were puppets. Anything that would skew the reality and give the otherworldly sense that I had gone through.

Ultimately, while going through so many ideas of how to tell my story, I always came back to the idea that the simplest one and most direct way would be the most effective. When I actually began working on the show, it became my working dictum. I was interested in reducing it to the elements of how I imagined theater must have begun, as people coming together at the end of the day and telling each other where they had been, and how those stories got passed on.

There was something that someone gave me at that time that became a guide. It was a book called *If You Meet the Buddha on the Highway, Shoot Him.* There's a chapter called, I believe, "Disclosing the Self." It was about man's ability to examine where he's been, where he is now, and where he wants to go. It is the telling of the story and the revealing of the self that reveals the self to the individual, as well as forwarding the civilization a fraction of an inch. I became intrigued by that and made it a working guide in writing my piece, and the style in which it would be performed. And I found that it held up to be true. Each night, when I went out on the stage to tell my story as directly and simply as possible, there was something that came back to me, and something that the people in the theater left with me.

How and Why I Started

When I was in the hospital, just to combat boredom, I asked my father to get me what was then a really early laptop computer. In the first six months of what proved to be a four-year ordeal, I kept a detailed diary of dreams, of what was going on every day, of the treatment, just about everything. These were just notes. The laptop didn't have a printer. It wasn't till years later, when I was working on *Six Degrees of Separation*, that I went to the offices of Lincoln Center and asked them to print my notes out for me. I found some of it to be pretty intriguing, pretty fascinating. I started to write things up, the first five pages or so, and showed it to people at *Six Degrees*. I showed it to Peter Maloney, who was a writer, and to John Guare. And I got encouragement.

At the same time, Naked Angels was doing something called Tuesday Nights at Nine, where people could bring five or ten minutes of stuff they were working on. Eventually I got my nerve up and read the first five pages. It was about ten minutes' worth. I got a response that was far better than I ever could have imagined. People howled with laughter and at the same time became appalled at what they were laughing at. That set the tone. I realized that that was the roller-coaster ride I wanted to take people on.

The literary background that I had prior to this piece was that I had worked extensively as an actor on new plays in developmental situations. I had six summers at the Sundance Playwrights Laboratory as an actor. I had been around and listened to and heard a lot of the concepts that stuck with me. Things like: It's better to show than to tell. Reveal the story through dramatic action rather than description. Dramatic action comes through conflict. Put the characters into conflict with each other or give them obstacles to overcome, and then show how they do that.

The interesting task for me became, since I'm sitting there and talking by myself, how do I dramatize or show anything dramatically? Everything was description. But I found that there was a way, even within a first-person monologue.

One thing I discovered was that by inhabiting the characters and having them talking to each other, I could create a present-tense engaging section. I gave the piece a two-act form. Within the two acts, I broke it up into scenes. Each of the scenes revealed specific elements of the story. I gave a lot of thought to structuring the play.

My Agenda

I had many agendas in the play. I wanted to show what existed behind the elegant façade of major institutions. I particularly wanted to expose Sloane-Kettering Institute, which was relying on a reputation it had earned three decades earlier. The point was, most people don't know what many of these institutes are like on the inside, unless they've been there. There is no Zagat Guide for hospitals or doctors.

I also wanted to show people that there was more than one way to go through the experience. People are entitled to stand up and fight. I felt a lot of what I went through was a microcosm for the way one decides to go through his life. Most people feel that they're not entitled to all that much, that you must please those in authority and follow the rules.

My play is about one person who had excelled by refusing. The theme of my play is that the world around you tends to demand mediocrity. If you decide to do something to an excellent degree by yourself, there will be a lot of resistance. Today I perform my piece for medical conferences, symposiums, stuff like that. I go to places like Stanford in California, or a conference of four thousand people at the Sheraton in Washington.

Developing the Piece

Going back to the beginnings of the piece: As I mentioned, Naked Angels was doing Tuesday Nights at Nine, where they would assign a topic each week, like religion or money or family. I realized that for any topic they came up with, I could still write about this experience in my life. It was like my weekly soap opera. I went every week with another chapter of five to ten minutes. I didn't work on it every day. But when I did, it could be a six-hour work session. I sat down and wrote. You have to also realize that I had been telling these stories for years prior to the actual sitting down and writing of them. My standing joke was that I'm writing the oral history of me as told to myself. Like any legend or story that's told over and over, I just, in conversation, had honed it and exaggerated it or pinpointed it. Like what you do as an actor, I'd inflate the reality and the drama of the situation without bursting the balloon and going over the line of it being untrue. I would recite it as I read it, as I wrote it. I would recite it over and over, trying to make it fit in my mouth, trying to make it the best story that I could.

So at one point Naked Angels said, "Do you want to do a ninety-minute show?" They suggested that I put my pieces together to make one cohesive play. I had a deadline. I had three to six months to do it. I knew the story I wanted to tell, so I started work on the whole play.

I had a clear outline in my head about the shape I wanted it to take. I wrote the whole story down; that was about ninety pages. What I discovered at those Naked Angels nights was that people most wanted to hear what I least wanted to reveal. I discovered that if you're willing to push beyond the bounds of honesty of what most people are willing to give, you've got an edge up on getting their attention and in gaining their respect and interest.

Anybody just telling his personal stuff is not what I'm talking about. You have to find a way to do it that is interesting. I realized that the more personal, honest—and I mean scathingly honest, even toward myself—that I made this, people would respond.

When I reached the end of the story, when I was up to today, was when I realized it was ready. When I went to Marcia Jean Kurtz [the director] with the ninety pages, we began to edit it, and we ended up cutting it in half.

Rehearsals and Rewrites

The way we rehearsed was, I would just start reading the piece. And she would say, like, I don't get this, or, what about this? Or, why am I hearing this? Or, you're using too many words. So I started to realize that saying something four different times, no matter how cleverly, is not valuable. It's better to pick the most clever of the four and get rid of the rest. This is really about being concise and succinct. I discovered that I was willing to be a ruthless editor of my own stuff. Marcia Jean is one of the best editors I've ever worked with. Marcia Jean was my eyes and ears on the outside. I did rewrites every night at home.

What was interesting about the developing of the piece—the ending kept changing. It seemed that what was going on in my life would suddenly become the ending of the piece. It was like a gift was given. I thought, "Well, there you go, I just lived the ending of the piece."

So then I invited everyone I'd known or thought I'd want to know in the theater world to the Naked Angels readings—four nights. From that, I was offered the Second Stage Theatre production.

Between the Naked Angels readings and the Second Stage production, there were some more rewrites. I felt there were a couple of things missing from the text. I incorporated them into the new productions. Then we tried to figure out, how do you put this on a stage, give people their money's worth? I wasn't interested in overproducing this. We started from the place of, I'm telling this story to a group of friends in someone's living room. Anywhere that I would stand up to act something out in that environment is where I'll stand up and act something out here. Wherever the story gets worked up enough for you to stand up, then you do. The idea was to keep the story as a story told, as opposed to putting on a show. If I thought something was funny about how someone moved or behaved, then I'd jump up off the couch. I never wanted the feeling, Okay, you're coming into a theater, the lights are going down, here's the musical introduction, now I'll take you away to Cancerland. In fact, I wanted to startle people with the simplicity.

At the beginning of the run there was experimentation. The producers felt there should be more. They felt, people are paying good money to see a show, we should give them something for their money. There was talk about getting another director whose strengths were in lighting and sound design. They felt we should just have "more." But many of their ideas were not what I wanted the piece to be.

I did it in two acts at Naked Angels, and that was very unusual for a monologue show. The joke that I used at the time about the piece was that I called it my "minimalist epic." The whole thing was really about defiance. So I got a kick out of defying what the norms were in the theater. Basically, I had decided that it would work the way I wanted it, despite the conventional wisdom saying it should be more conventional.

Out on a Limb

On a purely personal level, it was terrifying to go out there every night. It felt like I was putting myself much further out on a limb then I ever had before. I felt that if the people weren't liking it, essentially they weren't liking me. On the other hand, it made me feel prouder and more powerful than ever before, because every bit of its success was my success.

In the beginning I wasn't remembering all my words, so I had little cheat sheets in my pockets. It was a very massive thing. It was written with a literary sense. When I'd go up on my lines, as happened at the beginning, I'd just sit there for a moment, have a moment of terror, and then the next thing would come to me somehow. I'd take a sip of water or something. Mostly, the audience never knew that's what had happened. It became a matter of trusting that the words would come to me.

At the beginning, the Second Stage audiences weren't receiving the show very well. Carole Rothman, the producer, felt that it would work better if I told the audience a little about myself first, introducing myself, rather than digging right into the piece. We ended up with me on the edge of the stage, the lights coming up, and me actually introducing myself. A couple of times I actually started the show by saying, "Hi, I'm Evan." So I did adopt this new beginning of telling a bit about myself. I'd prepare the audience, let them know that this is supposed to be funny, and that it's supposed to be horrible, and that it's okay to experience both.

At least 50 percent of the time at Second Stage Theatre, I performed the piece to near-total silence. What was odd was, the same piece at Naked Angels was a near-raucous laugh riot a lot of the way through. The Second Stage version deprived me of the experience that I wanted to have. But then people would come backstage and tell me how funny the show was. Jerry Zaks [the director] said, "My stomach hurt from holding back the laughs." I asked him, "Why did you?" And he said, "I don't know, it just seemed like what happened out there." It seemed like a great many people that I spoke to at that time were having a similar experience but wouldn't allow themselves to laugh out loud.

There were a lot of walkouts each night during previews. With an audience of fifty to seventy people, five to ten people would walk out each night. Many of these people were subscription audience people and weren't always aware of what they were coming to see. Many of these people don't want to see a one-person show, let alone a show about cancer. There was a very long preview period. Then the show opened, got this rave review, and sold out immediately. I noticed that once it got the review and people were coming because they wanted to see this particular play, then the response was far better. Every once in a while I would improvise a line or two during the show. If the audience responded well, I'd leave it in. Over the years there have been quite a few of these add-ons.

Advice to Writers

For writers everywhere, there is a constant choice to be made regarding those in power and your work. Whether it's a producer or editor or film studio people, you have to decide on what it is you want to say. You must decide how much you're willing to let them influence your choices. I don't mean that there is a constant danger, that these people are out to hurt you. But it is a constant choice to be made. You must decide if what they suggest is helping you to say what you're trying to say. Or is this something that that person wishes this piece was? You must decide, To what extent am I willing to compromise myself? There is a balance to be struck between saying what you have to say and allowing in genuinely good suggestions.

CHAPTER 27

shelly mars

© Tilden Patterson

Shelly Mars has had leads in the *Kids in the Hall* and in the HBO special *Drag Kings*. She has had featured and supporting roles in HBO's *Out There Hollywood* and the independent features *Scenes from a Plague Year* and *Drop Dead Rock*. Her shows *Mars Behind Bars* and *Whiplash: Tale of a Tomboy* have been performed at Dixon Place, the Grove Street Playhouse, and the Kitchen. She's also appeared in shows at Naked Angels Theater, New York Theatre Workshop (*An Evening with Shelly Mars*), Berkeley Rep, and the Performing Garage. She's appeared on *The Montel Williams Show, The Phil Donahue Show, Real Personal, The Richard Bey Show*, and *Sally Jesse Raphael*.

Chaser, Shelly's latest provocative new work-in-progress, explores the surreal, self-destructive world of sex-addicted gay men who knowingly give and receive the HIV virus. She recently acted in and coproduced a commercial for the Museum of Sex in New York City.

Amy Taubin in the Village Voice *has called Mars "An after-hours Lily Tomlin. Mars . . . tells all through precise and subtle body language, tippy-toeing between irony and lewdness."*

John Karoly of Cab Magazine *has said, "Mars can time a deadpan stare to just the perfect comedic length or let a darker emotion creep subtly across her face during beautifully choreographed pauses in dialogue . . . Mars will thrill, infuriate and arouse anyone who gets to see her work."*

Pushing the Envelope

I started out over fifteen years ago in San Francisco. I was taken to this bisexual bathhouse. There was a striptease contest going on there, and my friend dared me to enter it. I did and won the prize. I saw that they did massage in this place. I was like nineteen years old, and so I lied to the owner of the place and told him I was older and that I did massage.

So I started working at this bathhouse and started doing shows there. These were crazy, striptease, performance-art kind of shows. Actually, I had more clothes on than most of the people in the audience. They had, like, towels on them. I had studied acting and dance and martial arts, and had incorporated it into my act. I was always a mimic and a character type. People whom I found intriguing, I'd mimic and create them as characters.

I was writing to some degree, but mostly just performing and retaining, learning while I was doing. At this time, I didn't sit down like a writer and write. I would usually make up things and bounce it off other people. I incorporated music and dance in my shows, too.

By the time I was twenty-one I had developed my own show, which I was doing in a lesbian bar. The show was about Mistress S., a dominatrix. As it developed, it was scripted, but really basic. At this time I was pretty wild and pretty out there, so my show naturally reflected that. I was extremely rebellious, and the show reflected that too. People would say, You have to do this or that, and I'd just do whatever it was that I wanted to say at that time. My stuff was very political, very gay. I was exploring gender. I was exploring how repressed gay women were. This was a time when "lipstick lesbians" weren't allowed to exist. I was very opposed to the political correctness of that time. I started doing my male impersonation then. My stuff had a lot of sexual content in it and it really upset lesbians a lot. I always pushed the envelope.

Basically, what I've always tried to say is there are all these variations of the human existence and we're all screwed up. There are all these genders and we need to take on these labels to feel comfortable. I still am talking about that in my present show; it's just a lot more sophisticated now.

Developing My Process

I work with a video camera. That came into my process about eight years ago. I work with directors and they'll fish things out of me. I'll be in a persona of a character, and I'll let that persona respond and channel through me into that character. Sometimes things happen in improvisation, and then I'll transcribe it. Then we'll make it into something, give it a structure. The artist as editor will decide what works and what sucks.

The director is very important in my process these days. When I was younger, the director was less important. The last few years, I've been working with Janice Diner. She's a writer and a film director. She's been important to my writing and helps me with making sense of structure. Her input is very important. She helps things make sense by asking me questions.

Mistress S. was one of my earliest shows. There were other characters, other actors. Now I do a one-person show with many characters. I guess I do about ten characters, all different ages. For instance, Martin is one of my oldest characters. He is a Wall Street, Merrill Lynch, middle-management type. He is a misogynist. My characters evolve with time. What's happening in pop culture affects how they change.

Originally the characters were more broad. They became more specific as they evolved. Owning yourself as an artist really affects your work. Saying "This is what I do" very much affects the work. I ask myself questions like, "Why are these characters here, and why do I want them to be here?"

As my work progressed, there were lots of *An Evening with Shelly Mars* kinds of shows. Then came *Invasion from Mars; Whiplash: Tale of a Tomboy;* and *Mars Behind Bars,* some of my more recent shows. In *Whiplash: Tale of a Tomboy,* I play my mother, my father, my therapist, and myself. It's the story of how I got to where I'm at. *Mars Behind Bars* evolved from that show. That was about your dreams, how you think your life is going to be. It starts out how I grew up in Ohio in a small town, being the only Jewish kid. And how I got the hell out of there when I was seventeen and hitchhiked to South America. Part of the show was about my hitchhiking experiences, how I was raped, then later fell in love with this French girl, Briget. I act all of this out, including the rape.

My work continued on being about my life story and what I thought of it. In the last three years, my work has been much more autobiographical. I now let people know more of who I am, rather than all of the wild personas.

I rehearse a piece a lot. I'll work with the director, do it for him, then call some friends in, do it for them. Everything is scripted now, all my shows. It seems more professional. You can go into a theater and give the production people the script and they can see what happens where, technically. It's very helpful to them. I think you should workshop your piece a lot.

What's Theater For?

The audience is very much a part of the process. Once your homework is done, it really takes life in front of an audience. You can learn so much about what you've created. I'm performing my new work out of town more often these days. Before you get reviewed, you want to hone it down and make sure that it's ready. You don't want too much attention on a new piece until it's ready. Yet you need people there. It's a catch-22 kind of thing.

There is a part of me that really knows how to shock people, get their attention that way, push buttons. But there is another part of me that looks really normal, like the girl next door. These personas constantly fight each other. Anger has pushed me for a long time. As I've gotten older, the anger has mellowed, and I find myself more compassionate. But I feel that as an artist, you really have to dig in the closets. You've got to let it out. That's what theater's for.

Many years ago, I wanted very much to be an actress. I was studying theater, working on scenes, and doing monologues that other people wrote. I hated doing all this stuff [the monologues] that had been done for years. I wanted to do my own thing. I also wanted to do my own thing as a calling card to get recognized. I wanted to be more of a crossover artist, like Lily Tomlin and John Leguizamo.

CHAPTER 28

brian dykstra

Besides his one-man show, *Brian Dykstra: Cornered and Alone*, his screenplays include *Joints, V.I.R.T.U.E., Amazombies, Fight Game, Un-Coupled, Baggage Claim, Double Down*, and adaptations of his plays *A Sane Policy* and *Forsaking All Others*.

As a playwright, Mr. Dykstra most recently saw a production of his play *Hiding Behind Comets* at 29th Street Rep after its world premiere at Cincinnati Playhouse in the Park, and *That Damn Dykstra* and *STRANGERHORSE* at the Access Theater in New York. Before that, *Forsaking All Others* opened in London at the Pentameters Theatre and in New York at the Access Theater. This same play was a Dramalogue Critic's Choice, and *L.A. Times* and *L.A. Weekly* Pick of the Week for the production at the Powerhouse Theatre. Brian's other plays include: *Silence*, commissioned and performed at the College of the Holy Cross in Worchester, Massachusetts; *I Am/Lot's Wife* at the Harold Clurman Theater in New York City; *A Sane Policy*, commissioned by the New York Shakespeare Festival at the Public Theater; *Spill The Wine*, and his latest plays, *Clean Alternatives* and *A Play on Words* are being workshopped at the Lark Theatre.

As a columnist, Brian was able to express his political and social commentary during his tenure at the award-winning webzine *Urban Desires*. His column, "The Rant," covered everything from the annoyance of baby carriages on the sidewalks of New York to the lunacy of Marla Maples, Nike, Al Sharpton, and Joey Buttafucco.

Brian has worked with at-risk high-school students at the Dakota Young Playwrights Festival in Fargo, North Dakota, producing and directing student-written one-act plays. He has directed high-school students at the Pittsburgh Public Theater in their Shakespeare Intensive Program and acting classes for the past four years.

Tom Sellar of the Village Voice *has said of Brian Dykstra's solo show,* Cornered and Alone, *"Brian Dykstra is working hard to turn ranting into a new genre, and if he succeeds, comedy may not be safe. . . . Verbal flights take off in psychological, political, and just plain pathological directions—leaving some badly skewered subjects in their wake . . . rising into an obsessive-compulsive delirium . . .*

Phillip Hopkins wrote on Theatermania: *"Seinfeldian comedy with this kind of intelligence and edge would be right at home on the sharper satiric cable shows. Fans of* The Daily Show with Jon Stewart *will be pleased."*

What Led Up to It?

In my case, I was pushed. Gently pushed, but pushed nonetheless. There was an evening of one-act plays that I'd written, *That Damn Dykstra (the boxed set),* and the director (Margarett Perry) thought it might work to have me come out and talk to the audience, or perform some of my poems between some of the plays. The evening was wonderfully reviewed by the *Voice,* so we invited Lou Viola, who was scouting for the Aspen Comedy Festival, to come look at it. He said he liked it, but that he wasn't about to pitch this evening of six actors going to Aspen. He mentioned that his favorite part of the evening was the talking to the audience, and suggested that if I got rid of all the plays and wrote something just for one person, he might be interested in that. He said, reacting to some of the political aspects of what I was talking about, "I'd be interested in watching you talk about the fall of Rome." So, I started culling together my most political slam poems and writing about the political climate. Naturally, with somebody as destructive as monkey-boy in the White House, a lot of the stuff wrote itself. I guess if you're going to write something like this, to have an opinion like "The President is a dangerously stupid monkey" helps immensely and easily informs everything I'm trying to say.

Career Control Awareness

I started working on a one-man show a bunch of years ago after hearing Bill Maher mentioning something about his fortieth birthday running him down like a Mack truck and feeling like he had to do something to take control of his career. I got started maybe six years ago and wrote a thing or two that made it into this show, but it languished on the hard drives of three different computers for a long time. At that time I thought I was going to do a show about "deconstructing" one-person shows. Some of it was really funny, but I couldn't figure out where to take it when I was still outside of the political arena, so it just laid there. I suppose the impetus was a kind of a career-control awareness, but it wasn't so desperate that I actually finished anything until much later.

Talking about Whatever I Want

For the most part, as in playwriting, I just let the character—in this case, me—talk about whatever I wanted. I knew it was political. I knew I still wanted to hang it all on that first deconstructed idea. I knew I was writing to the last slam poem "Just Say No." With all that in place, it's easy to let yourself alone and explore freely, because, at least sub-consciously, you're exploring all the themes and goals you'd like to explore, without that obsessive need to make everything directly tie in. All the good stuff, both in plays and this one-man show, came out of the freedom to realize later that it might not be going into the final product. All that other planning leads to pressure. Pressure leads to blocks. Unless there's a deadline involved. And with one-person shows, there is so rarely a real deadline.

This was a kind of trickling out. I started writing monologues, which I like writing anyway, and wanted to see how outrageous I could get with the deconstructed stuff. Then, it all had to really sound like a human being talking (and not just any human being, but really like me) because I knew it was going to get highlighted with spoken word. Which is almost like doing songs in the middle of this one-man thing. Ultimately, it started to feel like a hybrid of monologue, stand-up, and spoken word.

Politics, Elections, and the News

When it's political and it's just before an election and the election has torn a rift in the country so wide, we Blue State people couldn't even recognize our Red State brothers and sisters, the topical nature of what I'm talking about can really bite you in the ass. If Bush or Cheney said something particularly galling, it had to go in. If Kerry couldn't make a point about whatever he was trying to make a point about that day, it has to get dropped in. The Democratic National Convention started to fade out of audience memory. The Republican National Convention was going on during my show, so I had no choice but to watch it and comment. The New York audience was depressed after the Republican convention and the bounce Bush got in the polls, so the show was more difficult, and of course I had to address their mood and the convention. They were giddy after Bush did so poorly in the debates, and just saying hello was funny to them.

I had to access whatever was topical, and slowly let go of stuff that had begun to fade. There were certain go-to topics—the environment, the prison abuse scandal, the President's I.Q.—but if I were doing this particular show again, a whole ton of material would have to be reworked or cut out entirely. Sure, I can talk about a specific terrorist or cabinet member, but if the day ever comes when they catch the guy or there's another resignation, the very next moment anything I had to say about him would have to be changed. It's the nature of doing political material. It was a lead-up to the election; afterward, it's a completely different animal. I understood that going in, and that's fine with me. Bush getting elected might be good for future shows, but I'd have gladly given that up for a more sane leader in the White House.

The truth is, self-censorship must be overcome, as it is the greatest enemy of this kind of expression. I remember a teacher I had in college. She was a terrific actress, and somebody asked her how she got so brave with her choices in rehearsal. Her answer was that it's not bravery if you don't care if you look like a fool. I believe we're living in dangerous political times. I believe we're being represented by some of the worst our country has to offer. It's easy to go to the wall when the alternative feels like capitulation to a religious fanaticism we recognize as evil in other parts of the world, but are self-righteous about at home. I'm sure some people reading this consider those thoughts foolish. I don't care.

Rehearsal

Half the time I rehearsed by myself, half the time with my director. It's a tough question to answer because as I look back, it seems impossible that I did rehearse the piece. I mean, it was just me for eighty-seven minutes and I talk fast up there. The idea that one could pick up the script and even just memorize that much verbiage is daunting in even that simple task. I guess I rehearsed as I wrote, in pieces. By the time I was working on what I was going to say at the end, I was already pretty well into what I was doing in the beginning. Also, I got booked into a couple alternative comedy venues to try out the version that Lou Viola was trying to take to Aspen. I did a forty-minute version, then a thirty-minute version, then twenty-seven minutes at one point. I didn't get into Aspen, but after that, the next thought was, "Now let's see what it would be if there's no time limit." That's how I ended up with the eighty-seven-minute version I performed at The Triad.

Margarett, my director, was smart enough to look for humor when I wanted to bask in hopelessness and despair. I found, fairly quickly, how to mitigate some of the darkest material. As I wrote more, it was with a comic slant whenever possible. It just feels better when they're laughing. Plus, it's more fun to cut through the laughter when it does get serious, and with the nature of what I was talking about, it necessarily has to get serious. Or, rather, I necessarily have to get serious.

The First Performance . . . and the Aftermath

There was a day we were inviting the first audience, and we opened with what we had. Fortunately, it was ready "enough."

Well, the first time was like a long march to the gas chamber. There is a particular terror that is only available to solo performers who write their own material. What is there to hide behind? I can't blame the playwright for the material, I'm the playwright. I can't blame the actor for screwing up my play, I'm the actor. The sensation of drowning doesn't go away until walking off stage. The first time felt like crap. The second time felt less like crap. The third time felt even less like crap. Then, somehow, slowly, it started to be about as much fun as you can have onstage. The change is so gradual you can't calibrate it. Just, all of a sudden, it's on!

When your show is well received in the press, there is an expectation that what you have to say is somehow worthwhile. Audiences were so warm and eager to show how much they enjoyed the show. That is, except for the people who couldn't wait to demonstrate how much they *hated* it! Politics is divisive, especially now. I got hate mail like you wouldn't believe, really nasty stuff. I got people who couldn't wait to make a big show of walking out.

I got really vocal support, which is actually more difficult to deal with. With a standard heckler, you can just treat them like the standard heckler. When they're wrecking the show for everybody around them by being so vocal in their support, how to shut them down in a nice way is something I'm still dealing with. I realize talking to the audience is incredibly inviting to them to talk back. But people in the back who can't hear them, get annoyed. If they're yelling from the back, it's very rare that anyone up front can really make out what they're saying. So, the job is to get the audience, who mostly are happy to be there, to keep quiet without them feeling like I'm telling them to shut up. Because that's not only a laugh-killer; it undermines the intimacy I hope to have developed all through the evening.

Finding the Funny

I think I look to the absurd earlier now. I think I try and find a way to poke fun at this insane world for as long as possible. But I always want to continue to push until it doesn't hold humor any more. It's like doing a production of any good play. There's nothing wrong with finding the humor everywhere you can. The play will tell you when to stop. There will come a time, in everything but comedies, when the play won't hold the humor any more. *Macbeth* and *The Crucible* stop being funny more quickly than, say, *Dinner With Friends*. The play will tell you. I try to write these as comedies, and trust the material will run up against a wall and will insist on some other, darker take. At least, that's been true in the past. Maybe next time, I'll be doing straight stand-up because I want to get a sitcom. But I doubt it.

Passion

As I go over my answers to the previous questions, I am stuck with an awareness that I have a passion for the material. Ergo, my advice would be to have a passion for the material. This is not always totally true when writing plays. With a play, I might really love a character, or an event, or a psycho-logical reality that I think I'm beginning to understand. But when it's going to be me, alone, on stage, speaking my words, in the character of me—remember, I'm not talking about character-driven monologists—I'd better have a passion for the material that will drive me to think this is important enough to spend the kind of time (and often money) that will get it to a point where people are coming to see it. It's a ton of work, a *ton*, don't be fooled, and not just the writing of it. You have to learn it, rehearse it, help produce it, market it, and live it for as long as it's going on. It's not like you can really do a whole bunch of other things when you're speaking for eighty-seven minutes every night. It has to be worth it. That, for me, means it has to feel like it might be important. It doesn't have to be important to a whole committee—that way lies madness—but it has to feel important to me. If other people come along for that ride, later, then that means I might have been right about it. But the passion for the material is paramount. Can you do it without that passion? I guess. But I'd hate to have to try.

CHAPTER 29

penny arcade

© Lisa Tomasetti

Penny Arcade debuted at the age of seventeen with Johnny Vaccaro's explosive Playhouse of the Ridiculous. She was a teenage superstar for Andy Warhol's factory, featured in the Morrissey/Warhol film *Women in Revolt*. She has worked with many of the greats of American experimental theater, including Jack Smith, Jackie Curtis, Charles Ludlam, H.M. Koutoukas, and Tom O'Horgan, among others.

She began her solo work in 1982. Some of her shows include *While You Were Out* (P.S. 122), *A Quiet Evening with Sid and Nancy* (Chelsea Hotel, En Garde Arts), and *Based on a True Story* (La MaMa). Her highly acclaimed show *Bitch! Dyke! Faghag! Whore!* had an international run, playing such places as Switzerland, Ireland, Scotland, Austria, Germany, England, and Melbourne, Australia, as well as an extensive run at the Village Gate in New York City. *An Evening with Penny Arcade and Quentin Crisp* was performed at the Vienna Festival as well as in New York.

Penny recently teamed up with singer and songwriter Chris Rael to create *Rebellion Cabaret*. She workshopped the piece over the over the past two years at Ars Nova and the Gershwin Hotel. It will receive its World Premiere at the Sydney Opera House in Australia.

> *Jan Hoffman in the* Village Voice *said of* True Stories: *"Ms. Arcade exudes the wry confidence and facility of a veteran downtown performer. . . . Jagged, remarkable, unexpected. And mesmerizing."*
>
> *Patrick McDonald in* The Advertiser *called* Bitch! Dyke! Faghag! Whore! *"a powerful message wrapped in a challenging package of inspired comedy and gaudy erotica."*

Trying to Get a Job

I found myself going out on auditions and the casting directors saying that I was the most original person they'd ever seen in months and months. They said that someday, people would be clamoring, "Get me a Penny Arcade. Get me someone like Penny Arcade." After I was told that for about a year and a half, and after getting insignificant roles, I realized I just didn't have time to wait around for people to give me work.

This was around 1981. The performance art scene at that time was wide open, particularly for women. There was no money in it, but no parameters of what you could and could not do. So, at that time I realized I didn't want to write plays, but I wanted to write stuff that I could perform.

Eventually, I began to write some very large performance pieces, some with as many as thirty people at a time. But I started out just writing for me. I was in a play called *Tinseltown Tirade* at Theater for the New City. The play starred Hibiscus, a famous downtown drag performer. The part that Hibiscus wrote for me was of a Warhol superstar. But he actually didn't know any Warhol superstars. I found that what he wrote was very wooden and unreal. So during rehearsal, for the amusement of other members of the cast, I would improvise on Andrea Whipp, who was a Warhol superstar of the 1960s. Eventually he came to me and said, "That's so much better than what I had. Would you mind writing that, and we'll give you credit?" I went home and looked at a blank piece of paper. I learned that there's a big difference between improvising and writing things. I finally called a friend of mine who was a professional writer and said, "I've been sitting here for four hours and I'm in horrible pain, and the sheet is still blank." And he said, "Oh, yeah, you're writing."

I continued to do "Andrea" for a long time. People were always requesting me to do her. I'm a precision mimic for people who I'm interested in mimicking. I can't do anyone on demand, like Pamela Anderson, or someone. I have to really want to mimic them.

Phase Two

I was at a performance art piece at St. Marks in the Bowery. I really hated the piece. So I was in the lobby pacing back and forth, smoking cigarettes, and ranting about how bad it was. Chris Kraus, who was the curator, came up to me and said, "You're fantastic; would you like to do a show here?" I looked at her and said, "What would I do?" And she said, "I hear you write your own material." So I said, "I perform it, I don't write it." She said, "That's fine with me." She gave me a booking.

In my real life, I'm always imitating people that I run into. So friends suggested that I do some of those characters on stage. So I did. I actually didn't start writing things down until as late as 1990. The reason I finally did write something down was because I was invited to do one of my monologues at Lincoln Center at a big benefit with Glenn Close, Peter Allen, and all these famous people. I was told that I had ten minutes. Now, I'd never had to time anything, so that's when I decided I had to write this particular monologue down.

The Type of Artist I Am

People often say I'm a political artist. But I'm not a political artist, say, like Judith Malina [The Living Theatre]. A political artist to me is someone who has a political vision that they want to communicate to the public. So they will write theater in order to use that as a vehicle of communication. I'm a political person, so my politics invariably come out in my writing. But that's not my first goal. But ironically, at this time of life, everything is political. If you flush your toilet, it's political. What kind of bottles you choose to buy your drinks in is political.

Today, I feel that the only reason that I perform is to alleviate human suffering and break down self-delusion and isolation.

Originally, I would tell the same story and the same idea to everyone that I'd come into contact with during the course of a day. That idea came from a sentence I once heard about selling a film treatment. The thought being, if you couldn't pitch your idea in ten minutes, if you couldn't keep someone's interest in that short a time, then you didn't have anything. So, pitching the idea to ten or twenty people in a day and seeing how they were responding was how I kind of formed my work. As I said, I started my work by improvising. I have a prodigious memory. So I'd remember most of what I did from night to night.

Bonding with the Audience

Very early in my career, about 1986–87, I started to feel a tremendous bond with my audience. It was at that time that I was developing my work only in front of an audience. All my work was unrehearsed, unscripted, live, in front of the audience. I felt that from night to night, whatever stayed in my memory from the show was worth remembering.

When I started working with other people, however, they insisted that I write things down for them. That became the difficult part. I'd write for them, but not get around to myself. So they would be fully scripted and my monologues would be fully improvised.

In 1989, I was commissioned by Anne Hamburger [En Garde Arts] to do a piece at the Chelsea Hotel. I chose to do a piece about Sid Vicious and Nancy Spungen. That was the first time I had a piece with other actors. They needed a script to work with. That was a very painful day. I had to write out the entire script for both them and me. It was difficult. I was so used to improvising.

Bitch! Dyke! Faghag! Whore! ran for a year at the Village Gate. I was able to improvise every night, and was able to change it around. At that time I worked with a dramaturge, Steve Zehenter. He showed me where I was repeating myself. He helped me to develop and shape the show. Ironically, he had no background in theater whatsoever. He's an architect. It was a sensibility that he had.

I believe the audience is a major player in my work. I often tell them, "I can do nothing for you." I always talk directly to the audience. I always include the audience. I don't feel like I'm more intelligent than my audience. I feel they're pretty much like me. I feel like we're doing it together. They're holding out an end of the tightrope, and I'm at the other end. If they believe it, I believe it. If they don't believe it, I don't believe it. Let's face it, people who have an overriding need to perform are not the healthiest people in the world. It's an ego lack. And I like to admit this to the audience. What I get from an audience is a tremendous feeling of acceptance. I'll sometimes tell an audience, "A lot of you might not like me now, but that might change."

Although it might seem self-indulgent, I'm really looking for a transformation for myself and my audience every night. I know that I look for a rigorous inquiry when I go to the theater. I expect the same for my audience. You go to the theater to experience what you are unwilling or unable to experience in real life.

Self-Censoring

About self-censoring, sometimes it's intuitive and not even conscious. You have to always look at "Why am I saying something? What's the real reason?" I always hold myself up to an audience. I'm braver in front of an audience, more honest. Quentin Crisp said a very funny thing. He said, "At a certain point, I had to decide how much I was putting on to please myself and how much I was putting on to annoy my mother."

One thing that I learned from Steve [Zehenter] was that by tightening up certain areas, it gave me more room to improvise the rest of the time. If I just group the like-minded thoughts together, then I'd have more room to improvise. I don't rehearse. If I'm in one of my shows with other actors, they rehearse.

Whatever Works

My advice to other writers of their own material is to use whatever process works for you until it proves otherwise. Even if that process isn't sensible to anyone else. If you start to feel that that process is a copout or a way of hiding, then it's no longer working well for you.

I remember one way that I used to work was to play specific music over and over. I'd play the same song maybe thirty times in a row. This would put me in to kind of a meditative state that was useful to what I was trying to evoke out of myself.

After a while, however, I started to have more respect for the reason why I was doing this, and my process changed. I started to include more people, give up a lot of my unhealthy control. I started to listen to what people said about my work. I'm a very internal person. I think a lot. Then I talk to people about it in my daily life. Then finally, I get on stage and talk to the audience. Now I also include feedback from Steve and Eric, my director. That's how I develop my work. My advice to your readers is talk to us about what you're afraid for us to know about you.

CHAPTER 30

kate clinton

© Carol Rosegg

In 1993, Kate Clinton's first one-woman show, *Out Is In*, debuted in Los Angeles to sold-out crowds. The show then moved to New York for a three-month run off-Broadway. In 1995, her next one-woman show, *Impure Thoughts*, debuted in Los Angeles. Her next show, *All Het Up*, toured the country in 1996. Ms. Clinton joined *The Rosie O'Donnell Show* as a television writer, seeing them through their initial launch and rollout period. She has appeared on Comedy Central, *Good Morning America*, *Nightline*, *CNN*, *C-SPAN*, *Entertainment Tonight*, *The Arsenio Hall Show*, the Food Network, FX, and PBS. She also hosted *In the Life* and collaborated on *The World According to Us*, which aired as three specials on the Lifetime network. Ms. Clinton has five comedy albums to her credit. Her book, *Don't Get Me Started*, was published by Ballantine, and is presently in its fourth printing. She writes a monthly column for *The Progressive*, and has written pieces for the *New York Times*, *The Advocate*, and *George* magazine.

Kate Clinton recently released her new CD, *The Marrying Kind*. It is a wild, free-associating, dot-connecting romp through presidential selections, stem and terrorist cells, the Fox of War, Patriot action, Homeland Insecurity, the Axis of Medievals, Mad Vow Disease, and Bush-Free Daze.

> *Ben Brantley in the* New York Times *has said, ". . . while Ms. Clinton may exude a raffish professional polish that fits comfortably within a conventional talk-show format, she never forsakes a certain sunny subversiveness. Metaphorically, she always carries a knife: only a dinner knife, perhaps, but its edge is never blunt."*
>
> *Sharon Schatz of the* Los Angeles Times *has said, "[Clinton's] quick wit and hilarious antics, combined with an endearing maternal style, make even the potential homophobes in the audience want to take her to lunch by show's end."*

Starting in Stand-Up

My material is topical and occasional. What I mean by "occasional" is that it's for different occasions. I write a lot of political stuff. Generally, the political material is at the beginning of each routine. It usually changes with almost every show.

I started out in 1981. I was doing these readings with this women's writing group I was in. I would intentionally go for laughs to help with the maudlin aspect of some of the heavy stuff a lot of these ladies were writing. At that same time, I had been talking about trying to do stand-up comedy. I think I told my best friend too many times that I wanted to try stand-up, because she booked me into a club. It was a club in Syracuse. She called me and said, You're on in a month. That's how I started. That first piece was just to amuse, to see if I could get laughs. I like to say I was translating Adrienne Rich into one-liners. In case you don't know who she is, she's a wonderful but definitely very serious feminist writer. Rich had written a huge piece about compulsory heterosexuality. I condensed it into one line about a penis with a mind of its own.

What Teaching Taught Me

Because I had been a high-school English teacher, I had developed a way of working. I wrote and clipped and cut material for my shows, just as I had in school. Also, I would try out the material with people at dinner. And I'd read things to my partner. I discovered that although I'd written a two-page piece of material, after performing it once, I could cut it down to one or two lines, based on a person's or audience's reaction. I would watch to see how people reacted to my material, and that was a strong determining factor of how it would change. So, to be precise, I'd write it down first, and then I'd take it out into the field and try it out. The tryout phase for new material would usually be about a year.

The first piece I performed publicly was thirty-three minutes long. I called one hundred and eighty of my closest friends and trusted codependents to come see it. It went fine. They were all the people I had amused at parties, except now they had to pay.

Actually, the second show that I did was more revealing to me. It was in Boston at an alternative theater space. These were people that I didn't know. What was interesting was that two weeks before, I had gotten uproarious laughs at a particular line, but that night there was dead silence. From teaching, I knew not to panic. I just kept going on. Again, there was another line that two weeks before I had gotten a lot of laughs on. But that night, again, nothing, silence. I must have had a stricken look on my face, because I heard a voice from the audience say, "You're on your own, darling." The lesson, of course, is, You *are* on your own, and you just must keep going.

The Arc of a Show

Within six months of that first show, my shows were running ninety minutes. My material is arranged like a newspaper. I always start out with a kind of welcome in the beginning. I next locate where we are, a comment on the hall itself. I like to spy on the crowd as they're coming in. I'll talk about them. It's a way of locating us. After that, I discuss the news of the day, front page. There's sports, there's media, culture comments, editorials, science news, etc.

Because I wasn't performing in comedy clubs, I wasn't gearing my material with jokes and punch lines. I worked more with anecdotes, observations, that kind of thing. I always end my show with some sort of farewell material, which has varied during the years, but generally is a more serious material. In the beginning, I worked a lot in church basements. Later on, I moved upstairs in the church. I must say, the Unitarian's really moved my career along. I've also worked in coffeehouses. Now I do concert halls. The way that I used to rehearse was, I worked in front of my blue couch. I picture imaginary people sitting there. My best friend was there; I'd imagine Lily Tomlin, Dorothy Parker, all kinds of folks. I'd rehearse my material to them, imagine their reactions.

Topical Anthropologist

These days in my show, I'm talking a lot about mergers, how everything's merging. Banks are merging, oil companies are merging, like that. I mention how gay and straight people seem to be merging. And also I mention that I've noticed how the world is going very fast these days. Maybe because of everyone drinking too much coffee. Money, media, and sports interest me, and I also include those subjects in my shows. I often feel like I'm an anthropologist.

My new show feels particularly like that. When I think of my process of working on material, I think of the way I developed my work as a teacher. When I first started teaching I would write out almost everything, word for word, what I was going to say in class. But by the time I stopped teaching, years later, I was lucky if I wrote just one or two words to remind me what I'd be teaching the next day. I'd stopped writing out everything and would just wing it. At the beginning of my monologue work, I wrote out every sentence. That eventually evolved to just a simple set list of what I was going to talk about. There was a real script for me, which I'd automatically memorize. If there's a lot of new material, I'll put a set list down, which I take with me on the stage. I no longer rehearse with imaginary people on a blue couch. They've sort of become internalized now. As I said, I try things out on people all the time. I depend totally on the audience for feedback. I don't have a director; I never have.

A Natural High

For me, performing my material is a legal high. I did a show at Town Hall [New York] once that was spectacular. I remember getting off that stage and going, "Yes!" I still see people on the street who say to me, "I was at the Town Hall show." And I'll say to them, "Well, then, you saw the show." They know exactly what I mean. I felt like I had actually levitated during that show—that's how high it made me feel. It's like you do all the hard work, you prepare, and then sometimes, like on that night, it felt like it was just coming right through me. My timing was wonderful. Everything seemed to work perfectly.

I don't do characters, say like Lily Tomlin. But every so often when I'm on stage and I hear myself doing voices, I know something special is happening out there. The material is taking me somewhere. I don't write character monologue material per se. But in the stories that I tell, I will sometimes deliver a line as the character. I do sound effects, though. I find myself doing them to enhance a story. I've always loved doing sound effects, even as a kid.

Talking about audiences, I'd like to go back to how teaching affected my work. When I was a teacher, on some days I'd teach like five classes. Three of those classes might be the same thing. If something went really well in the first class, I'd try to do it in the second and it would just fall into place, because it had now become spontaneous. And what I learned there was, you can't have any expectations, you have to go with what's presented to you. You present and then you get a reaction, and that's what you can't predict. In performing, I find that also true. I find that if I'm prepared enough, I can improvise from what I've prepared.

Changing the System

In the show I'm now working on, I'm at a point where I'm just taking notes. This show feels like it will be transitional. I'm making myself write more personal things. I'm working with these blue index cards that are all over my desk. They are notes of interesting phrases or historical things that have occurred. Right now I'm in a process of discovery and serendipity. I make myself work on the material for four or five hours every day. I'll sit around and think about what I want to say, then I'll write out some of the thoughts, and then I'll go to my computer and type it up and then print it out and take a look at what I've got. There will be things on the page that kind of vibrate, visually. And when that happens, I know it's something I want to pursue. So I'll underline those things. I'm interested in entertaining people, but I'm also interested in the political scene. I'm interested in changing people's minds about things. I hope that when I'm much older, I'll still be talking about things that will change the system a bit.

CHAPTER 31

ann randolph

© Stephen Najera

Ann Randolph is a writer/performer who began her career by writing a play with the patients at the Athens State Mental Hospital while attending Ohio University. After her parents gave her a one-way ticket to Alaska for graduation, she spent the next year teaching playwriting at Prince William Sound College in Valdez, Alaska. After two years in Alaska, she moved to Boston, where she performed in various improv groups and toured with the Boston Arts Group. She then moved to Santa Fe, New Mexico, where she staged her first solo show.

She moved to Los Angeles where she joined the Groundlings. She performed weekly with the company, and then quit to perform her own solo shows. Her second solo show, *Loveland*, was optioned for television and headlined the NYC Word Fire Fest. Her third solo show, *Miss America*, won her the prestigious *L.A. Weekly* Theater Award for best solo show. Her fourth solo show, *Squeeze Box*, was produced by the late Anne Bancroft, and ran off-Broadway. A feature film is now in the works with Randolph and Bancroft as the screenwriters and Mel Brooks producing. Excerpts from her various shows have been featured on NPR and PBS.

The New York Times *has said, "Now* Squeeze Box *has come to New York, and it's clear what Ms. Bancroft, the show's producer, saw in it. Ms. Randolph has a definite talent for sketch comedy"*

The New York Sun *has said: "Such warmth and frankness are in short supply in the theater, so go and bask while you can. Her piece has been optioned for film rights, and this off-Broadway run may catapult her to bigger and better places. If you go now, you get a bargain. You want to see her after she's a star? That, as Brandy would say, will cost extra."*

From Broadway.com: *"This combination of compassionate storytelling, humor and frank confessions makes for an enjoyable evening of theater."*

From NYTheater.com: *"*Squeeze Box *is a simple piece of theatre and Randolph is funny, gawky, and poignantly touching. There is no political agenda* *to the play, no terminal disease, no screaming battle—just the contribution of a life, dealing with real issues, insecurities, and passions. I encourage you witness this refreshing experience on the New York stage."*

The Freedom a Solo Show Allows

I think the main reason I started writing solo shows was the freedom it allowed me as a writer/performer. In the past, I was involved in sketch comedy groups like the Groundlings, and I always felt confined creatively. My beginnings as a writer were in comedy, but I always felt pulled to explore a darker deeper side of myself, and solo shows allowed me to do that. I also loved the idea of being able to set up shop anywhere—meaning I could just show up on a stage with nothing but myself and do an evening of theater. And, of course, there was this incredible desire to express so much of what I was witnessing in the world and in my community.

I started writing by asking myself a very deep life question that would then lead me down a road I had not gone down before. In writing, I hoped to learn something of my own truth. For example, in *Squeeze Box*, I started out with the question of, "Why am I not progressing in my life, and why have I lost my faith?"

I always try to just allow myself to explore freely. It was difficult in the beginning because I wanted to impose a structure on the piece, but I had a wonderful teacher, Terri Silverman, and director, Alan Bailey, who encouraged me to just let the piece evolve organically, and I did.

Journaling and Music

I just started writing. I found that journaling helped me a great deal and that what I wrote in my journals seemed to make its way into my piece. I also do a lot of characters, and I like to play in front of a mirror and see who comes out. I then have the different characters address the theme from their point of view. And of course, all the characters are exaggerated parts of my contradictory self. Another element that is most important to me is music. I like to weave music throughout my pieces in ways that one might normally not do so. For example, in *Squeeze Box*, I wanted to show how music was inspiring and revelatory, so I chose to have the climax of *Squeeze Box* at a concert of Aaron Copland's *Appalachian Spring*. In the show, I sit to listen to the music, and then I begin to describe exactly what I'm hearing, and as the music shifts in emotion, so do I. It's rather complicated to explain, but quite fascinating on stage.

Rewrites, Rewrites, Rewrites, and Mel Brooks and Anne Bancroft

I booked the theater and that made me have the piece ready. That was the first step, but I knew from my structure when it was finished. I had set up a structure where the beginning would also be the ending, so

I knew where I was headed. However, I didn't know this until halfway into writing the piece.

When I finished the show in 2001, it was two and a half hours long with the intermission. That's quite long for a solo show, but it did quite well and was awarded best solo show by *L.A. Weekly* and the Los Angeles Ovation Award for best solo show. However, when Mel Brooks and Anne Bancroft came to see it, they suggested that I cut it down to seventy minutes before they would open it off-Broadway.

For the next year, I did six major rewrites. Each time I did a rewrite, I thought it was the best, but it wasn't. Plus, I had the added pressure of showing Mel and Anne the rewrite in front of an invited audience at whatever coast they happened to be on. It was very difficult. For example, they would say that I needed to fly to New York City to show them the latest rewrite, and I did. When I flew into New York City, I would tech the same day of the show and then perform that night in a space I'd never been in.

Also, I was responsible for packing the house. They had their friends, but I always had to come up with about two hundred people. This was hard because I knew very few people in New York City, but my L.A. friends were incredible and e-mailed all their New York City friends. I can honestly say that I would never have made it this far without friends and e-mail. Mel and Anne also flew up to Minneapolis to see me perform the show in the Midwest. I thought that was amazing. They showed up at this funky little theater attached to a bowling alley and snuck in through the back door. They wanted to see how Midwest audiences responded. That's how committed they were to the project. Finally, after a year, I got the rewrite they were looking for.

Self-Doubts

I can't think of an occasion where I have ever felt inclined to censor myself in my writing, but I sure have had lots of doubts in my actual performance. I continue to deal with self-doubts before, after, and during the performance. I've found that meditation and acknowledging my fears are the most helpful ways of dealing with performance anxiety. I can tell you that coming to New York City and opening off-Broadway was the scariest thing I've ever done.

I had been working the graveyard shift at a homeless shelter for mentally ill women for the past ten years because I loved the work and it allowed me the freedom during the day to write. I also had my weekends free to perform. However, to make the transition from working fifty hours a week at a shelter for eight bucks an hour to Broadway was quite a big leap, and I was so excited and scared at the same time. Also, *Squeeze Box* is about my work in the shelter and my loss of faith in progressing and being successful in life.

Every night is completely different. Somehow, I thought doing an off-Broadway show eight nights a week would start to seem routine, but it hasn't. I still get nervous every night, and the energy from the audience is so different from night to night.

Rehearsals

I rehearsed mostly at home by myself. My director would come and give me notes, and then I would go off and practice by myself. My director was with me from the first ten minutes of the piece. Whenever I had a new chunk of material, I would read it to him, and he would give his feedback. He was extremely positive and encouraging and was fantastic about helping me edit the material. He also was super organized. I would have my script written on scraps of paper and scribbled writing, and he would organize it all. He also did not impose a way to tell the story, but allowed me to discover the way, and then he would help me bring out the emotional beats of the piece.

The first time I performed the piece, I felt like I was speaking so fast that nobody could keep up. I was so nervous and I only thought about performing from a writer's point of view instead of a performer. Gradually, I was able to take my time with the piece and really live it. That took about three years.

Some Advice for Actors

Find a writer's group and put your material up weekly. When you have a solid ten-minute chunk, go to an open-mike night and perform it in front of a live audience. Whenever I could get stage time, I would. It wouldn't matter if it was in some dive or a friend's salon—just get the material out and do it.

PART III

interviews
with
directors
of one-person
shows

These were the general questions that I asked of all the directors that I interviewed. Some additional questions were asked depending on the director's individual response.

- What drew you to directing the first one-person show you worked on?
- As you started rehearsing, what differences did you notice between working on solo shows and on a regular play? Were there any things that came up that you hadn't anticipated?
- How would you describe the relationship between you and the actors in the solo shows you've worked on? How was it different from working on a regular play?
- Can you describe the way you like to rehearse and develop these plays?
- How did you shape the material with the actors you worked with? Did that change much from performer to performer?
- How do you decide when the material is ready?
- What similarities and differences have you noticed between the solo shows you've worked on?
- From a director's point of view, what advice do you have for actors who are thinking about writing their own solo shows? Any other comments that you'd like to make regarding solo shows?

CHAPTER 32

peter askin

© Joan Marcus

Peter Askin directed and developed the award-winning off-Broadway productions of John Leguizamo's *Mambo Mouth* and *Spic-O-Rama*, and Dael Orlandersmith's *Beauty's Daughter*. Other off-Broadway directing credits include *Reality Ranch, Beauty Marks, Reno*, and the New York and Pasadena Playhouse productions of *Down an Alley Filled with Cats*. He directed *The Gimmick* at the McCarter and the Sundance Film Festival, and the highly acclaimed rock musical *Hedwig and the Angry Inch*. For television, he directed the HBO production of *Spic-O-Rama* and was the supervising producer for John Leguizamo's Fox comedy series *House of Buggin'*. He also collaborated with Mr. Leguizamo on the Comedy Central's *The Talent Pool*.

Mr. Askin co-wrote *Smithereens*, Susan Seidelman's directorial film debut. He has directed Sigourney Weaver, John Turturro, and Woody Allen in *Company Man*, a film he co-wrote with Doug McGrath. *Mambo Mouth* won an Obie and Outer Critics Award, and *Spic-O-Rama* won the Drama Desk Award and several Cable Ace Awards, including Best Direction of a Comedy Special (TV). *Beauty's Daughter* won the Obie and *The Talent Pool* won a Cable Ace Award. He wrote "What Are You, Stupid?" for HBO's *Peace: Live It or Rest in It*. Most recently, he directed Eve Ensler's one-woman show, *The Good Body*, on Broadway and *Privilege* at the Second Stage Theater.

Clive Barnes in the New York Post *has said, "Spic-O-Rama has been expertly directed by Peter Askin, who is also credited with 'developing' the show, so presumably had some creative hand in the deal. Don't miss it!"*

Ben Brantley in the New York Times *has said, "Under Peter Askin's slick direction, Mr. McGrath emerges as an agile, confident performer, capable of shifting roles with ease."*

Peter Marks, also in the New York Times, *has said, "[In] Hedwig and the Angry Inch, Michael Cerveris is superbly directed by Peter Askin."*

How to Talk to Actors

My first one-person show was a play called *Reno*, with Paul Zimmerman. I directed it at the West Bank Cafe and later on at the Acme Bar and Grill. I was very attracted to the material. It had a dark bite to it, dark, dark humor. One thing I learned working on that show was how to talk to actors. I had been a directing student with Wynn Handman, and was now learning to apply some of my new skills.

Prior to this I had been a writer. So what I brought to directing was a writer's eye in terms of structure. The thing I still bring and concentrate on initially is dramaturgy. I feel that it is such a luxury to work one-on-one with the writer-actor. You can focus on minutiae both in performance and on the page. The goal, at least for me, is to get it as close to what I think it can be on the page. Then, when you start rehearsal, you have a stronger platform.

The Difference Between a Regular Play and a Solo Play

Dramaturgically, I don't think there is that much difference between a one-person play and a multi-character play. Both still need structure. One of the pitfalls authors of one-person shows have is that their stuff is not always in dramatic form—it's too narrative and expositional. To make things dramatic, you have to place things in the present tense. You have to look for conflict.

Since there are just the two of you in development of a one-person show, the actor has to trust you. In a play, the actors in rehearsal feed off each other. A one-person show is a much lonelier proposition, particularly for the actor. He's in a much more vulnerable position. Actors in a regular play rely on each other to create; in the one-person show, the actor only has the audience as his partner. If the actor in a multi-character play is off or flat in a certain beat or moment (especially in the beginning), another actor can rescue him.

It was always interesting to watch John Leguizamo, who, like many actors, relates to laughter like food. The shows would vary from performance to performance, depending on the audience's response, in itself always a variable. *Spic-O-Rama* could be shortened by as much as two or three minutes if the audience wasn't responding that night. John would go faster because he was not getting the laughter he wanted. His performance would get a shade angrier, which would also speed things up.

Directing John Leguizamo

I first saw the show at Intar on 42nd Street. It had elaborate costumes and changes could take five minutes between monologues. It was mainly a question dramaturgically of shaping, condensing, combining, and eliminating redundancy. I worked with him on shaping the monologues so they'd have an arc. We worked to illuminate the monologues, to find what a monologue was really about. The best example of this was "Crossover King." It was the last monologue of the evening, as a Japanese businessman. Originally, I believe the fun for John was playing a Japanese character. What seemed obvious to me, though, after we read it through two or three times, was that this was about a Hispanic, who put on the guise of a Japanese businessman. His dilemma was that the Japanese corporate shell could not contain the emotions of the real person, the Hispanic, from bursting through at moments. Once we realized that, then it was easy, because that's what it was about.

To make the transitions interesting in *Mambo Mouth,* I hit on the silhouette idea. The characters would finish a monologue behind a scrim. And as John changed costumes, he'd keep talking behind the scrim as the end of one character fed into the beginning of the next monologue. The order of the characters, to some extent, depended on those transitions.

I wanted *Mambo Mouth* to have some kind of common thread, if possible. So we imposed a network of relationships. It was mainly for us, but the cross-references helped unify the evening's landscape.

I mainly want to tell a story in a one-person show, rather than just have an actor showing his craft. With *Spic-O-Rama,* we created a family. John was still going to do different characters, but now there was an event, the marriage of one of the brothers. The precocious kid who opened the show introduced us to all of his family members. He provided the through-line. Each monologue reflected on the event.

The way the stage was used was determined by the story or the play. John, like Eric Bogosian, could have done *Spic-O-Rama* in street clothes. But he enjoyed using costumes. The most important thing for me was speed between scenes. *Spic-O-Rama* had a much more ambitious set, kind of a warped reality, representing elements from the Gigante life.

Working on *Political Animal*

Another one-person show I directed was Doug McGrath's *Political Animal.* That show used video. Once again, the story dictated the set. It was a political satire involving a television interview with a particularly greasy Republican presidential candidate. So we used the idea of the television interview. We taped Doug doing the candidate being interviewed. That was the thread throughout the play because we kept coming back to that interview. There were four TV monitors on the stage. As Doug began another character, we'd go to the television video of that character. We'd begin a scene on those monitors. As soon as he was in costume change, we'd go from the monitors to him live. *Political Animal* was one story with twelve characters.

Hedwig and the Angry Inch

I had never seen *Hedwig and the Angry Inch* before, although they had done several performances before I got involved. I also had never worked on a musical before. I was struck by the intelligence of the writing, a combination of broad standup and very smart storytelling and songwriting. Still, the first thing again was dramaturgy. It was kind of all over the place, hard for the audience to follow. I worked on clarifying it. We broke it down into two acts. Once we did that, it was easy to build toward the end of each act.

Dael Orlandersmith

Working with Dael Orlandersmith was different because she's primarily a poet. We worked together very closely on developing her pieces. She writes very close to the bone, based on her own experience. The three pieces we worked on were *Beauty's Daughter, Monster*, and *The Gimmick*. Her writing can be repetitive; she comes back to the same themes. What freed Dael up was when I introduced her poetry into *Beauty's Daughter*, then found this poetic narrative voice, a form she is writing in now which is unique to her. It has all her strengths, and she writes much more freely.

How the Rehearsal Processes Varies

The rehearsal process with John Leguizamo was fascinating for me. I learned so much about acting from him. It was simply a question of having an idea, communicating it to him, and then watching him make it his own. You just watch it grow. He has the tools, these extraordinary gifts as an actor. Not only is he a comic, but he's also a stunning dramatic actor.

Doug is a highly skilled writer and one of the funniest people alive. I did a lot less dramaturgical work with Doug, and when I'd give him an idea, he'd grasp it very quickly. He grew a great deal as an actor during rehearsal.

Dael is a powerhouse, a force of nature. We trust each other and are friends. But I'm much tougher on Dael than anyone else. What was a bit more difficult with her was that she was always writing and memorizing during rehearsal. It was a slower process. She's a very strong actor and, once she has an idea, she has the capacity to build on it.

John Cameron Mitchell is an extremely bright actor and writer. *Hedwig* was an ambitious play, drawing inspiration from elements as diverse as Plato's *Symposium*. John and Stephen Trask had lived inside of it too long and simply needed a fresh perspective they could trust.

Knowing When It's Ready

The way you know when the one-person show is ready is similar to knowing when a regular play is ready. Does it build? Are there flat moments? Is there redundancy? Is it clear?

When those questions are answered, you get a sense of where the piece is. It's a living thing, like any play. It's going to be a lot different in the third week than the first. If the actor's still trying to solve writing problems in previews, then the he'll never have a chance to be able to expand it, play, and grow.

My Advice to Actor-Writers

For actors who want to write their own shows, the only advice I have is, think hard and long about the story you want to tell. Spend a lot of time on the written part of it. I know that a lot of actors like to work out of improv. If that's the case, you still have to develop your story; it's just a different methodology. You need someone with you whose eye you trust. It doesn't have to be a director—just someone who can help clarify the story, the through-line, or the structure. Break the piece into three acts and give each a structure. If you want to write characters, find the story you want to tell with these characters. Think of each character as a dramatic, comedic story. Tell the story in the present tense. Find conflict within the monologue.

CHAPTER 33

jo bonney

© Paula Cort

Jo Bonney directed the highly acclaimed premiere of Diana Son's *Stop Kiss* at the Public Theater in New York. She also directed Danny Hoch's *Jails, Hospitals & Hip-Hop* at P.S. 122, Philip Ridley's *The Fastest Clock in the Universe*, and the premiere of Seth Zvi Rosenfeld's *The Flatted Fifth* at The New Group. She directed Eric Bogosian's *Suburbia* at the Studio Theatre in Washington, D.C.; Karen William's *How I Got to Cleveland* with Robert Olen Butler's *Fairy Tale* at P.S. 122; Patrick Breen's *Midnight and Morning Rain*; and Warren Leight's *Stray Cats*, both at Naked Angels. She directed Eric Bogosian's *Funhouse; Sex, Drugs, Rock & Roll; Pounding Nails in the Floor with My Forehead*; and his current work in progress. At the Public Theater, she directed Danny Hoch's *Some People*. Ms. Bonney is the Associate Artistic Director of The New Group in New York City. She is the recipient of the Obie for Sustained Excellence in Directing. Most recently she directed Neil LaBute's *Fat Pig* for the MCC Theater and Christopher Shinn's *On the Mountain* for Playwrights Horizons.

Of Ms. Bonney's direction of Eric Bogosian's Wake Up and Smell the Coffee, *Robert Hurwitt in the* San Francisco Examiner *said: "Bogosian's solos (as opposed to plays like* Talk Radio) *seem both carelessly thrown together and crafted with exquisite care by the writer-performer and his director, wife, and longtime collaborator, Jo Bonney."*

Michael Feingold in the Village Voice *said of Bonney's direction of Danny Hoch's* Some People: *"It's in these complex pieces that Jo Bonney's discreet direction comes subtly into play."*

Visual Artist to Director

I didn't come out of theater. I came out of visual arts, arts and design. So I didn't make a decision to direct my first solo show. I had started working with Eric Bogosian. I had hired him to do a voiceover for a short film I was making. It was around 1980. He had just started creating his solo shows. It was a particular time when a lot of people were making solo shows. So I started directing his work simply because we were working on a lot of projects together at that time. I directed all of his shows, from *Funhouse* to *Sex, Drugs, Rock & Roll* to *Pounding Nails in the Floor with My Forehead.*

Even though I started out in visual arts, I had always worked in graphics, so I had done some work in TV and video. I had directed shorts, many using actors. So working on a one-person show was very manageable for me. Also, I spend a lot of time on these shows as an editor-dramaturge. I don't come in at the end, when the piece is already written. I come in at ground zero, at the beginning, when the piece is just starting to be written. That's how I've always worked with Eric and Danny [Hoch]. For me, that's always half the pleasure. For me, directing, that is, blocking a piece, is only about 25 percent of the work. The rest of the work is working with the dialogue. I know a lot of other directors of one-person shows who come in when the piece is already written. They help by editing and staging it. It really just depends on who you're working with, the relationship you have established, the trust, the sensibilities, etc.

The Difference between Solo Shows and Ensemble Pieces

I would say the main differences between working on a solo show and a regular play has to do with whether the piece is scripted (as in most plays). With a scripted play, you just apply your vision to the piece. As I mentioned, with a solo piece, I come into the collaboration very early on, at the beginning. My work is similar when working on a new play and working on solo material. In both cases, I help develop the material. I'm part of the creation of the show.

I worked on a play [for The New Group] that was already completely scripted. It was a very different process than working with a play's development. I personally love the interaction, the collaboration, with the writer in a play's growth.

When you're working with an actor in a solo piece, they're also the writer, the originator of the material. There's a lot of conversation as to, perhaps, the tone is off, or the structure isn't working, etc. You have to split the writer from the performer. The writer is in love with the words, and the performer is in love with the audience. My job, I've always felt, is tempering both inclinations so that they can work together. With the writer, you just have to be ruthless and just eliminate where the writing isn't working. If they trust you, they'll go with your choices and what you're seeing. They know that my job is just to make them look better. My work with the writer-performer is to make them look fabulous on that stage, so that I just disappear into the woodwork.

In ensemble work, the director's hand is more at the forefront. Working with solo performers is very intense, very mind-to-mind. If you like that other mind, it's really fun; you're both in the sandpit together. I'm very selective about who I work with on solo work because it's a very demanding commitment. It's a shared sensibility. These pieces can take nine months to complete. There's the editing, the workshops, then out on the road, then you bring them in for a run—a lot of time and energy.

I should mention that I'm very writer-oriented. I want the pieces to read as really strong literature on the page as well as in the performance. That's not the case with all solo work. A lot of solo work is very body-oriented or dance or cabaret or performance art. I mainly work with people who come out of a theater tradition.

Staging a Solo Show

One of the main areas that I work with technically, in solo work, is lighting. The work that I do uses minimal set and props. This isn't always the case with other artists' solo shows. There is a huge range of solo work. Some are very prop-, costume-, and set-intensive. Some use video screens, multimedia, etc.

What I like about the solo work that I do with Eric and Danny is the quick change from character to character, and the quick change in body language and voice; you're suddenly in another place and time with another character. The less clutter there is around that, the more amazing the transformation.

A solo piece is a very delicate piece. It's really about the energy and personality of the performer. And more than anything, it's about the energy between the performer and the audience. So actually, I spend a lot of my time once we have gone through the sitting in a room, you know, scanning the writing and ideas, out in the back of the audience. I watch the audience as much as I watch the performer. I try to gauge where it's connecting and where it's reading and where it's going off, and what the audience's reaction is.

Working with Eric Bogosian and Danny Hoch

Danny, Eric, and I have a similar work situation. Both of them came out of theater as actors, not as writers. Initially, when they were both doing their work, they'd get up on stage, unscripted. Much of the work was in their heads, and they'd improvise. When I started to work with Eric, and then later with Danny, I told them, "I can't direct you if I don't have something on paper, it's way too ephemeral." So at a certain point, they both started scripting their pieces, transcribing them, writing down work that had simply existed in their heads before.

Before we actually go to a rehearsal room, we'd just meet and discuss what's on the page. In some cases, it may be a fully birthed character. Then I'll just say, "Let's see him on his feet." Then I'll watch and decide whether I felt it needed cutting or something, or whether it didn't need any playing with. For another character, in a whole page of writing, I might find that there may be just one fabulous line of writing. So you start from that and say, "This line makes sense and the rest should just go. The rest is just punching in the dark." Then we'd play around with that, improv on that, and then they'd go away, do some more writing.

In the past, Eric has used a tape recorder in order to feel more spontaneous. He felt he might not get that spontaneity if he was sitting, just writing. Then I'd listen to the recording and see if there was a line or direction that seemed interesting. Eric hasn't worked, however, with a tape recorder in a number of years, but at one point he felt it was useful.

One thing I've noticed about Eric and Danny over the years is that they've become better and better writers. So the flow from the brain to the hand has become almost as organic as if they were really saying the line. Another thing [is] Eric and Danny will both jot things down as it comes to them, stuff that they might want to look at later. It's a very free-fall kind of process. They'll improv, they'll write, they'll show me stuff, put it up, go back, I'll do some editing, they'll write some more, they'll workshop it, then there's a point where they'll put it up in front of people. It's not a clean-cut, black-and-white kind of process. It's very circular.

Developing the Piece in Front of an Audience

We never sit and decide, "This piece is ready now." What we do is, we get to the point where we arbitrarily decide a time to set it up and put it in front of an audience. We'll put it up at P.S. 122, or at the Knitting Factory or at any space. The criterion is you decide that you have an hour's worth of work that you're ready to have seen. We make it clear to our audience at that time that this is a work in progress. The first workshops are just the embryos. You might see some characters, some ideas. But as the workshops continue in the course of a few months, you'll see them grow. Some characters might drop out completely; others may suddenly appear.

Sometimes I'll see something in one piece, then something in another that isn't quite there. But if you put the two pieces together you can create a more complex character. The way you know when it's set is that the character is satisfying to you, the show has the shape and the arc that you want it to have, the piece has the right rhythms from the beginning to the end. You just have to trust your instincts.

The beginning and end, characters are often quite tricky to decide on because you're trying to find what dynamic you start and finish on. You also want to make sure that whatever you lead with really sets your audience's mind in a particular place. In Danny's show, *Jails, Hospitals & Hip-Hop*, there's a rap piece that used to be at the end, but then we finally decided that it should be at the beginning. We realized that its message was too heavy, that it was more interesting at the top of the show.

Things to Keep in Mind

By the end of the show, where do we want to take the audience? How do we get there? Like a dance or music piece, there is a rhythm to a show. It's how you hear it, see it. You're juggling a lot of things when deciding which piece goes when. Pacing also is a factor to consider. There are different dialects and languages in these shows that the ear has to catch up to. You also have to give the audience's ears a chance to relax because it's often such a diatribe coming at them, a wall of words. There's also comedic versus dramatic pieces to consider. There are so many factors to constantly keep considering in the formation of the whole evening.

Solo shows are a personality-driven form. It's difficult to mention rules because it's so individual. If your interests or personality go toward a more mythical-fantastical storytelling, then that's the kind of show you should make. If you have an ear for urban dialect, and you get off on those rhythms, then you should go toward creating characters. It should always have an energy that's about theater. The worst kind of shows are where a person is just telling the story of their life, where they think people will be interested in their paranoias or dilemmas.

As far as directors doing these shows, you must really love that intense one-on-one collaboration with another artist. You must be the kind of director who can sit on your ego in the end, because it really does, in the final moment, become the phenomenon of the solo performer.

My advice to actors is, if you're working on your own material, you should find a director that you really trust to work with you at some point. It's very difficult to do this kind of work all alone. Having an objective eye on your work can be immensely helpful.

CHAPTER 34

christopher ashley

Christopher Ashley's solo shows include Anna Deavere Smith's *Fires in the Mirror* at the New York Shakespeare Festival, Claudia Shear's *Blown Sideways Through Life* at New York Theatre Workshop and the Minetta Lane Theater, and Dario Fo's *Tale of the Tiger* at New York Theatre Workshop and the Minetta Lane Theater. Other New York credits include *The Most Fabulous Story Ever Told* at the New York Theatre Workshop and the Minetta Lane Theater; *Jeffrey* at the WPA and Minetta Lane Theater; *Communicating Doors* at the Variety Arts Theatre; *Li'l Abner* for Encores! at City Center; *Das Barbecu* at the Minetta Lane Theater; *Bunny, Bunny* at the Lucille Lortel; *As Thousands Cheer* for The Drama Department; *The Naked Truth*, and *The Night Hank Williams Died*; as well as numerous plays at the WPA.

Regionally, he has directed at the American Repertory Theatre, Center Stage in Baltimore, Cincinnati Playhouse in the Park, George Street Theater, Goodspeed Opera House, Intiman Theater, Long Wharf, Williamstown Theatre Festival, Los Angeles Theater Center, New York Stage and Film, Philadelphia Theatre Company, the Royal George in Chicago, and Shakespeare & Company. Westside Arts in Los Angeles. His film work includes *Blown Sideways Through Life* for *American Playhouse* (PBS) and *Jeffrey* (for Orion Classics). Mr. Ashley won the Lucille Lortel Award for Outstanding Direction of *Fires in the Mirror* and *Jeffrey*. For *Jeffrey*, he won an Obie award, two Dramalogues, and a San Francisco Bay Area Critics Award. He recently directed Paul Rudnick's off-Broadway *Valhalla* and *All Shook Up* on Broadway.

> *Clive Barnes in the* New York Post *said of* Blown Sideways Through Life, *"Ms. Shear has what used to be called the gift of gab . . . aided, abetted, developed, and directed by the extraordinarily talented Christopher Ashley . . ."*
>
> *Frank Rich in the* New York Times *said,* "Blown Sideways *may not be a play, exactly, but it merits the elegant full-dress production that it has received from the director Christopher Ashley."*

Fires in the Mirror

The two most well known one-person shows that I've done are *Blown Sideways Through Life*, written by and starring Claudia Shear, and *Fires in the Mirror*, written by and starring Anna Deavere Smith. I directed both of these shows at almost the same time, but I believe *Fires in the Mirror* came first.

I believe *Fires in the Mirror* was the first piece in Anna Deavere Smith's documentary-type series. I didn't know Anna before I was asked to do that piece. For me, the hook there was the material; it was so interesting, so fresh, so innovative. Also, her way of working was so interesting. This whole thing happened during Joanne Alkalitis's tenure at the Public Theater. I had assisted Joanne on one of those TCG NEA grants a couple of months before. Anna had done a workshop of *Fires in the Mirror* and was hunting around for a director. I didn't see the original workshop that Anna had done at the Public.

Originally there were, believe it or not, about nine hours of material for *Fires in the Mirror*. Plus, there were hundreds of hours of other interviews that hadn't been used yet. Some of her material was written out and some was on tape. It was kind of a huge hodgepodge. Added to all this, they only gave us two and a half weeks to work; that was our deadline. So there was this huge push to edit down and select the best and most workable material. It was not an easy job, believe me. But it was fascinating.

The main thing Anna Deavere does when she's working with people is to wear a Walkman during her interviews with them. She tape-records everything. A lot of what we did was make an index card for each individual interview. Then we'd move the pieces around and figure out what structural questions were significant. Generally, people are going to say what they're going to say during the interviews, so we had to be selective as to what worked best for the interview, and what worked best for the play. We were kind of making up the rules as we went along.

Fires in the Mirror is about the Crown Heights riots, both from the Jewish and the African-American perspective. There were many questions during the interview about identity. Many of the questions focused on, How do you define yourself? If someone asks you who you are, do you pull up race? Do you pull up gender? Do you pull up your job? Do you pull up where you live or who your parents are? Clearly, everything exploded in Crown Heights around issues of difference. Then we had to deal with why those two communities found it necessary to define themselves in a way that was in direct opposition to each other.

My favorite way of working with a solo piece is starting from the seed of an idea with the actor-writer. As I mentioned, in this case, with Anna, she had already had a previous workshop, so it was a bit of a different process. One thing, though: Every solo show that I've worked on, the actor-writer is always hungry for input and dramaturgical assistance.

A lot of our discussions were about the reality of the piece. All of the decisions were about there being an actual person who was going to be portrayed by Anna on the stage. The editing decisions were all based on what was said during the interviews. Inevitably you have to change some of what they've said. But the secret is, you must remain truthful to the core of who they are. You really have to listen to what they're trying to say and see how it can filter into what the needs of your piece are.

There are a lot of interpretative decisions to be made that you have to tussle out in rehearsal. The hardest thing in that piece was that everybody was either happy or interested. Nobody was furious at all. Because Anna is African-American and a woman, we had to deal with things like, How are you going to portray a Jewish male? How would you do his dialect without stereotyping him? When you're playing a man, what are you trying to hold on to as to what's masculine for that character, without being too overt?

Blown Sideways Through Life

In *Blown Sideways Through Life,* Claudia [Shear] and I developed the piece over about three years. There were many readings and small productions around the country prior to it settling in at the Cherry Lane Theatre in New York. The piece started with an idea that Claudia had. She said, "There are things in my experience that I think could make a show. Would you help develop it with me?" She'd write material and then we'd talk. Then she'd write some more and we'd discuss that. It went on that way.

About two months into working this way, we decided she'd structure it around the jobs that she'd had. She'd bring material to me and we'd cull it, reshape it, and try it out over a couple of years. Claudia wrote every word, but structurally we developed together. When we first showed the piece, it was around thirty minutes. Eventually it ran sixty-seven minutes. At one point it went as long as an hour and a half, but we pulled it back down.

Because this was the first thing Claudia had written, it was at times like a roller coaster ride for her. Like, "Wheeeee! What am I doing?! How do I write?!" She was figuring out where her voice was as she was writing. With Anna Deavere Smith, she had taught a lot and had written other plays, so the experience was quite different. Anna had a lot more self-awareness of what type of voice she would be writing in.

Table Work and Physical Life

Both pieces would have like a weaving in and out of rehearsing, followed by dramaturgical table work. We'd rehearse for about an hour and then we'd take a break back at the table, where we'd edit down and reorganize. The way we rehearsed was, the actresses would get up and work on the text. There'd be some blocking, some physical stage work. They both worked on a set of some kind. We'd figure out what the physical life was and how the pacing would go. We'd work on how we were defining the characters at every given time. With Anna, there was a lot more character work. With

Claudia, there was a dance element to the piece. Also in *Blown Sideways*, there were these rapid-fire lists that sometimes went on for a minute or two. Early on we decided that there would be like a stunt quality to these lists. They were going to go so fast and yet every element of the list had to be specific. That took a lot of memorizing and attaching specifics to them. We had to at first work very slowly. You'd look at each element of the list and ask, "How do you feel about it? What's the action attached to it?" Then we'd take it at one-half speed, then three-fourths speed, then all the way.

There are certain similarities between both pieces. Both Anna's and Claudia's pieces have a play structure to them. In both cases, the writer/primary creator is performing them. What I do is shape the production around the core of who both of them are and what their instincts are. In a regular play where you cast actors, I feel like they're working for me. The writer and I have created a framework that the actors are acting within. But in both of these two one-person shows, I'm creating a production that's faithful to the actors. I try to never hide or cover up what's particularly interesting about them. Both actresses are completely exposed in their shows. It's their instincts, they thought of it, they're doing it, it's their piece.

One thing I find myself saying to one-person performers a lot in rehearsal is, "Don't hide from the audience." Especially with Claudia's piece, which is all directly addressed to the audience, you cannot allow yourself to hide. There is a subtle but really important difference in those kinds of pieces, actually talking "at" the audience or talking "to" the audience. You certainly have to fake that in rehearsal because I, the director, am the only one who's there. But once you're in front of an audience you have to really talk to them. With Claudia, I remember, we constantly discussed at which point she would grab a specific person in the audience and talk to them. We also discussed when she would talk to the audience as a whole. At other times there would be a subtle kind of fourth wall up, where she would do her own thing. It was very plotted out. People who come from an improv background especially like when the audience does stuff while looking at them; the actors respond to it.

Individually Tailored Directing

One of my favorite things about one-person shows is that how you work and what the show is comes organically right out of the person who is performing in it. You have to reinvent a way of working each time for the person who is performing it. You have to find a vocabulary and method with each individual person, whereas the director on prewritten plays has a more regulated way of working that generally works all the time.

As far as the director's ego gratification, on one extreme end of the continuum is Shakespeare. New plays, with the writer in the room, are somewhere in the middle. And for me, in general, one-person plays are the most humbling experience for a director. Because if you direct very aggressively, kind of in-your-face, let the audience see your direction, I think you're making a terrible mistake.

About the relationship between the director and the solo performer, there is nobody throwing input into that process besides the two people working on the play. It's just the two of you in a very intense work situation. This really makes it a sort of marriage. It's very difficult from the outside to know how much the director did. Some directors do very little, justifiably, on a piece. In those cases, the actor uses the director like a friend who gives them feedback. But in other cases, the director is an absolutely central collaborator on the show.

What Makes a Good Solo Show

In a one-person show, that one person is the center of everything. The tech that surrounds him should not overwhelm him. A lot of times, in blocking and transitions, I never want that person to go off stage if I can help it. I know that some actors do leave the stage during the performance, especially when playing multiple characters. But you always have to let the audience be in connection with that performer.

With Anna, one of the things we discovered in rehearsal was, anytime there was a transition time, say, to change characters, it would kill it. We developed this thing where the last words from the previous piece and the first word of the next piece would be butted right up against each other. She would do whatever costume change or prop change, or go to a new area in the text. Everything was totally fluid; there was no edge. We had technical run-throughs to deal with these things. There was zero transition time allowed.

One of the thrilling things about one-person shows is that the good ones reinvent the form. The thrill of writing a one-person show is that you get to invent a new kind of theater for yourself. It's a great form for breaking the rules. Actors should ask themselves, "What does the show that's inside of me have that hasn't been seen before?" At some point in the evening, I think every one-person show has to get really honest about who that person is. That is, what they think, what they feel, etc. Because you don't have dynamics between two characters in a one-person show; what you have is interesting, gutsy, honest acting.

As a writer of a one-person show, you have to conquer the problem of where variety is coming from. Because you're not going to have multiple voices or people, you have to take care of your audience in terms of creating differences for them to look at and feel. Arc is really important in one-person shows. You must have a beginning, middle, and end, and you have to arrive somewhere different from where you started. You have to set up a problem. And although you don't have to resolve it, you have to work through it. In a one-person show, directorially, less is generally more. The director must be really interested in the actor he will be working with, because mostly your job is to serve him up to an audience. The director must bring that interest in the actor to the audience.

One of my favorite things about one-person shows is how much it empowers the actor. The actor is in control of his own destiny. But don't do it unless you really have something to talk about. One thing you should ask yourself is, "Is there something about what I've lived through that people need to hear?"

CHAPTER 35

marcia jean kurtz

© Bob Newey Photos, NYC

Marcia Jean Kurtz directed the critically acclaimed productions *Time on Fire* by Evan Handler at Second Stage and *Uncle Philip's Coat* by Matty Selman starring Larry Block at HB Playwrights Theater and the American Jewish Theatre. As an actress, Ms. Kurtz received an Obie for her performance in Donald Margulies's *The Loman Family Picnic* at the Manhattan Theatre Club and an Obie and Drama Desk nomination for her performance in Martin Sherman's *When She Danced* at Playwrights Horizons. Ms. Kurtz was a member of Peter Brook's C.I.R.T., Jerome Robbins's American Theater Lab, and Joseph Chaikin's Open Theater. She is currently a member of the Ensemble Studio Theatre and the Lincoln Center Directors Lab.

Lawrence Van Gelder in the New York Times *said, "Here are three names: Larry Block, Matty Selman, and Marcia Jean Kurtz. They are the three talented principals behind* Uncle Philip's Coat, *the funny, insightful, and often touching play at the American Jewish Theatre."*

Michael Feingold in the Village Voice *said, "[Under] Ms. Kurtz's self-effacing direction . . . the production elements are almost threadbare, the emotions are deep, and the interplay of ironies and images are complex."*

The Words Should Be Wonderful

The first one-person play I directed was called *A Thread in My Head* by Frederica Meister. It was for E.S.T. (Ensemble Studio Theatre) for Octoberfest. I learned quite a bit while working on that piece.

It's interesting; I really don't see much difference between working on a solo piece and a regular play. The main thing is that the person who has written and is performing the piece is talented. The thing that matters most to me is that the text is wonderful. I noticed that Meister's piece had theatricality. There are some pieces that are only meant to be read, not to be acted out. You just know that those pieces don't have that vibrancy that you need to have someone standing in front of you and telling you something that has immediacy and vibrancy and imagery that you find with any playwright. If the dialogue within the monologue is something that needs to be told in the theater, it's there whether it's a monologue or any play.

The thing that I have found is that I assist by being the editor and developer of the material. No one comes to me with a fully formed piece. Everyone comes to me with a bunch of material. It's very much a collaborative effort, making the piece a play. It's very much like being a literary manager, a dramaturge; at least, that's my experience. The piece changes immensely during the rehearsal process.

If there's a sentence that absolutely defines the moment, reaches the audience, is active, that's what I'll want to keep. If there are ten other sentences after that that are boring, then, like any editor, you'll get rid of them. If there are parts of the story that aren't fleshed out, where you feel more needs to be told, you'll encourage the writer-actor to develop that.

If the piece needs to be more dramatic, or funnier, you'll point them in that direction. It's really very similar to what a book editor does when a novelist comes to him with a piece of writing.

I think some of my instincts were developed just by being an actor and knowing what words you want to speak. If I pick up a script and start speaking the words, and I feel exhausted immediately, I know that it stinks. Yet I know if I'm having fun, if it engages me immediately, that I want to act it. I feel that a lot of my ideas come from being an actor, as well as being a great reader all my life.

Working with Movement

I studied dance and music. I was a choreographer at Juilliard. All of those things come together when I work with someone. When I get bored, when I feel myself zoning out, I realize everyone else will too. Bottom line, you have to hook into what you feel is the story that you think this person wants to tell. It's a constant process. As the actor-writer comes to you each day and you rehearse, it's a constant chipping away, reshaping. You must get the writer to make the piece sharper, clearer. It's like Michelangelo chipping away at the marble until the sculpture reveals itself.

Quite often you see in one-person shows a lot of movement. There is a tendency in some directors to keep the actor moving, keep the eye going. I think that if the words are conveying the images clearly enough, the audience will be immediately entranced because they will be transported by what the actor is talking about. When the moment cries out for something to be physicalized, the actor usually knows it. It's not something that I impose.

People start moving when they start talking. From the little movements, the little human gestures that you see. Perhaps because of my work as a choreographer, I'm very aware of all the movements the actor is making. You can selectively make them more emphatic, larger, smaller, put them in to emphasize, etc. I think the performer shows you the way to what the physicalization of the piece will be.

I've worked as an actor with Peter Brook, Joe Chaikin, and Jerome Robbins. I've worked with some wonderful people. I remember when Peter Brook walked into the first day of rehearsal. He had everything marked out like little toy soldiers where everyone would go. All of a sudden, he looked up on the stage and said, "What's happening up there is much more interesting." He then threw out his blueprint. Most of the really good directors that I've worked with, I've noticed their inspiration came from who was up there in front of them, and what they were doing.

Overproducing a piece is the trap. There is that tendency to try to do too much with a piece. Both Evan Handler and Larry Block moved so well on stage. Their every gesture communicated so much. Even if stillness is at the center of the gesture, I'm always looking for the gesture of grace, the gesture of communication. It all comes down to one's style. I wouldn't want anything on the stage that wasn't eloquent.

How I Rehearse

I don't have a set way of working on a piece; I hope that I never do. At the first day of work, you just start with the first sentence of the piece and away you go. I personally like to work on a piece in sections. You watch what the actor is doing. And you say, "You know, when you did that, that was great, let's remember that." It's like having a discussion with someone about the piece.

You don't want to go through the whole piece the first day; it's too exhausting. Since for the most part, most solo writer-performers have said these words a hundred times while writing it, I don't think it's necessary to sit at a table and discover the text. I have to say that on all the pieces that I've worked on, the writing, doing, honing, and developing of it all seem to happen at the same time.

How do you know when the piece is ready? When it has a great beginning, middle, and end, and I'm not falling asleep at any point. I want to be engaged, moved, from moment to moment. If I'm not, then something isn't working yet. Little by little, you bring people in (whose opinion you trust) and you get their input. You can gauge what's working and what's not by just having a couple of smart friends come by and watch the piece.

The wonderful thing is that every time a writer-actor brings you something new, you start fresh. You have a new world to explore. I try to find out how I can go there with them, to illuminate it. I think you really have to be pretty brave to trust the words, let the words do the job.

CHAPTER 36

david bar katz

David Bar Katz cocreated, produced, and was head writer of the Emmy-nominated Fox show *House of Buggin'*. He coproduced and wrote *The Pest* for Tristar Pictures and developed as well as directed John Leguizamo's show *Freak*. He is also the co-author of the book *Freak*, which is based on the show. His novel *The Heaviest God* is published by Crown Publishers. Mr. Katz is the cofounder (with John Leguizamo) of Lower East Side Films. He is presently writing a screenplay of the science fiction novel *The Uplift War*.

Regarding Freak, *Alexis Greene of* In Theater Magazine *said, "David Bar Katz keeps the pace energetic, and ultimately you are grateful that no scenic abracadabra competes with Leguizamo's blade-sharp comic timing."*

Clifford A. Ridley in the Philadelphia Inquirer *said of* Freak, *"The show's director . . . tempers Leguizamo's natural ebullience with some welcome quiet moments."*

Creating a Freak

The way it started out was that John [Leguizamo] and I were writing *Freak* together; that's how the process began. John had actually wanted to do more of a stand-up show, as opposed to his previous one-man shows. He wanted to do like a Richard Pryor in concert kind of thing. So at the beginning, we were writing almost stand-up type material. The rehearsal process and the writing process were like one and the same. Actually, even after we opened, we never stopped writing it, tweaking things.

Previously, on his other shows, John would come out in costume and do a character for about fifteen minutes. But in this show we weren't relying on costumes. In one five-minute scene of our show, John could be doing five or six characters, in the same costume, switching from character to character. What we worked on in rehearsals was the way the transitions would occur. They needed to be seamless.

The way we actually worked on a day-to-day basis was we'd go over the script, discuss what the scene was about, the problems and the issues, and then would just start reading through it. John liked to put it on its feet as soon as possible. So much of his work was just getting comfortable with the physicality. We'd break down the scene into bits. We'd work on the comedy bits first, and then on the dramatic bits. I'll give you an example of what I'm talking about. There was a scene where he's wrestling with his father, obviously playing both characters. We'd have to figure out the positioning of his body, just where his body is and how he can, in an instant, split to become his father's character. Stuff like that took a lot of work. Every now and then, just to get the right physical truth, I'd be a stand-in for his father in that scene.

We worked on *Freak* for a year and a half. We'd do readings all over the place, just to get audience reactions. My primary concern for the whole beginning part of the process was just the text, and working on the script. I knew that in relation to the staging of it, that would come later. What we were trying to do was something very difficult, a marriage of intense drama and broad comedy. We needed to find a balance there.

I was the publicist on John's show, *Mambo Mouth*. We became good friends. We eventually cocreated the TV show *House of Buggin'*. We've been best friends, so working together was great, truly like a marriage, a good one. John and I think in similar ways, and we have a great trust.

Finding the Drama

John's initial agenda, as I mentioned, was that this was going to be a comedic show. One of my biggest contributions was helping him find the more dramatic levels in his material. Ostensibly, it was an autobiographical show about John, so it was at times like a process of psychoanalysis. There were places that John didn't want to go because they were too painful, and I had to keep pushing him, urging him on.

Characters came and went in the developmental process, and that would sometimes be difficult. Two characters were cut two days before we opened, and that was really tough. They were female characters, and his audiences love to see him do female characters. And although they were audience-pleasers, they just didn't work in the play, structurally.

From the very beginning, our goal was to get to Broadway with the play. We didn't know if that was going to work out, but that was our goal. John had done two off-Broadway shows. So my view directorially was that everything had to be taken up a notch. John has a huge amount of energy; I felt we could use his energy and be as unconventional as we could on a Broadway stage. I felt we could utilize the space of a Broadway stage and fill it with John's tremendous energy in an organic way. We would even break the proscenium and have him climb the wall of the theater and go into the balcony. In another scene, he jumps back and forth covering the whole stage. We wanted it to have a sense of just John alone in the theater, playing. We wanted to break that wall between him and the audience.

The show was extremely tightly blocked. Because John is such a good actor, each audience thought they were seeing him move around at random, like for the first time. The hardest thing in the show was making it seem like it was improvised.

At first we just did readings at P.S. 122, then we workshopped the play as a work in progress at the Goodman Theatre in Chicago, then we did six weeks at Theater on the Square in San Francisco, then six weeks at the Atlantic Theater in New York, and then ended up at the Cort Theater on Broadway.

The first reading was almost three and a half hours long. It was epic. We certainly cut a lot of material. The feeling was never that we were trying to get it perfect, but rather, How good could we get it? It was always an ongoing process. If the deadline wasn't for another year, we'd still be working on it. My feeling is, you can always find a better line, you can always set a scene slightly better. Since you're an artist and are constantly changing, so will your work. What you did six months ago isn't always the same truth that you might have today.

In *Freak*, we, the audience, discover John's search for an individuation in his work, a search for his own identity. His work is about his own search in his life. I feel his earlier shows like *Mambo Mouth* were saying things like, "I'm here, I'm Latin." I feel that was more like a statement. *Freak* is more of a textured work; it is more nuanced, which perhaps makes it more ambiguous as well.

Displaying Your Passion and Your Pain

My advice to your readers is that they must search themselves and find out what they're passionate about. Too many people decide to do one-person shows because they want to get an agent or jump-start a career. You must be brutally honest with yourself. What makes these kinds of shows interesting is the confessional quality they must have. You must be able to discern what is being just indulgent and what is of some interest to an audience. For any artist to be effective, you must be aware that what is amusing or moving to you may not be the same for an audience.

The problem with so many actors is that because they're so taken with themselves, they have trouble discerning what is effective. That's one major reason why you must find a director whom you trust, who can help steer the way for you. That director must be able to comfortably tell the actor, "What you're saying there isn't interesting, but what you said over there is."

I think anything can work in these kinds of shows if they're done well. I tried to do things in *Freak* that don't traditionally work in this kind of show. There was an aspect of like a Tennessee Williams sort of thing in our show. We'd go back into John's childhood, and suddenly John would become a narrator. In sort of a Proustian way he'd take in the scene of his childhood while being John Leguizamo the narrator. It was a way of looking at the past and dreading it in some way, and yet there was a longing for it. And all the time he was narrating this.

I don't know if that all makes sense to you, but the way it played was very effective. Normally, a lot of directors would say, "Just do the scene." But we found this way of showing it much more effective. This type of narration would say, "This is who I am now, and this is what I'm feeling. Let me show you a little bit of what created who I am." If it feels fake, the audience will sense that.

APPENDIX A

artist colonies where you can develop your solo show

This section lists artist colonies where solo artists can escape to do their work in a tranquil and (usually) idyllic surrounding. Artists are offered a getaway opportunity where they can avoid life's pressures and annoyances. The fees for this dream working vacation are small or nonexistent, depending on the residency you apply to. Many of these residencies offer housing to artists in different disciplines. The deadline dates may change, so please always check with the residence that you're interested in before the deadline listed.

Blue Mountain Center
P.O. Box 109
Blue Mountain Lake, NY 12812
Tel: (518) 352-7391
Web site: *www.bluemountaincenter.org*
Contact: Ben Strader

This residence is located in the Adirondacks. The available dates are between mid-June and October. They provide free room and board. Primarily the colony looks for work that is appropriate for a general audience and deals with social issues. Send a SASE (self-addressed stamped envelope) or visit their Web site for guidelines. The deadline is February 1. You'll be notified by early April.

Byrdcliffe Art Colony
The Woodstock Guild
34 Tinker Street
Woodstock, NY 12498
Tel: (845) 679-2079
Fax: (845) 679-4529

E-mail: *wguild@ulster.net*
Web site: *www.woodstockguild.org*
Contact: Artists Residency Program

This colony offers a four-week residency between June and September at its three-hundred-acre colony in the Catskill Mountains. The residence is ninety miles from New York, near Woodstock. It offers private rooms and a space at Viletta Inn, a lovely mountain lodge. The residents provide their own food and cook in a common kitchen area. There is also a common living room where you can meet with some of the other artists. Aside from monologue writers, Byrdcliffe offers residencies to screenwriters, play-wrights, librettists, and translators. To stay at Byrdcliffe, you must pay a $500 fee per session. To be eligible to stay here, you must prove that you are a serious solo artist. Byrdcliffe looks for commitment to your work as a chief criterion. Send a SASE or visit their Web site for more information on the application process. The deadline is April 1.

Centrum Artist-in-Residency Program

Fort Worden State Park
P.O. Box 1158
Port Townsend, WA 98368
Tel: (360) 385-3102
Fax: (360) 385-2470
Web site: *www.centrum.org*
Contact: Sally Rodgers, Residency Program Facilitator

The residence is located on the 445-acre Fort Worden State Park. It offers self-contained cabins, plus a separate studio space to write in. There is no charge for facilities. The program looks for writers who show a clear sense of direction in their work and have some accomplishments. Please check with Centrum or visit their Web site for more information on the length of stay, application process, and deadlines.

Hedgebrook

2197 East Millman Road
Langley, WA 98260
Tel: (360) 321-4786
Web site: *www.hedgebrook.org*

This residence is for women of different cultural backgrounds. Hedgebrook offers cottages on Whidbey Island, surrounded by a wooded area. Room and board is free. Any woman writer is invited to apply. Send a SASE or visit their Web site for application. Hedgebrook requests that you return the application with a work sample, a description of the solo material that you're working on, and a $15 fee. If you'd like to stay there in the winter or spring, submit the required material by October 1. If you'd like to stay there in the summer or fall, contact the colony by April 1. Generally, you'll be notified in a couple of months.

Isle Royal National Park Artist-in-Residence
  800 East Lakeshore Drive
  Houghton, MI 49931
  Tel: (906) 482-8753
  Fax: (906) 482-8753
  Web site: *www.nps.gov/volunteer/air.htm*
  Contact: Greg Blust

This residence offers a two- to three-week stay between June to September, in a cabin on a very quiet island near Lake Superior. Only one artist is housed at a time. There is no electricity, and you must provide your own food. The program expects the artist selected to be able to exist in this natural environment and to donate time for work in the park. Isle Royal National Park requests that you complete an application and include a description of your project, your résumé, and a sample of a project that you've worked on. The deadline for this residence is February, and you're notified by mid-April.

New York Mills Arts Retreat
  24 North Main Avenue
  P.O. Box 246
  New York Mills, MN 56567
  Tel: (218) 385-3339
  Fax: (218) 385-3366
  E-mail: *nymills@kulcher.org*
  Web site: *http://kulcher.org/html/artsretreat.html*
  Contact: Heather Humber Price, Arts Retreat Coordinator

This residence operates year-round. Housing is offered to one artist at a time for a two- to four-week stay. The residence is part of a small farming community. Jerome Foundation Fellowships stipend of $1,500 for a four-week residency or $750 for two-week residency. Special emphasis for artists of color. The artist is expected to work in the community for at least eight hours per week during his stay. Those interested must complete an application, which is available online. The deadlines for this residence are October 1 and April 1. You'll hear from the retreat about eight weeks after the deadline.

Studio for Creative Inquiry
    Carnegie Mellon University
    College of Fine Arts
    Pittsburgh, PA 15213-3890
    Tel: (412) 268-3454
    Fax: (412) 268-2829
    E-mail: *mmbm@andrew.cmu.edu*
    Web site: *www.cmu.edu/studio*
    Contact: Margaret Myers

This residence offers two different types of residencies, year-round. The first, the shorter one, is for two weeks to three months. The longer residency is from six months to three years. A studio facility and any necessary equipment are provided in Carnegie Mellon's College of Fine Arts building. The College assists artists in finding housing. A stipend is provided. The college requests that you send a work sample and résumé. The deadline for this residence is open. Generally you'll hear from the studio in a couple of months.

The Hall Farm Center for Arts and Education
    392 Hall Drive
    Townshend, VT 05353
    Tel: (802) 365-4483
    E-mail: *info@hallfarm.org*
    Web site: *www.hallfarm.org*
    Contact: Scott Browning, Director

Hall Farm offers a one-week to one-month residency for solo performers. They accept four to five artists per session. They request a work sample, a project description, a letter of recommendation, a résumé, and a $20 fee. The deadline is February 1. You'll be notified by April.

Montana Artists Refuge
    P.O. Box 8
    Basin, MT 59631
    Tel: (406) 225-3500
    E-mail: *mar@mt.net*
    Web site: *www.montanaartistsrefuge.org*
    Contact: Joy Lewis, Coordinator

Montana Artists offers a one-month to one-year residency for three to five artists. Residents pay $450 to $550 per month (meals not provided). Send SASE for guidelines and application, or you can download them from the Web site. They will want a work sample and a project description. The deadline is August 15 for January to April, January 15 for May to August, and May 15 for September to December.

APPENDIX B

theaters that accept solo material

This appendix includes theaters that you can submit your material to. Be selective about where you send your work. It's important to read the general information about the theater. If they're interested in solo material that is unusual or surreal, don't send your naturalistic monologue. If they say not to send unsolicited material, don't.

Always include a letter of inquiry and a synopsis of the monologue when writing to potential theaters.

Actors and Playwrights Initiative Theater
P.O. Box 50051
Kalamazoo, MI 49005-0051
Tel: (616) 343-8310
Fax: (616) 343-8310
Contact: Robert C. Walker

Unsolicited material is not accepted. The theater only wants to hear from writers living in Illinois, Indiana, Michigan, Ohio, Wisconsin, and Ontario. The theater will, however, accept a synopsis of your show. Also include a résumé and a letter of inquiry with a SASE for response. Actors and Playwrights Initiative is particularly interested in gay material and provocative social and political work. The best time to submit is May through October. Generally you'll get a response in two to six months. The remuneration is negotiable.

Actors' Theatre
P.O. Box 780
Talent, OR 97540-0780
Tel: (541) 535-5250
Contact: Chris Sackett

This is a community, nonprofessional theater. The theater requests that you send a query, a synopsis with about ten pages of dialogue from your show, a résumé, and a SASE. Please do not send unsolicited scripts or tapes of your show. The Actors' Theatre creates tours of solo shows, and likes the unusual and bizarre as well as family fare. You may have to wait a month or two for a response.

Actors Theatre of Louisville
316 West Main Street
Louisville, KY 40202-4218
Tel: (502) 584-1265
Fax: (502) 561-3300
E-mail: *actors@aye.net*
Web site: *www.actorstheatre.org*
Contact: Michael Bigelow Dixon or Amy Wegener

Unsolicited videotapes/scripts are accepted for their Flying Solo and Friends Festival, an important venue for solo artists. Actors Theatre reads about 2,500 scripts a year and produces twenty to forty (not including the Flying Solo Festival). You can submit your material year round, but check when their deadlines are for the solo festivals.

Adirondack Theatre Festival
P.O. Box 3203
Glen Falls, NY 12801
Tel: (518) 798-7479
E-mail: *atf@ATFestival.org*
Web site: *www.atfestival.org*
Contact: David Turner

They prefer professional submissions. The best time to submit is from August to January. You'll hear back from them in about six months.

American Music Theater Festival
123 Broad Street, 18th floor
Philadelphia, PA 19109
Tel: (215) 893-1570 or (800) 318-AMTF
Fax: (215) 893-1570
Contact: David McCane

Do not send unsolicited material. Only submissions through agents are accepted and new and experimental work is preferred. Generally your agent will hear from American Music Theater Festival in about four months.

Arena Stage
1101 Sixth Street SW
Washington, D.C. 20024
Tel: (202) 554-9066
Fax: (202) 488-4056
Web site: *www.arenastage.org*
Contact: Cathy Madison

Unsolicited material is not accepted, only a synopsis of your material, bio, and letter of inquiry. Arena Stage is specifically interested in material from women, writers of color, disabled, and other non-mainstream artists. If you send a letter, the theater will respond almost immediately. Scripts can take up to six months for a response. The best time to contact Arena is in the late summer to early fall.

ART Station
5384 Manor Drive
Stone Mountain, GA 30086
Tel: (770) 469-1105
Fax: (770) 469-0355
E-mail: *artstation@mindspring.com*
Web site: *www.ARTstation.org*
Contact: Jon Goldstein

Unsolicited material is accepted. ART prefers that your show has not been professionally produced before. ART is especially looking for material from Southern artists or plays with Southern themes. The best time to contact the theater is between June and December. It generally takes about two months for the theater to respond.

Asolo Theatre Company
Asolo Center for the Performing Arts
5555 North Tamiami Trail
Sarasota, FL 34243
Tel: (941) 351-9010
Fax: (941) 351-5796
E-mail: *brodge@worldnet.att.net*
Web site: *www.asolo.org*
Contact: Bruce E. Rogers

Unsolicited material is not accepted. Asolo does accept a one-page synopsis of your piece and a letter of inquiry. Don't forget the SASE for a response. The best time to submit material is June through August. Generally you'll hear back in two to six months. The remuneration is negotiable.

Attic Theatre Centre
5429 West Washington Boulevard
Los Angeles, CA 90016
Tel: (323) 525-0600
Web site: *www.attictheatre.org*
Contact: James Carey

Unsolicited material is not accepted, but you can send a synopsis of your work with your résumé and a letter of inquiry (with a SASE) for a response. Minority subjects are preferred. You can submit your material year round. You should hear from Attic in a few months.

Bailiwick Repertory
1229 West Belmont Avenue
Chicago, IL 60657-3205
Tel: (323) 883-1090
Fax: (323) 525-2017
Web site: *www.bailiwick.org*
Contact: David Zak

Send a SASE or visit their Web site for guidelines for submissions. Bailiwick likes women's, gay, deaf, and political material. You can submit all year round. You'll hear from Bailiwick in about nine months.

Bay Street Theatre
P.O. Box 810
Sag Harbor, NY 11963
Tel: (516) 725-0818
Fax: (516) 628-0906
Web site: *www.baystreet.org*
Contact: Mia Grosjean

No unsolicited material accepted, only agent submissions. Bay Street Theatre likes innovative material that is interesting as well as entertaining. Your agent can submit year-round, but the theater prefers submissions in June through January. Generally, you'll hear back from them in three to six months.

Berkshire Theatre Festival
P.O. Box 797
Stockbridge, MA 01262
Tel: (413) 298-5536
Fax: (413) 298-3368
E-mail: *info@berkshiretheatre.org*
Web site: *www.berkshiretheatre.org*
Contact: Kate Maguire

Agent submissions only. Provocative, cutting-edge material preferred. The best time for contact is October through December. Generally, you'll hear from them in about three months.

Bristol Riverside Theatre
P.O. Box 1250
Bristol, PA 19007
Tel: (215) 785-6664
Fax: (215) 785-2762
Web site: *www.BRTstage.org*
Contact: David J. Abers

Unsolicited material is accepted. The theater likes innovative, cutting-edge material. You should contact them in January. If you send a letter, you'll hear from Bristol in four to six months. If you send your material, expect a response in six to eighteen months.

Cleveland Public Theatre
6415 Detroit Avenue
Cleveland, OH 44102-3011
Tel: (216) 631-2727
Fax: (216) 631-2575
E-mail: *cpt@en.com*
Web site: *www.cptonline.org*
Contact: Randy Rolliston

Cleveland Public Theatre prefers a letter of inquiry and a synopsis of your solo material. If you want, you may also send a ten-page sample of your work. The theater is adventurous in its taste; it prefers experimental or provocative material, as well as works from gay people, people of color, and women. Contact Cleveland Public Theatre from February through October. For certain festivals, a $10 submission fee is charged. You'll hear back in about six weeks (letter) to nine months (sent material).

GALA Hispanic Theatre
P.O. Box 43209
Washington, D.C. 20010
Tel: (202) 234-7174
Fax: (202) 302-5041
Web site: *www.galatheatre.org*
Contact: Hugo J. Medrano

Unsolicited material is accepted, but a synopsis and letter of inquiry is preferred. GALA is especially interested in hearing from Hispanic-Americans (writing either in English or Spanish), solo pieces by Spanish writer-actors, and work that reflects the Hispanic-American experience. The best time to contact GALA is April/May. You'll hear back in about a month (for a letter) and in about eight months if you send your material.

John Drew Theater
158 Main Street
East Hampton, NY 11937
Tel: (516) 324-0806
Fax: (516) 324-2722
Contact: Josh Gladstone

Unsolicited material is not accepted. You can send a one-page synopsis of your piece. You can contact John Drew all year round. Generally you'll hear back in three months. Remuneration is negotiable.

La MaMa Experimental Theater Club
74A East Fourth Street
New York, NY 10003
Tel: (212) 254-6468
Fax: (212) 254-7597
Web site: *www.LaMama.org*
Contact: Ellen Stewart

La MaMa accepts unsolicited videos of your show (with synopsis). However, it prefers a professional recommendation. As the name implies, La MaMa prefers experimental, surreal, innovative work. The theater has a "One Night Stand" series where writers can perform their own work. You can contact La MaMa year-round. You'll hear from them in two to six months.

New York Theatre Workshop
79 East Fourth Street
New York, NY 10003
Tel: (212) 780-9037
Contact: Kate Spencer

New York Theatre Workshop doesn't accept unsolicited material. Send a query letter and a résumé. New York Theatre Workshop looks for socially relevant material and large and minority issues. The theater is especially interested in language and form. New York Theatre Workshop looks for long-term collaborative relationships. Proposals for performance projects are accepted. The best time to submit is in the fall or spring. You'll get a response in about six months.

The Wooden O Drama Studio
2207 Federal Avenue
Los Angeles, CA 90064
Tel: (310) 477-2199
Contact: the Producing Director

This theater accepts unsolicited material. It requests that you send a query, a synopsis of your show, and a SASE. Wooden O is particularly looking for material that deals with the human condition.

Woolly Mammoth Theatre Company
641 D Street NW
Washington, D.C. 20004
Tel: (202) 234-6130
Fax: (202) 667-0904
Web site: *www.woollymammoth.net*

Unsolicited material is accepted. Woolly Mammoth is especially looking for unusual, offbeat, and surreal material. You can submit all year round. Expect to hear back in four to six months. The remuneration is negotiable.

APPENDIX C

publishers of
solo material

Having your solo piece published is certainly one way to feel validated and get some type of recognition for your work. But before you submit your manuscript to anyone, it is in your best interest to find out something about the publisher you're submitting your manuscript to. You'll want to be sure that your work will be presented in the best way. You should feel confident that you are dealing with a reputable and honest publisher.

The Author's Guild
31 East Twenty-Eighth Street, Tenth Floor
New York, NY 10016
Tel: (212) 563-5904

The Council of Literary Magazines and Presses
154 Christopher Street, Suite 3C
New York, NY 10014-2839
Tel: (212) 741-9110
Web site: *www.clmp.org*

Request their *Directory of Literary Magazines.* This publication lists hundreds of magazines.

The Dramatists Guild
1501 Broadway, Suite 701
New York, NY 10036
Tel: (212) 398-9366

By being a member of the Dramatists Guild, you will have access to many of the publications and theaters that feature solo artists. The Dramatists Guild meetings and events are a great way to network with other playwrights and solo writers.

Dustbooks
P.O. Box 100
Paradise, CA 95967
Tel: (530) 877-6110

Their *International Directory of Little Magazines and Small Presses* costs $35.95 for paper binding and $55 for cloth binding, plus $7 for shipping and handling.

You can also write to some of the publishers listed below and ask them for sample copies or catalogues:

Contemporary Drama Service
Meriwether Publishing, Ltd.
885 Elkton Drive
Colorado Springs, CO 80907
Tel: (719) 594-4422
Fax: (719) 594-9916
Web site: *http://contemporarydrama.com*
Contact: Arthur L. Zapel

Unsolicited material is accepted. Meriwether publishes books of original monologues. It publishes material that is suitable for high schools, teenagers, the college market, church groups, and community theaters. It is especially interested in authors with name recognition. Generally you'll hear from Contemporary in about one month. The remuneration is royalty up to buy-out figure. Be aware that the publisher holds the copyright.

Dramatic Publishing
311 Washington Street
P.O. Box 129
Woodstock, IL 60098
Tel: (815) 338-7170
Fax: (815) 338-8981
E-mail: *plays@dramaticpublishing.com*
Web site: *www.dramaticpublishing.com*
Contact: Linda Habjan

Dramatic Publishing accepts unsolicited material. It publishes books of monologues and prefers works that have been produced. The readership is stock, amateur market, professional, community, and college. The remuneration is the standard royalty plus ten complimentary copies. Response time is two to four months.

Earth's Daughters
    P.O. Box 41
    Central Park Station
    Buffalo, New York 14215
    Tel: (716) 837-7778
    Web site: *www.earthsdaughters.org*

This is a feminist literary and art periodical published three times a year. It accepts unsolicited material with a SASE. The remuneration is two complimentary copies. Response time is about two months.

Encore Performance Publishing
    P.O. Box 95567
    South Jordan, UT 84995
    Tel: (801) 282-8159
    Web site: *www.encoreplay.com*

Encore doesn't accept unsolicited, but you can send a synopsis and production information about your piece, with a letter of inquiry. The best time to make contact is May through August. You'll hear back in a few weeks. Encore publishes ten to thirty plays a year. You should have had at least two amateur or professional productions. The publisher especially looks for family, religious, and holiday material. The remuneration is 10 percent for book royalty and ten complimentary copies. Encore prefers that your material has no profanity in it and that it doesn't misuse the name of God. It does, however, like subjects of a controversial nature (if handled with discretion).

Kalliope, a Journal of Women's Literature and Art
    Florida Community College
    3939 Roosevelt Boulevard
    Jacksonville, FL 32205
    Web site: *www.fccj.org/kalliope*
    Contact: Mary Sue Koeppel

This journal, published three times a year, looks for work by women. It does accept unsolicited material. Kalliope requests that your solo work be less than twenty-five pages long and not of an erotic nature. It wants material that is original, not trite. Remuneration is two free copies or a free one-year subscription. It will take three to six months to get a response.

The Kenyon Review
    104 College Dr.
    Gambier, OH 43022-9623
    Tel: (740) 427-5208

Fax: (740) 427-5417
E-mail: *kenyonreview@kenyon.edu*
Web site: *www.kenyonreview.org*
Contact: David H. Lynn

This literary journal generally publishes about two plays (including solo works) per year. It is published four times a year. It accepts unsolicited material as long as it's unpublished and unproduced and a maximum of thirty pages. They will either pay you with a cash payment or two complimentary copies. Submit from September through April (with SASE). Generally you'll get a response in about four months.

Lamia Ink!
P.O. Box 202
Prince Street Station
New York, NY 10012
Contact: Ms. Cortland Jessup

This magazine looks for short monologues and especially performance art pieces. It is published three times a year. It prefers that the material not exceed five pages, and accepts unsolicited material with a SASE. The response time is at least three weeks. If your material is accepted, you'll get four free copies.

Players Press
P.O. Box 1132
Studio City, CA 91614-0132
Tel: (818) 789-4980
Contact: Robert W. Gordon

This company publishes all sorts of theater-related books. The readership is worldwide (with special interests in theater-related material). It accepts unsolicited submissions with verification that your work was produced. Send a copy of your material with a résumé and SASE. It may take up to six months to hear from them.

Smith and Kraus
P.O. Box 127
Lyme, NH 03768
Tel: (603) 669-7032
Fax: (603) 669-7945
E-mail: *sandk@sover.net*
Web site: *www.smithandkraus.com*
Contact: Marisa Smith

This small publishing company publishes monologue books and other solo work. It will give you ten complimentary copies or an agreed-upon royalty. It doesn't accept unsolicited material. Send a letter of inquiry regarding your work. You'll hear back in a few months. The best time to contact Smith and Kraus is mid-August.

Speert Publishing
P.O. Box 2281
New York, NY 10019
Tel: (212) 979-7656
E-mail: *espeert@speertpublishing.com*
Web site: *www.speertpublishing.com*

This company establishes fees on a per-project basis. It is important to understand that Speert publishing is a self-publishing producer. For more information about what this means, you can go to their Web site. They publish plays for regional theater, stock, and professional and nonprofessional markets. The response time is generally about a week.

playwriting competitions that accept solo material

Another potential source for income from and exposure for your monologue play is playwriting competitions. These nationally held contests offer cash prizes and in some cases production opportunities to winners. A few things to keep in mind before entering your monologue/solo work:

1. **If a competition requests that you send for guidelines, do so.** These guidelines give specific instructions for that particular contest. In some cases, they even request that you fill out an application form to send with your material.

2. **Send your material in earlier rather than close to the deadline.** Most of us wait until the last minute to send things. In this case, that choice could work to your disadvantage. If you send the material earlier, your chances of getting a good read of your material are better. By deadline time, the judges are quite often exhausted and just want to get through the material as fast as they can.

Also, be aware of the entrance fees for some of the competitions. Supposedly, these are to aid in the cost of running the competition. Always send a SASE with your material.

The Annual Nationwide Blank Theatre Company Young Playwrights Competition & Festival
1301 Lucile Avenue
Los Angeles, CA 90026
Tel: (323) 611-9827
Fax: (213) 661-3903
Web site: *www.youngplaywrights.com*

To enter this competition, you must be nineteen years old or younger. Send your monologue/solo material with a cover sheet that has your name, address, phone number, birth date, and the school you attend. The deadline is April. The nine winners of this competition are given a production as a prize. Winners are notified a month later. Note: Do not send a SASE. Scripts will not be returned.

Center Theater International Playwriting Competition
1346 West Devon Avenue
Chicago, IL 60660
Tel: (312) 508-0220
Contact: Dale Calandra

This competition offers a $300 award to the winner. Your solo material cannot have been published, previously produced, or presently under option. The Center requests that you send a SASE for guidelines and application form. There is a $15 fee to enter this competition, and your script will not be returned. The deadline varies from year to year.

The Cunningham Commission for Youth Theatre
DePaul University
2135 North Kenmore
Chicago, IL. 60614-4111
Tel: (773) 325-8938
Fax: (773) 325-7920
E-mail: *Igoetsch@wppost.depaul.edu*
Web site: *http://theatreschool.depaul.edu/programs/prize.htm*
Contact: Lara Goetsch

The prize given to the winner of this competition is $5,000! The contest requests that you live in the Chicago area to apply (i.e., within one hundred miles of downtown Chicago). The competition requests that you send for specific guidelines. The kind of work that is sought "affirms the centrality of religion, broadly defined, and the human quest for meaning, truth, and community." The deadline is December. You'll be notified by March of the next year.

Playwrights' Center of San Francisco Dramarama
P.O. Box 460466
San Francisco, CA 94146-0466
Tel: (415) 626-4603
E-mail: *playctrsf@aol.com*
Web site: *http://playwrightscentersf.org*
Contact: Sheppard Kominars

There is a $25 entry fee. The award is $500. Your entry should not have been published or previously produced (except in a workshop production). They request that you send a SASE for guidelines. The deadline is March 15, but Dramarama requests that you don't enter before January 1.

Inner City Cultural Center Competition
1605 North Ivar Avenue
Los Angeles, CA 90028
Tel: (213) 962-2102
Fax: (213) 386-9017
Contact: C. Bernard Jackson

There is a $45 entry fee. This contest offers a $1,000 prize to the winner. The second prize is $500, and the third prize is $250. The competition also offers internships with major Hollywood studios to the winners. Your play should be ready and fully mounted. Inner City Cultural Competition will provide the entire technical backup to produce it (lighting, crew, sound, etc.). Your piece cannot exceed forty minutes! Send SASE for guidelines. The deadline is March. Response time is a couple of months.

Jane Chambers Playwriting Award
c/o Division of Theater
Southern Methodist University
P.O. Box 750356
Dallas, TX 75275-0356
E-mail: *gesmith@mail.smu.edu*
Contact: Gretchen E. Smith, Administrator

This competition offers a $1,000 first prize with a possible staged reading of your work. There is also a student award of $250, as well as five finalists and fifteen honorable mentions. The contest prefers that those submitting have works that experiment with form. The authors must be women! Works that "reflect a feminist perspective" are sought. Send a SASE for guidelines. If you have a videotaped recording of your piece, send it with your application. The deadline is February 15. You'll be notified by June 15.

Marvin Taylor Playwriting Contest
Sierra Repertory Theater
P.O. Box 3030
Sonora, CA 95370
Tel: (209) 532-3120
Fax: (209) 532-7270
Contact: Dennis Jones

The award for this competition is $500 with the chance of a possible production. Your work must be unpublished, and you cannot have had more than two productions. Sierra Repertory requests that you send a copy of your monologue with a SASE. The deadline is August 31, with winners announced in March of the next year.

Mildred and Albert Panowski Playwriting Award

Forest Roberts Theatre
Northern Michigan University
1401 Presque Isle Avenue
Marquette, MI 49855
Tel: (906) 227-2553
Fax: (906) 227-2567
Contact: James A. Panowski

The award for this competition is $2,000! The competition also provides transportation and room and board for a one-week residency for a production of your work. Winners will also be entered in the Kennedy Center American College Theater Festival (if they're eligible). Your play must be unpublished and previously unproduced. Send for guidelines and entry form (with SASE). The deadline is November 21. You'll hear back by April of the next year.

The Mill Mountain Theatre New Play Competition

The Norfolk Southern Festival of New Works
1 Market Square SE, Second floor
Roanoke, VA 24011-1437
Tel: (540) 342-5730
Fax: (540) 342-5745
Web site: *www.millmountain.org*
Contact: Jack Parrish

The remuneration is $1,000. Mill Mountain also may do a staged reading of your monologue and a possible production. They'd provide travel and housing accommodations. Your piece must be unpublished and previously unproduced. Send SASE for guidelines. Your piece must be either submitted by an agent or with a professional recommendation. The deadline is January 1. You'll hear back by August. Please do not submit your work before October 1.

Theodore Ward Prize for African-American Playwrights

Columbia College Chicago
Theatre/Music Center
72 East Eleventh Street

Chicago, IL 60605
Tel: (312) 344-6136
Fax: (312) 663-9591
E-mail: *chigochuck@aol.com*
Contact: Chuck Smith

The first prize for this competition is $2,000! Transportation and housing are provided for the winner for a production. Second prize is $500 and a staged reading, and the third prize is a staged reading at the Goodman Theatre. You must be a United States resident of African-American descent. Your piece cannot have received a professional production. Write for guidelines (with SASE). The deadline for this contest is July 1, but please do not submit before April 1. The winners will be notified in November.

applying
for grants

Another source of financial assistance for solo artists is grants. Most of the time, grants are authorized to institutions (such as theaters) rather than individual artists. The awards from the grants provide for commissions, development, and production costs.

Since most of the grants offer huge financial remuneration, attaining them can be quite competitive. I suggest that you apply as early as possible. If you have any questions or need advice regarding the grant, make sure to contact the organization directly. They can be very helpful in what is sometimes a complicated process.

Do the best that you can in completing the application in an intelligent and thoughtful manner. Neatly type and answer all questions to the best of your ability. You are permitted to apply for as many grants as you wish, and I recommend that you do. You'll notice that once you have completed a grant proposal, it's not that difficult to adapt it for other grants.

What follows is a mere sampling of the many opportunities for solo artists in this area. I've listed only ones that I've heard about from solo artists. For a far more detailed listing, get a copy of the Dramatists Sourcebook (Theater Communications Group, 520 Eighth Avenue, New York, NY 10018-4156).

National Endowment for the Arts International Partnerships
    1100 Pennsylvania Avenue NW, Room 618
    Washington, D.C. 20506
    Tel: (202) 682-5429
    Fax: (202) 682-5602
    Web site: *www.arts.gov/partner/international/index.html*
    Contact: Pennie Ojeda, International Coordinator

CEC ArtsLink
    12 West Thirty-Second Street
    New York, NY 10001-4415

Tel: (212) 643-1985
E-mail: *al@cecartslink.org*
Web site: *www.cecartslink.org*

Although the grants for this organization may be up to $10,000, generally they are about $4,500. You must be a U.S. citizen or resident and be willing to work with this organizations counterparts in Eurasia, Russia, and central Europe. The deadline is January 15. You'll be notified by April.

The Playwrights' Center Grant Programs
2301 Franklin Avenue East
Minneapolis, MN 55406-1099
Tel: (612) 332-7481
E-mail: *pwcenter@mtn.org*
Web site: *www.pwcenter.org*
Contact: Carlo Cuesta

The following grants and fellowships are offered through the Playwrights' Center:

Jerome Playwright-in-Residence Fellowship
This annually offered fellowship offers five one-year fellowships of $9,000. The Center is looking for emerging artists (not more than two full productions of your work) willing to spend a year at the Center to develop their work. Send for SASE. The deadline is September 15. You'll be notified by January of the next year.

Many Voices Playwriting Residency Awards
This award is offered yearly (depending on availability of funds) to African-American residents of Minnesota. The award is given to eight artists. It includes a $1,250 stipend, a scholarship to playwriting classes, ongoing assistance by a dramaturge, and public readings. Send SASE for guidelines. The deadline for application is July 1. You'll be notified by September 15.

McKnight Advancement Grants
These yearly grants offer three awards of $25,000. You must be a United States citizen and have been living in Minnesota as a legal resident since May 1997. The grants are given to accomplished artists who have had at least two professional productions produced by a professional theater. The recipient must be willing to spend two months at the Center to participate in ongoing programs. Send SASE for guidelines. The deadline is February 1. You'll hear from the Center by May.

The Mark Taper Forum, Kirk Douglas Theater, Development Programs
601 West Temple Street
Los Angeles, CA 90012
Tel: (213) 972-8033
E-mail: *scripts@ctgh.org*
Web site: *www.taperahmanson.com*

New work festival. The remuneration varies. Send them five to ten pages of an unproduced solo work, a synopsis, and a brief summary. The deadline is March.

APPENDIX F

literary
agents

Literary agents can be very helpful in getting your material to the best theaters (and the top readers) for your specific type of play. Although they primarily deal with regular plays, it's certainly worth your while to try to find an agent who believes in your monologue play.

It's been suggested that you should only contact a couple of agents at a time. Most literary agents request that you first send a query letter describing your piece. You should also enclose an updated bio with the letter and any press material or past reviews of your work. If you find a theater or club where you can perform your work, make sure that you contact any agents who have expressed interest in your work.

For further information on finding the right literary agent for your material, contact the Association of Authors' Representatives, 10 Astor Place, Third Floor, New York, NY 10003. Send the AAR a check or money order for $7 and a SASE (60 cents) for its brochure.

Alan Brodie Representation Ltd.
211 Picadilly
London W1V 9LD
England
Tel: 011-44-171-917-2871
Contact: Alan Brodie or Sarah McNair

They prefer recommendations by professionals known to their agency.

Alliance Talent Agency
1501 Broadway, Suite 404
New York, NY 10036
Tel: (212) 840-6868
Fax: (212) 840-7237
Contact: Carole Davis

Send Carole Davis a copy of your monologue play or a synopsis and query letter.

Agency for the Performing Arts
888 Seventh Avenue, Suite 602
New York, NY 10106
Tel: (212) 582-1500
Contact: Leo Bookman

Ann Elmo Agency
60 East Forty-Second Street
New York, NY 10165
Tel: (212) 661-2800
Contact: Mari Cronin or Letti Lee

Ann Wright Representatives
165 West Forty-Second Street, #1105
New York, NY 10036-2501
Tel: (212) 764-6770
Contact: Dan Wright

The Ann Wright Representatives prefer that you send them a query letter with a SASE.

Barbara Hogenson Agency
165 West End Avenue, #19C
New York, NY 10023
Tel: (212) 874-8084
Fax: (212) 362-3011
Contact: Barbara Hogenson

Bret Adams, Ltd.
448 West Forty-Fourth Street
New York, NY 10036
Tel: (212) 765-5630
Fax: (212) 265-2212
Contact: Bret Adams, Bruce Ostler

Curtis Brown, Ltd.
28 Haymarket
London, SW1Y 4SP England
Tel: 011-44-171-396-6600
Fax: 011-44-171-396-0110

The agency prefers that you send them your monologue play.

Don Buchwald and Associates
10 East Forty-Fourth Street
New York, NY 10017
Tel: (212) 867-1200
Fax: (212) 972-3200
Contact: Theatrical Department

A query or synopsis along with a bio is preferred.

Douglas, Gorman, Rothacker and Wilhelm
1501 Broadway, Suite 703
New York, NY 10036
Tel: (212) 382-2000
Fax: (212) 719-2878

Send them ten pages of your monologue, a résumé, and a query letter.

Duva-Flack Associates, Inc.
200 West Fifty-Seventh Street, Suite 1008
New York, NY 10019
Tel: (212) 957-9600
Fax: (212) 957-9606

Flora Roberts
157 West Fifty-Seventh Street
New York, NY 10019
Tel: (212) 355-4165
Fax: (212) 246-7138
Contact: Flora Roberts, Sarah Douglas

They are looking for playwrights with outstanding credits. Send a query with a résumé.

The Gersh Agency
130 West Forty-Second Street, Suite 2400
New York, NY 10036
Tel: (212) 997-1818
Fax: (212) 391-8459
Contact: Peter Hagen, John Buzzetti, Mike Lubin, Scott Yoselow, Kara Young

The Gersh Agency prefers a professional recommendation or a query letter with SASE.

The Graham Agency
311 West Forty-Third Street
New York, NY 10036
Tel: (212) 489-7730
Contact: Earl Graham

Harden Curtis Associates
850 Seventh Avenue, Suite 903
New York, NY 10019
Tel: (212) 977-8502
Contact: Mary Harden

Letters of inquiry are preferred.

Helen Merril, Ltd.
425 West Twenty-Third Street, Suite 1F
New York, NY 10011
Tel: (212) 691-5326
Contact: Patrick Herold

Impulse Dramatists
3131 S.W. Sherwood Place
Portland, OR 97201-2254
Contact: Ed Udovick

Ed Udovick accepts unsolicited scripts.

International Creative Management
40 West Fifty-Seventh Street
New York, NY 10019
Tel: (212) 556-5600
Contact: Bridget Aschenberg, Sam Cohn, Arlene Donovan, Mitch Douglas

The Joyce Ketay Agency
1501 Broadway, Suite 1908
New York, NY 10036
Tel: (212) 354-6825
Fax: (212) 354-6732
E-mail: *ketay@aol.com*
Contact: Joyce Ketay, Carl Mulert, Wendy Streeter

They prefer you to contact them only through referrals.

Judy Boals, Inc.
208 West Thirtieth Street, Suite 401
New York, NY 10001
Tel: (212) 868-0924
Contact: Judy Boals, Agent

Ms. Boals prefers letters of inquiry or recommendations from professionals whom she's familiar with.

The Lantz Office
888 Seventh Avenue, #2500
New York, NY 10106
Tel: (212) 586-0200
Contact: Robert Lantz, Dennis Aspland

Literary Artists Representatives
575 West End Avenue
New York, NY 10024
Tel: (212) 787-3808
Fax: (212) 595-2098
Contact: Madeline Perrone

Mark Christian Subias Agency
331 West Fifty-Seventh Street, #46
New York, NY 10019
Tel: (212) 445-1091
Contact: Mark Christian Subias, Agent

Mr. Subias prefers letters of inquiry or professional recommendations.

Peregrine Whittlesey Agency
345 East Eightieth Street, #31F
New York, NY 10021
Tel: (212) 737-0153
Fax: (212) 734-5176
Contact: Peregrine Whittlesey

Peregrine Whittlesey prefers that you send a query with résumé. They're only looking for "original writing."

Rosenstone/Wender
3 East Forty-Eighth Street
New York, NY 10017

Tel: (212) 832-8330
Fax: (212) 759-4524
Contact: Ron Gwiazda, Howard Rosenstone, Phyllis Wender

The Shukat Company
340 West Fifty-Fifth Street, Suite 1A
New York, NY 10019-3744
Tel: (212) 582-7614
E-mail: *staff@shukat.com*

Susan Shulman Literary Agency
454 West Forty-Fourth Street
New York, NY 10036
Tel: (212) 713-1633
Fax: (212) 581-8830
E-mail: *schulman@aol.com*
Contact: Susan Schulman

Susan prefers a professional recommendation or a query letter.

Talent Representatives
20 East Fifty-Third Street, Suite 2A
New York, NY 10022
Tel: (212) 752-1835
Fax: (212) 752-7558
Contact: Honey Raider

The Tantleff Agency
375 Greenwich Street, #700
New York, NY 10013
Tel: (212) 941-3939
Fax: (212) 941-3948
Contact: Jack Tantleff, Charmaine Ferenczi

Writers and Artists Agency
19 West Forty-Fourth Street, Suite 1000
New York, NY 10036
Tel: (212) 391-1112
Fax: (212) 575-6397
Contact: William Craver, Greg Wagner

They prefer that you don't send your queries by fax.

Greg Ziegler
160 East Ninety-Seventh Street
New York, NY 10029

Greg Ziegler prefers that you send a synopsis with a short sample of your monologue and a query letter.

APPENDIX G

recommended books

Alterman, Glenn. *The Perfect Audition Monologue*. Lyme, NH: Smith and Kraus, 2003.

Alterman, Glenn. *Two Minutes and Under*. Lyme, NH: Smith and Kraus, 1993.

Alterman, Glenn. *Two Minutes and Under, Volume 3*. Lyme, NH: Smith and Kraus, 2004.

Beard, Jocelyn. *The Ultimate Audition Book, 222 Monologues 2 Minutes and Under*. Lyme, NH: Smith and Kraus, 1997.

Friedman, Ginger Howard. *The Perfect Monologue: How to Find and Perform the Monologue That Will Get You the Part*, Pompton Plains, NJ: Limelight Editions, 1990.

Goldberg, Natalie. *Writing Down the Bones: Freeing the Writer Within*. Boston: Shambahala, 1986.

Lamott, Anne. *Bird by Bird: Some Instructions on Writing and Life*. New York: Knopf Publishing Group, 1995.

McCullough, L.E. *Ice Babies in Oz*. Lyme, NH: Smith and Kraus, 1995.

Muir, Kerry. *Childsplay, A Collection of Scenes and Monologues for Children*. Pompton Plains, NJ: Limelight Editions, 2001.

Poggi, Jack. *The Monologue Workshop*. New York: Applause Books, 1990.

Ueland, Brenda. *If You Want to Write*. Saint Paul, MN: Graywolf Press, 1987.

APPENDIX H

internet resources

Today, just about every theater and theater-related organization has an Internet presence. Knowing the address of these sites can be of value to you as you attempt to market your solo show. What follows are just of few of the many sites available to monologists. For further information on Internet sites, go to the Dramatists Sourcebook.

PLAYS AND PLAYWRIGHTS
http://groups.yahoo.com/group/playsandplaywrights

This site offers a discussion group of 325 members who discuss the craft of playwriting (including monologue work), grant writing, submission information, and opportunities for theater writers. The discussions receive anywhere from 45 to 350 messages per month. You can also have these online discussions e-mailed to you if you wish.

PLAYWRIGHTS ON THE WEB
www.stageplays.com/writers.htm

This site offers an international database for playwrights and their Web sites. The site also offers a playwrights' discussion group and a link to the Internet Theatre Bookshop.

THEATER CENTRAL
www.playbill.com

This is a theater portal site. There are many related links that you may find of value in promoting and submitting your piece.

YAHOO THEATER INDEX
http://dir.yahoo.com/arts/performing_arts/theatre

This is an index of many valuable contacts for monologue playwrights. Just within the playwriting site, there are thirty-seven different subjects, which include playwrights and plays.

WWW VIRTUAL LIBRARY FOR THEATRE AND DRAMA
www.vl-theatre.com

This site is a library of international theater sources. The site has daily updates. The many links offered here include links to plays in print, monologues in print, conferences for theater scholars, electronic plays online, theater books in print, and general resources.

PERMISSIONS

Spalding Gray

Excerpt from *Swimming to Cambodia*, © 1985 Spalding Gray. Published by Theater Communications Group, Inc., 355 Lexington Avenue, New York, NY 10017. Reprinted by permission of the author.

Excerpt from *Gray's Anatomy*, © 1993 Spalding Gray. Published by Vintage Books, a division of Random House, Inc. Reprinted by permission of the author.

Evan Handler

Excerpt from *Time on Fire*, © 1996 Evan Handler. Published by Little, Brown and Company. Reprinted by permission of the author.

Charlayne Woodard

Excerpt from *Pretty Fire,* © Charlayne Woodard. Published by Penguin Press. Permission granted by the author.

Shelly Mars

Excerpt from *An Evening with Shelly Mars*, © Shelly Mars Reprinted by permission granted by the author.

Quentin Crisp

Excerpt from *An Evening with Quentin Crisp*, © 1998 by Quentin Crisp. Reprinted by permission of the author.

Dael Orlandersmith

Excerpt from *Monster*, © 1998 Dael Orlandersmith. Reprinted by permission of the author.

Penny Arcade

Excerpt from *True Stories*, © 1989 Penny Arcade. Reprinted by permission of the author.

Danny Hoch

Excerpt from *Some People*, © 1998 Danny Hoch. Reprint permission granted by Villard Books/Random House.

Excerpt from *Jails, Hospitals & Hip-Hop*, © 1998 Danny Hoch. Reprint permission granted by Villard Books/Random House.

Kate Clinton

Excerpt from *Comedy You Can Dance To*, © Kate Clinton. Reprinted by permission of the author.

Mary Louise Wilson and Mark Hampton

Excerpt from *Full Gallop*, © Mary Louise Wilson and Mark Hampton. Reprinted by permission of the authors.

Glenn Alterman

Craig from *Two Minutes and Under, Volume 3*, © 2004 Glenn Alterman. Published by Smith and Kraus. Reprinted by permission of the author.

Bernice Weinstein from *Two Minutes and Under, Volume 2*, © 2002 Glenn Alterman. Published by Smith and Kraus. Reprinted by permission of the author.

Sal from *Street Talk, Character Monologues for Actors*, © 1991 Glenn Alterman. Published by Smith and Kraus Publishers. Reprinted by permission of the author.

Anastasia Traina

Excerpt from *The Eternal Pyramid*, © Anastasia Traina. Reprinted by permission of the author.

Bashore Halow

Except from *I'm Breathing the Water Now*, © 2003 Bashore Halow. Reprinted by permission of the author. Rights available through the author. E-mail: *bhalow@yahoo.com*.

Ellen Lewis

Excerpt from *The Sun and the Moon Live in the Sky*, © 1990 Ellen Lewis. Reprinted by permission of the author.

Taylor Mac

Except from *Safe*, © 2005 Taylor Mac. Reprinted by permission of the author.

ty adams

Excerpts from *The Finger Hole* and *Master of the Stale*, from the play *The Dark String*, © 1998 ty adams. Reprinted by permission of the author. For permission to perform, contact ty adams, P.O. Box 1256, Woodstock, NY 12498. E-mail: *tyadams@casablancalane.com*

Joe Pintauro

Except from *A Kiss to Build a Dream On*, © Joe Pintauro. Permission to reproduce given by the author. For permission to perform, contact Ron Guiazda, Rosenstone Wender, 38 East Twenty-Nineth Street, New York, NY 10016.

ABOUT THE AUTHOR

GLENN ALTERMAN is the author of *The Perfect Audition Monologue, Two Minutes and Under* (and Volumes 2 and 3), *Street Talk (Original Character Monologues for Actors), Uptown, Promoting Your Acting Career, The Job Book—One Hundred Acting Jobs for Actors, The Job Book 2—One Hundred Day Jobs for Actors, What to Give Your Agent for Christmas, Two-Minute Monologs,* and *An Actor's Guide—Making It in New York.*

Two Minutes and Under (Volumes 1, 2, and 3), *Street Talk, Uptown, Creating Your Own Monologue, Promoting Your Acting Career, One Hundred Acting Jobs For Actors, Two Minutes and Under,* and *An Actor's Guide—Making It in New York City* were all "Featured Selections" in the Doubleday Book Club (Fireside Theater and Stage and Screen Division). Most of his published works have gone on to multiple printings.

His recent book, *The Perfect Audition Monologue,* was honored by the National Arts Club in New York City.

His plays *Like Family* and *The Pecking Order* were recently optioned by Red Eye Films (with Alterman writing the screenplay).

His latest play, *Solace,* was produced off-Broadway by Circle East Theater Company, and presently has several European productions. *Solace* was recently optioned for European TV and is to be produced as a feature film in the United States.

Nobody's Flood won the Bloomington National Playwriting Competition and was a finalist in the Key West Playwriting Competition.

Coulda-Woulda-Shoulda won the Three Genres Playwriting Competition twice, including publication of the play in two separate editions of the college textbook published by Prentice Hall. It has received several New York productions.

He wrote the book for *Heartstrings: The National Tour* (commissioned by the Design Industries Foundation for AIDS), a thirty-five-city tour that starred Michelle Pfeiffer, Ron Silver, Christopher Reeve, Susan Sarandon, Marlo Thomas, and Sandy Duncan.

Other plays include *Kiss Me When It's Over* (commissioned by E. Weissman Productions) starring and directed by Andre DeShields, *Tourists of the Mindfield* (finalist in the L. Arnold Weissberger Playwriting Competition at New Dramatists), and *Street Talk/Uptown* (based on his monologue books), produced at the West Coast Ensemble.

Goin' Round on Rock-Solid Ground, Unfamiliar Faces, and *Words Unspoken* were all finalists at the Actors Theatre of Louisville. *Spilt Milk* received its premiere at the Beverly Hills Rep/Theater 40 in Los Angeles and was selected to participate in the Samuel French Short Play Festival on two separate occasions. It's had over twenty productions. *The Danger of Strangers* won Honorable Mention in both the Deep South Writers Conference Competition and the Pittsburgh New Works Festival, and was also a finalist in the George R. Kernodle Playwriting Contest. There have been over thirty productions of this play by theaters including Circle Rep Lab, the West Bank Cafe Downstairs Theater Bar (starring James Gandolfini), the Emerging Artists Theatre's One-Act Marathon, and, most recently, at the Vital Theater Company on Theatre Row in New York.

His work has been performed at Primary Stages, Circle in the Square Downtown, the Turnip Festival, HERE, La MaMa, the Duplex, Playwrights Horizons, and at several theaters on Theatre Row in New York, as well as at many other theaters around the country.

He is one of the country's foremost monologue and audition coaches, having helped thousands of actors search for and prepare monologues, as well as create their own material for solo shows.

Glenn has lectured and taught at such diverse places as the Edward Albee Last Frontier Theater Conference (Valdez, Alaska), Southampton College, Governor's School for the Arts (Old Dominion University), the School for Film and Television, Western Connecticut State College, Star Map Acting School of Long Island, the Dramatists Guild, The Learning Annex, the Screen Actors Guild, the Seminar Center, and in the Boston Public School System, as well as at many acting schools all over the country.

In 1994, he created the Glenn Alterman Studio (*www.glennalterman.com*), and through its auspices has worked privately as a monologue and audition coach and at colleges, universities, and acting schools all around the country.

He lives in New York City, where he is working on a new commissioned play, developing a recently optioned screenplay, coaching actors, giving seminars, and occasionally working in film and TV. His latest book of original monologues, *101 One Minute Monologues* (Smith and Kraus) will be published in early 2006. He presently can be seen on TV in a series of commercials for American Express.

INDEX

Books from Allworth Press

Allworth Press is an imprint of Allworth Communications, Inc. Selected titles are listed below.

An Actor's Guide—Making It in New York City
by Glenn Alterman (paperback, 6 x 9, 288 pages, $19.95)

Promoting Your Acting Career, Second Edition
by Glenn Alterman (paperback, 6 x 9, 224 pages, $18.95)

Acting: Advanced Techniques for the Actor, Director, and Teacher
by Terry Schreiber with Mary Beth Barber (paperback, 6 x 9, 256 pages, $19.95)

Acting Is a Job: Real Life Lessons about the Acting Business
by Jason Pugtach (paperback, 6 x 9, 224 pages, $19.95)

Improv for Actors
by Dan Diggles (paperback, 6 x 9, 256 pages, $19.95)

Movement for Actors
edited by Nicole Potter (paperback, 6 x 9, 288 pages, $19.95)

Acting for Film
by Cathy Haase (paperback, 6 x 9, 224 pages, $19.95)

Acting That Matters
by Barry Pineo (paperback, 6 x 9, 240 pages, $16.95)

Mastering Shakespeare: An Acting Class in Seven Scenes
by Scott Kaiser (paperback, 6 x 9, 256 pages, $19.95)

The Art of Auditioning
by Rob Decina (paperback, 6 x 9, 224 pages, $19.95)

The Best Things Ever Said in the Dark:
The Wisest, Wittiest, Most Provocative Quotations from the Movies
by Bruce Adamson (7 1/2 x 7 1/2, 144 pages, $14.95)

Please write to request our free catalog. To order by credit card, call 1-800-491-2808 or send a check or money order to Allworth Press, 10 East 23rd Street, Suite 510, New York, NY 10010. Include $5 for shipping and handling for the first book ordered and $1 for each additional book. Ten dollars plus $1 for each additional book if ordering from Canada. New York State residents must add sales tax.

To see our complete catalog on the World Wide Web, or to order online, you can find us at
www.allworth.com.